DATE DUE

Sport Club Management

Matthew J. Robinson, EdD

University of Delaware

Human Kinetics

Library of Congress Cataloging-in-Publication Data

Robinson, Matthew J.
  Sport club management / Matthew J. Robinson.
     p. cm.
  Includes bibliographical references and index.
  ISBN-13: 978-0-7360-7596-1 (hard cover)
  ISBN-10: 0-7360-7596-8 (hard cover)
  1. Athletic clubs--Management. I. Title.
  GV563.R56 2010
  796.06'9--dc22

                                2009036253

ISBN-10: 0-7360-7596-8 (print)
ISBN-13: 978-0-7360-7596-1 (print)

The Web addresses cited in this text were current as of August 26, 2009 unless otherwise noted.

Acquisitions Editor: Myles Schrag; **Developmental Editor:** Amanda S. Ewing; **Assistant Editors:** Christine Bryant Cohen and Casey A. Gentis; **Copyeditor:** Patsy Fortney; **Indexer:** Andrea Hepner; **Permission Manager:** Dalene Reeder; **Graphic Designer:** Joe Buck; **Graphic Artist:** Tara Welsch; **Cover Designer:** Keith Blomberg; **Photographer (cover):** © Human Kinetics; **Photo Asset Manager:** Laura Fitch; **Photo Production Manager:** Jason Allen; **Art Manager:** Kelly Hendren; **Associate Art Manager:** Alan L. Wilborn; **Illustrator:** Tammy Page; **Printer:** Sheridan Books

Printed in the United States of America   10   9   8   7   6   5   4   3   2   1

The paper in this book is certified under a sustainable forestry program.

Human Kinetics
Web site: www.HumanKinetics.com

United States: Human Kinetics
P.O. Box 5076
Champaign, IL 61825-5076
800-747-4457
e-mail: humank@hkusa.com

Canada: Human Kinetics
475 Devonshire Road Unit 100
Windsor, ON N8Y 2L5
800-465-7301 (in Canada only)
e-mail: info@hkcanada.com

Europe: Human Kinetics
107 Bradford Road
Stanningley
Leeds LS28 6AT, United Kingdom
+44 (0) 113 255 5665
e-mail: hk@hkeurope.com

Australia: Human Kinetics
57A Price Avenue
Lower Mitcham, South Australia 5062
08 8372 0999
e-mail: info@hkaustralia.com

New Zealand: Human Kinetics
P.O. Box 80
Torrens Park, South Australia 5062
0800 222 062
e-mail: info@hknewzealand.com

E4598

To Lynn, Cullen, Patrick, and Maggie, my reasons for being.

Contents

Preface

The need for well-organized sport clubs and strong club leadership is greater than ever. In the past, sports in America have relied on the interscholastic environment to offer participation opportunities and to develop future players; but school budgets are being cut; sports are being dropped; and qualified coaches choose not to coach because of low pay, long hours, and underappreciation. The emerging reality is that sport clubs are often where children are introduced to sport and taught how to play a variety of games. Sport clubs also have a major influence on the development of elite athletes and foster a lifetime commitment to sport participation and a healthy lifestyle for the well-being of both individuals and society. To play a part in creating this reality, sport clubs must be run efficiently in all aspects.

I became aware of the growing influence of sport clubs while developing and teaching a course on soccer club management for the National Soccer Coaches Association of America (NSCAA). In offering the course, I was impressed at how professional some soccer clubs were and the scope of services they offered. I was alarmed, however, at how little some managers understood what it takes to manage all aspects of a club effectively. This concern was the impetus behind writing *Sport Club Management*. Those who read and use this book will have at their disposal information that will enable them to develop, manage, and sustain highly organized, professional, and structured clubs.

In sports such as soccer, volleyball, swimming, gymnastics, and track and field, the sport club environment is more developed. In these sports, clubs in many cases consist of several thousand players, several dozen volunteer coaches, full-time staff, several hundred thousand dollars in revenues and expenses, and physical plants consisting of multiple outdoor fields and indoor complexes. In some cases sport clubs provide a social outlet for both players and their parents and are integral parts of the local community.

In the past, the majority of educational opportunities and materials have addressed coaching. Professional development opportunities directed at the people who manage and lead the organizations has been limited. It has become evident that sport clubs that adhere to sound business practices, provide qualified coaches and excellent facilities, offer a variety of experiences for players on the field and off, and demonstrate success in terms of victories and players moving on to higher levels of play thrive, whereas clubs that do not meet the needs of their members and do not contribute to the growth of players and the sport do not.

Sport Club Management intends to fill that void of knowledge for those working in this area. We hope this book will be on the shelf of club managers around the world and serve as a resource for those aspiring to club manager positions.

This book addresses issues ranging from developing more effective sponsorship proposals to developing a comprehensive facility assessment plan to writing clear job descriptions for employees.

Drawing on my experiences within the club environment and my research in the area of sport management, I have included theories, concepts, insights, and examples on how to manage a club so that it excels on the field and off. I have also enlisted professionals in the areas of player development, parent relations, club structure, and facility design to develop a comprehensive text on leading a sport club. The book addresses the following:

- ▶ Structuring a club (chapter 1). Should a club be structured as a nonprofit organization or a limited liability corporation?
- ▶ Developing effective club leadership (chapter 2). What forms of power are best suited for an individual club manager's leadership style?
- ▶ Practicing sound human resources strategies (chapter 3). What are the best questions to ask when interviewing a potential job candidate?
- ▶ Appreciating the importance of parental relations (chapter 4). Why is parental involvement in a club so important?
- ▶ Understanding the legal aspects of running a club (chapter 5). When is a club liable for the actions of its employees?
- ▶ Using effective business and marketing strategies (chapter 6). How do club managers use the five Ps of sport marketing to market their clubs effectively?
- ▶ Growing sponsorship and fund-raising opportunities (chapter 7). What are the benefits to a corporation from partnership with a club?
- ▶ Developing facility design and management plans (chapter 8). Who should be included on a design team, and what is each person's role?
- ▶ Implementing a long-term athlete development plan (chapter 9). What is the best strategy for developing a well-rounded athlete?
- ▶ Practicing ethics in sport club management (chapter 10). To what ethical theory does a club adhere, and why is it important to hire people with the same ethics?

The book will also offer perspectives on the future of club sports.

People in leadership positions in sport clubs often have a firm grasp of the sport but do not have a strong foundation in areas such as business operations, strategic planning, management, marketing, public relations, risk management, liability, facility management, and player development. *Sport Club Management* provides information and practical examples that are essential for ensuring the success of the club and ultimately the members of that club so that the club will continue to fulfill and expand its roles in offering participation opportunities, developing the talent of players, and growing the sport.

Each chapter includes an opening and closing scenario related to the content of the chapter. The opening scenario presents a problem, which is resolved in the closing scenario using the theories and concepts presented in the chapter. Each chapter also offers examples of models, documents, and forms that you can replicate for your own use. Successful Strategy sidebars present real-life stories that highlight the need for sound planning; a few of the sidebars show how a lack of sound planning can lead to an unsuccessful outcome. Finally, each chapter offers a running glossary of terms related to the concepts and theories presented in the chapter.

In the past, the prerequisite for leading a sport club was having been either a successful player or a coach. In today's environment, such experience is not enough to lead what in some cases are close to million-dollar businesses. By the same token an all-volunteer organization is unlikely to be adequate for providing the desire services to its members. Meeting the responsibilities of club management requires a knowledge and understanding of sound business practices rather than coaching knowledge, and these responsibilities cannot be met in an organization staffed solely by volunteers. *Sport Club Management* is a source of information for those in the sport club environment. In the end, all those involved with sport and sport clubs will benefit.

Acknowledgments

I was made aware of the impact and potential of the sport club through my assistance in the development of the Director of Coaching (DOC) course from the National Soccer Coaches Association of America (NSCAA) in 2005. The idea for the development of that course as well as this book came from Richard Butler, who works for the South Charlotte Soccer Club and who is on the national staff of the NSCAA. Richard saw that the club programs were the ones developing many of the top players in the country, and the leaders of those clubs constituted a significant percentage of the membership of the NSCAA. Richard thought that the club directors' needs were not being met and that many soccer clubs were not being operated in the best or most professional manner. Often those who led those clubs were versed in soccer but not in the management of (in some cases) million-dollar businesses.

Initially Richard and I discussed writing a book specific to the soccer club, but in conversations with the editors at Human Kinetics and through my work with the United States Olympic Committee (USOC), we realized that there was an audience beyond soccer. Other sports, such as swimming, track and field, and volleyball, already had a strong club culture; some sports had an emerging club culture, such as basketball and lacrosse.

I met leaders of national governing bodies in the United States who expressed a need for more education of sport club leaders. I had discussions with sport leaders from other countries who provided insights into the operations of successful sport clubs. I saw that the sport club was on the rise in the United States and there was a need for a body of information on the management and leadership of those sport clubs.

I worked on the book for close to two years. On a few occasions, I was sidetracked by faculty commitments at the university and my work with the USOC and the U.S. Department of State, but I believed in the importance of the book. I do believe the future of sport in the United States is in the sport club environment. Those clubs will be instrumental in developing our Olympic and professional athletes, promote healthy lifestyles and lifetime participation in sports, and shape the moral and ethical fabric of our future leaders. For those things to happen, sport clubs must be run in a businesslike manner with a clear mission and purpose. Clubs should focus on the long-term development of the athlete and provide opportunities for all, not just the select talented few.

On a project like this, there are always people behind the scenes who help make it happen. First and foremost I have to thank my wife, Lynn, who always has let me chase my dreams. I also thank my three children, Cullen, Patrick, and Maggie. They learned that if Dad was on the back porch with his laptop, he was working on his book and was to be left alone! I love you guys. I would like to thank Richard Butler. His recognition of the need for this book led to my approaching Human Kinetics about the project. Richard is one of the true believers. He is out in the trenches every day developing good soccer players and good people. Richard is the best at what he does, and I feel fortunate to count him as a friend. I would also like to thank the following colleagues who contributed to some of the chapters in this book:

- Dena Deglau, PhD, assistant professor in the department of health, nutrition, and exercise sciences at the University of Delaware
- Christopher A. Sgarzi, AIA, president of Sgarzi Associates, Inc.
- Richard Way, MBA, Citius Performance Corp. and Advanced Training & Performance Ltd.
- Istvan Balyi, MA, Citius Performance Corp. and Advanced Training & Performance Ltd.
- Richard Butler, director of the Charlotte Soccer Academy

I would also like to thank Myles Schrag at Human Kinetics for believing in the project and encouraging me to keep plugging along. Thanks to Amanda Ewing for all her work in the editorial stages of the book. I also thank the reviewers for their insights on the book. Finally, I thank all of the professionals in sport clubs who provide a positive experience for the athletes under their charge. They are my reason for writing this book.

I want to recognize my parents, who always supported me. I know I would not be the person I am today without their unconditional love.

Thanks to Dr. Rick Carpenter for giving me my break 20 years ago at Western Maryland College. To Dr. Sam Case for pushing me to become an academic and for being a role model for me. To Pat Massa for putting up with me as a player, rival coach, colleague, and friend for over 25 years. To Jeff Tipping for bringing me back into the soccer world five years ago through the NSCAA DOC course. To Avron Abraham and Jack O'Neill for talking me into coming to the University of Delaware eight years ago (Av, you still owe me my cheesecake, and Jack, I miss you). To my past and present sport management students who amaze me on a daily basis with their accomplishments and potential. To my friends around the world who have shown me their part of it in Ireland (Karl and Debbie), Senegal (Cheikh), India (Harish, K.K. Divya, and Yuvika), and Turkey (Emir, Cem, and Tugba). To my fellow Creek Road runners whom I inspire every day with my world-class running ability, and to Carolina Bayon at the USOC and my ICECP family for making me a better person and professional through working on the ICECP project.

Finally, I want to thank Bruce Springsteen for his inspiration all of these years and for encouraging me to go explore the darkness on the edge of town, not to sell my Challenger and for not letting me settle for sleeping in the backseat of a borrowed car.

Enjoy!

By the end of the chapter, the sport club manager will be able to do the following:

▶ Describe the various business forms a sport club can take

▶ Appreciate the importance of a board of directors and its composition in achieving organizational success

▶ List the elements in a sport club's articles of incorporation or constitution

▶ Appreciate the importance of the club having a clear vision and mission

▶ Develop goals that support the club's mission

▶ Develop a strategic plan for the club

▶ Differentiate between a simple and a complex organization

▶ Recognize the types of organizational structures

▶ Appreciate the importance of developing policies and procedures to provide structure for the club

1

The Club

Richard Butler

• • •

Bob Armstrong achieved great success as a volleyball player. He started out in a local church-sponsored league that was organized by his father. Bob had success at the high school level and earned a college scholarship based on his athletic ability. He was named All-American his senior year. Later he represented his country in international competitions and had a 10-year professional career overseas and competed on the beach volleyball tour for a number of years. In thinking about what he wanted to do after his playing career, he considered getting into college coaching, but opted not to. His dream was to offer youths the same opportunities he had had to compete in volleyball. His first thought was to offer his services to existing volleyball clubs, but he wanted to have one of his own. Bob has name recognition, money saved from his professional career, and the desire and passion to create these opportunities for others. Bob is looking into how best to proceed. His vision has excited others who are interested in both funding and working for or with him. The next step is bringing that vision to reality. As much as Bob believes in his dream, he has many questions about how to make it happen.

• • •

In recent years there have been many changes in the youth sport environment, especially in the United States. In the past, youth sport was primarily a volunteer-based initiative. Youth sports leagues were usually affiliated with civic, church, and municipal organizations. They were nonprofit entities organized and run by boards of volunteers, some with little experience in the organization of sport, and contests were held at public parks and school facilities. The coaches were the parents of the players; some had training, but many had no experience in or knowledge of the sport. Competition remained at the local level. As the players got older, they left the local organization to compete for the high school team. The lucky few would have the opportunity to compete at the college level and perhaps earn athletic scholarships.

In recent years the model of youth sport has changed. Volunteer-initiated organizations have given way to individual and multisport clubs that have full-time staffs and six-figure and sometimes million-dollar budgets, and that service hundreds and even thousands of players a year who travel nationally and even internationally to compete and train. The reality is that sport clubs have become businesses, some nonprofit and others for profit, that are accountable to their players, members, and state and national governing bodies as well as the Internal Revenue Service. It is apparent that Bob Armstrong needs to look to the future instead of his past as he begins to chart a course for his new sport club.

Understanding why the club exists, what it aspires to be, and what goods and services it provides to its members is the foundation of the modern sport club. To thrive, a club must be able to secure and maintain human, financial, and physical plant resources. It must have realistic and measurable goals, a sound organizational structure and policies and procedures that support that structure, and a long-term plan to ensure its growth and viability. The objective of this chapter is to provide the outline for the structure of a model sport club.

The Club Plan

club plan—A written document that stipulates all aspects of a club's purpose and structure.

The **club plan** stipulates all aspects of the club's purpose and structure (figure 1.1). It communicates the philosophy, vision, and mission of the club, and it defines the services it provides and to whom, its goals, its business and organizational structures, the revenue streams and costs of operation, and the facilities it will need. This chapter addresses business structure, mission, goals, organizational structure, and policies and procedures. Later chapters address the other aspects of the club plan.

The club's plan makes a concept concrete. It is the blueprint for the club leadership, and it will attract investors and supporters for the club. Once developed, the plan should be followed, but it is a living document and should be reviewed as the club evolves. Software packages (see page 3) can assist in developing or refining a club plan, but the main elements are a philosophy, a vision statement, a mission statement, goals, policies and procedures, organizational structure, product and services offered, market analysis, and financial plan.

Figure 1.1   A club plan defines what the club is all about.

Developing a Business Plan

For those starting a club from scratch, the following Web sites are worth visiting to get ideas on how to develop a business plan. Also, Microsoft PowerPoint has a business plan model within the templates that can serve as a model as well.

www.sba.gov/smallbusinessplanner/index.html

www.score.org/template_gallery.html?gclid=CIaK54_G8JoCFQOaFQodFlrFJA

www.planware.org/businessplan.htm

Philosophy

The beliefs, values, and truths that define a person or organization constitute a **philosophy.** A philosophy distinguishes right from wrong and good from bad and defines success. The overall philosophy of the club has to be fashioned by the club's leadership and accepted by all staff and coaches, thereby enabling it to penetrate to the club's players and parents. Individual players and teams as a whole should know and accept the club philosophy. Bob Armstrong's coaching philosophy is shown on page 4. Club leaders creating a philosophy for a sport club can use similar language.

philosophy—The beliefs, values, and truths that define a person or organization.

Sample Coaching Philosophy

A club committed to promoting excellence in the educational, character, and physical development of adolescents by offering a rigorous and challenging athletic experience. Sport will be used to instill the qualities of leadership, teamwork, dedication, perseverance, loyalty, and fair play. These values will be tested and strengthened in the heat of competition. Participants will learn to cope with success and failure and to be humble in victory and proud in defeat, and will understand that the athletic competition is preparing them for the ultimate competition: life.

This philosophy statement communicates clearly Bob's belief that sport has the power to affect people and reaches beyond the playing field. These beliefs should drive all other aspects of the club. For the club to thrive, players, parents, the board of directors, coaches, and staff must buy in and live it on a daily basis.

Vision Statement

vision statement—A conceptual vision of what the club aspires to be, based on its philosophy.

A **vision statement** is a conceptual vision of what the club aspires to be, based on its philosophy. It presents the aspirations of the club and can address the size of the club in terms of participants and staff, the facilities, the programs, and the level of excellence that club leaders want to achieve. Bob Armstrong had a vision of a club that would have its own state-of-the-art facilities staffed by full-time coaches and trainers, where young athletes would train and compete at high levels but also be encouraged to grow as people away from the competition field. The vision statement ultimately communicates the aspirations toward which everybody associated with the club should be working.

Mission Statement

mission statement—A statement of intent that provides meaning, purpose, and direction to members, employees, and leaders of the club.

A club needs to know why it exists and its continuing purpose. The **mission statement** takes the beliefs and aspirations communicated in the philosophy and vision statement and turns them into a statement of intent (see the sample mission statement on page 5). The mission statement serves multiple purposes:

- ▶ It provides a snapshot of the club for potential employees and club members.
- ▶ It provides meaning, purpose, and direction to members and employees of the club.
- ▶ It provides direction for club leaders, guiding them in decision making.

As times change, the mission statement may change too.

The club sport scene is constantly evolving, and a club's purpose may change with the times. Organizational retreats are discussed in chapter 3. These annual functions offer a great opportunity for club leaders to revisit the club's mission and determine whether they are living up to the mission or need to modify it based on new opportunities and aspirations. In the end the club leadership must be clear about why the club exists, and that statement of purpose should be communicated to all who are affiliated or who wish to be affiliated with the club.

Scope of Club Services

The mission and vision statements are statements of purpose, intent, and aspirations. In addition to determining what the club is and should be, club leaders need to know what the club is not and should not be. Chapter 8 addresses the logistics of providing services, but before they can discuss such logistics, club leaders must know what those services will be. A sport club at its most basic level offers the opportunity to participate in sport. In chapter 6 we refer to this as the product that is offered to the consumer. But depending on the philosophy, vision, and mission, services beyond the basic service will vary from club to club. (For potential services a club can offer, see below.)

A club can consist of 12 talented basketball players who practice twice a week; play in a league; and participate in state, regional, and national tournaments. The players rent gym time at a local recreation center, and the club exists so that the players on the team can showcase their talents and earn college scholarships. Club leaders are not concerned about the academic status of the participants or about encouraging socialization among the participants and their parents.

Potential Services in the Club Sport Environment

- Competition
- Player development training
- Team training
- Free play
- Recreational play
- Sport-specific professional coaching
- Strength and conditioning coaching
- Out-of-season training and competition
- Special needs programs
- Sport psychologist
- Tournament hosting
- Tournament participation
- Camps and clinics
- Coaching education
- International travel
- Before- and after-school care programs
- Academic tutoring
- Facilities (e.g., pool, track, gymnasium)
- Multipurpose facilities (e.g., outdoor fields on which multiple sports can be played, a field house)
- Facility rentals (e.g., renting club facilities to outside groups to generate revenue)
- Social area (e.g., restaurant, pub)
- Social outings (e.g., bus trips to professional games)
- Speakers program (e.g., college coaches talking to players, coaches, or both)

Another club may be a multisport organization with a staff of 20 and teams with players of both genders and all age groups and skill levels. The club has teams that compete in state, regional, and national events as well as teams that meet once a week for instruction and games in which scores are not kept. The club has its own facility in which to hold practices and host contests, tournaments, summer camps, and clinics, and an area in the facility is used for social functions for the parents of participants. The club offers an after-school care program with academic tutors to oversee participants' homework, as well as strength and conditioning coaches to work with athletes. Every two years participants have the opportunity to travel overseas for an international tournament. The club also provides advisors to help participants in the college recruiting and selection process.

Both of these entities have the title *club*, but they are vastly different in terms of their reason for existing and the services they provide. Marketing sport clubs will be discussed in greater detail in chapter 6. Potential customers need to know what the club supplies to determine whether the club can meet their needs. What the club offers and does not offer is driven by its mission statement. If a club's mission is to produce high-level players and achieve excellence at the state, regional, and national levels, it may not offer an in-house recreation league. If the mission state-

SUCCESSFUL STRATEGY

Score More Athletic Club

Tucker Neale, executive director of the Score More Athletic Club (SMAC), had a distinguished basketball playing career. After earning First Team All-Ohio honors and setting numerous school records at Strongsville High School, he attended Colgate University, where he led the team to the NCAA tournament in 1995, the first time in the school's 96-year history. Tucker was twice named the Patriot League Conference Player of the Year. Tucker left Colgate as its all-time leading scorer (2,075 points) and had his number 20 jersey retired. After participating in tryouts with several NBA franchises and playing a season overseas in Germany, Tucker retired from playing and focused his energy on coaching and starting SMAC.

The Score More Athletic Club is entering its 11th year of providing young basketball players with a positive environment in which to develop their basketball skills. During those years, the club has grown to 62 teams and 650 participants. Past SMAC players have played professionally and at every collegiate level. During the 2007-08 season SMAC alum Rachele Fitz was named the 2008 Pepsi Metro Atlantic Athletic Conference Women's Basketball Player of the Year for her play at Marist College. In 2008 alone, 11 players received scholarships valued at $1.7 million.

The SMAC playing philosophy is to execute a simple system of man-to-man defense, motion offense, and a read-and-react fast break to teach players to make decisions and further their skills. SMAC also tries to ensure that players compete against some of the finest talent in the country in various tournaments across the Midwest predominantly. Tucker and the SMAC coaching staff strive to make each player's experience positive, challenging, and rewarding.

Along with SMAC player development, Tucker also trains professional players. His clientele has included or currently includes Calvin Booth (Minnesota Timberwolves), Keith McLeod (Utah Jazz), Cezary Trybanski (Phoenix Suns), and Andreas Glyniadakis (Detroit Pistons). He has worked with Paul Grant (Milwaukee Bucks) and Adonal Foyle (Golden State Warriors). His player workouts have been viewed by the general managers and player personnel directors of multiple NBA teams.

Information from www.smacsports.com.

ment addresses the development of sport in the area, then the club may conduct player camps and coaching clinics to introduce people to the game. This is the case with a sport such as lacrosse, which is expanding into new areas around the United States and the world.

Mission and vision statements help club leaders determine the programs and services they will offer and how to differentiate their club from the competition. They need to be clear about what their club offers, and participants need to know what they are getting.

Single-Sport Versus Multisport Clubs

Some clubs are structured to focus on only one sport, whereas others focus on multiple sports. There are pluses and minuses to each model. The multisport model is a common structure in Europe. Participants have a choice of a variety of sports under one roof and do not have to look for another club if they want to play another sport. This model encourages young athletes to try a variety of sports so that they develop as well-rounded athletes and don't get burned out on a single sport. The challenge is having the facilities and staff to address the sports offered.

Single-sport clubs have the advantage of specializing. The coaches know one sport well, and the club may have sport-specific facilities. Some are critical of the single-sport club model because such clubs have a vested financial interest in having athletes play the sport year-round. Registration fees are in many cases the main revenue stream for the club. This could be detrimental to younger players who may experience burnout from playing year-round, in addition to not having the opportunity to try other sports that may suit them better.

Goals

Goals are an extension of the vision and mission statements of the organization. Goals turn the concepts contained in the vision and mission statements into measurable outcomes that the club strives to meet. How does a club quantify being one of the most successful clubs in a region? A goal will define that. Goals can be applied to areas of revenue, membership, performance standards, facilities, and programs offered and can be applied to individual staff members as well as to the club as a whole.

Slack (1997) stated that organizations (in this case, sport clubs) can create different types of goals. Clubs can have **official goals** for public consumption that are tied to the mission. These goals are based on outcomes that the club would like to achieve based on fulfilling its purpose. These goals are still somewhat conceptual but are moving toward the concrete. The club may want to post these goals on its Web site and include them in promotional materials to communicate what the club wants to achieve, or the outcome of its efforts, for existing and potential members and employees. Official goals are statements about what the club wants to achieve.

Operational goals, on the other hand, are measurable and realistic and provide a time frame in which to be accomplished. These goals may apply to the overall club, as well as to subunits of the club such as the coaching staff and marketing staff. Some operational goals may not be for public consumption. They may appear

goals—Measurable outcomes that are based on the mission of the club.

official goals—Intended outcomes based on the mission that are developed for public consumption.

operational goals—Measurable, realistic, and time-sensitive outcomes developed for the club and individual units of the club.

in documents such as strategic plans, individual and subunit development plans, and annual reports to the board. These goals should be established with input from those who will be held accountable for achieving them. Doing so creates buy-in rather than imposing goals that people then have to follow.

Slack (1997) communicated that goals are invaluable to an organization because they assist in decision making, provide standards for performance appraisals, and reduce uncertainty in the members of the organization. Also, striving to achieve and achieving goals motivate staff. A club without goals is adrift and does not know whether it has accomplished anything.

Here is an example of how official goals and operational goals work together. The Downtown Basketball Club has the following official goals:

- Offer the largest in-house recreation league in the state
- Provide state-of-the-art training facilities for members
- Compete at the highest level in the state, as well as regionally and nationally
- Generate revenue through external sources to keep the cost to members affordable
- Make the club accessible to people of all races and abilities and both genders

Winning championship games is an operational goal; it is measurable, realistic, and can be done within a certain time frame.

Courtesy of the Brandywine Youth Club

To achieve these official goals, the club and the subunits within the club established these operational goals:

▶ Increase membership in the in-house recreation league by 40 percent by 2012 through increased marketing efforts.

▶ Raise $400,000 for facility renovation through a capital fund-raising campaign by 2012.

▶ Complete the renovation of the strength and conditioning area and the main gymnasium by June 2013.

▶ Win the boys' AAU state championship in three age groups by 2013.

▶ Win the girls' AAU state championship in three age groups by 2014.

▶ Win a national championship in one age group by 2014.

▶ Generate 30 percent of the operational revenue from the sale of corporate sponsorships and fund-raising initiatives on an annual basis.

▶ Secure $75,000 annually in local, state, and federal grants to offer an after-school basketball program for disadvantaged youth and a league for special needs participants.

These operational goals are realistic and measurable and can be accomplished within the time frame. The club must be committed to achieving the goals and allocating the human, financial, and physical plant resources to achieve them. It is easy to write goals; attaining them is the hard part.

When a goal is met, it is time to move on to new goals. If a goal is not met, the organization can reset the parameters of the goal or look at the organization to determine why the goal was not met and decide how to meet it in the future. If the club has not won a state championship in the time frame it determined, was it because the director of coaching did not hire good coaches, the best players were not attracted to the club, or the club does not have the facilities to allow players adequate practice time? Whatever the reason, decisions will have to be made.

Policies and Procedures

Once the club leaders understand the purpose and goals of the club, they must communicate what must be done and how it will be done. This is accomplished through the development of policies and procedures. Slack (1997) defined **policies** as general statements of organizational intent that may be both internally and externally focused. A policy does not state how the intent will be achieved; that is the purpose of procedures.

policies—General statements of organizational intent that may be both internally and externally focused.

Procedures make the actions of a club standardized. For example, the club may have a policy that an independent panel will oversee tryouts and select the players for a team. The panel will consist of five members—two coaches from another age group, the director of coaching, a board member, and the head coach. A majority of the panel is required for making a selection. The intent is to select teams based on merit, and the procedure ensures that all teams are selected in the same way.

procedures—Statements on how policies will be achieved that make the actions of a club standardized.

Establishing policies and procedures makes the decision-making processes easier on the staff and members of the club. Instead of having sole responsibility for player selection, the coach merely has to follow the established policy and procedure. The degree to which a club is formalized is left to the discretion of the club leadership. Some clubs are formalized and have policies and procedures for every aspect of their operation. Others are less formal, develop ad hoc policies based on circumstances, and have unofficial ways of doing things that have developed over time and become part of the organizational culture.

Policies and procedures can be created to address the following aspects of a club:

▶ Financial and budget

▶ Purchasing

▶ Travel

▶ Equipment purchase and inventory

▶ Facility operations related to scheduling for internal uses and external rentals

▶ Risk management

▶ Accident reporting

▶ Emergency plans

▶ Care and prevention of injuries

▶ Hosting special events

▶ Team selection

▶ Contest scheduling

▶ Marketing and media

▶ Public relations

Based on the formality of the club structure, the board may need to vote on policies and procedures. A policy and procedures manual may be beneficial in communicating the policies and procedures to employees and members. The sidebar on this page lists the potential contents of a policies and procedures manual.

Potential Contents of a Policy and Procedures Manual

1. Introduction
2. Vision and mission statements
3. Organization constitution
4. Official goals
5. Human resources
   a. Organizational chart
   b. Job descriptions
   c. Policies and procedures on hiring, evaluation, and termination
   d. Employee rights and benefits
6. Financial and budget policies
7. Travel
8. Equipment purchase and inventory
9. Facility operations
   a. Scheduling
   b. Internal uses
   c. External uses
10. Risk management policies and procedures
11. Emergency plans
12. Care and prevention of injuries
13. Special events
14. Team selection
15. Contest scheduling
16. Marketing
17. Media and public relations
18. Copies of forms

The Club Entity

A sport club will have one of several business structures. Each has its benefits and detriments (as summarized in table 1.1). Club leaders select a model based on how the club will be organized and administered. The models are sole proprietorship, partnership, limited liability corporation (LLC), 501(c) nonprofit, and franchise.

Sole Proprietorship

A **sole proprietorship** is a business owned by one individual. The club owner may have a staff, but the owner controls all decisions within the organization. The club manager/owner also receives all profits from the club venture and therefore is not subject to corporate income tax. The income is reported on the owner's personal income tax. The disadvantage of this model is that the club owner takes on a great deal of personal liability for debts as well as potential lawsuits associated with the operations of the club.

In the case of Bob Armstrong, he would start the club and run it as Bob Armstrong. He would generate income for himself and report what he made after expenses associated with the club on his personal income tax annually. Bob would have the power to make all decisions in relation to the club because he owns the

sole proprietorship—A business owned by an individual.

Table 1.1   Pros and Cons of Business Models

Model	Pros	Cons
Sole proprietorship	• Not subject to corporate income tax • Flexible • Individual has control of the club	• Individual exposure to liability • Lack of continuity if the sole proprietor leaves the business
Partnership	• Multiple individuals with varied strengths involved in the business	• Difficulty in dissolving the entity
Limited liability corporation (LLC)	• Control of club in the hands of the leader of the LLC • Protection from personal liability • Profit or loss passed on to personal income tax	• Limited oversight and input from the membership
501(c) nonprofit	• Tax exemption • Ability to secure grants as a revenue source	• Increased oversight of the club by the board and the state that grants nonprofit status
Franchise	• Use of the franchisor's brand name, advertising, name recognition, and reputation • Initial start-up time is relatively quick compared to starting a club from scratch • Learn the business more quickly with the help of the franchisor	• Limited autonomy in running the club • Must give up a percentage of the revenue

business. If a participant were injured or the club were not as financially successful as Bob had planned, Bob would be sued as an individual by the person who was injured, or creditors would seek payment from Bob. Thus, he could lose personal property not related to the club such as his house, savings, and other investments. Although this is the simplest business model, there are many risks associated with it. Many small sport clubs operate in this manner—for example, a coach selects athletes and enters the team in a league or tournament. This is fine, but the person leading this type of club should be aware that he is personally liable if something goes wrong.

Partnership

A **partnership** entails combining the resources of two or more people with the goal of providing services that will be profitable for the partners. This business structure is similar to a sole proprietorship, but it involves more than one person. The resources the partners bring to the partnership may came in the form of capital, expertise, or labor. The partnership agreement addresses control, ownership, sharing of profits and losses, and terms for dissolving the partnership. Those considering this option should consult an attorney to draft a contract that all partners can agree on.

In the case of Bob Armstrong, a prominent businessman may be willing to be a partner in terms of providing capital to start the club. Bob would provide the expertise and the name recognition and would be involved on a day-to-day basis. Bob would own 60 percent of the club, and the businessman would own the other 40 percent. By having the majority stake, Bob would have ultimate control of the business.

The ultimate goal of a partnership is to generate a profit; therefore, it must file an annual income return with the IRS to report income, deductions, gains, and losses. The partnership itself does not pay income tax; rather, any profits or losses are passed on to the partners, who report them on their individual income tax returns. The profit or loss is in proportion to the ownership stake of each partner. In the case of Bob, if the club generates a $100,000 profit, he would be taxed on $60,000.

As stated earlier, it is best to seek legal council to create a partnership. All terms should be clearly communicated in the partnership agreement. This ensures that all parties understand their roles. If the partnership does dissolve, the agreement will make it an easier process for all involved.

Limited Liability Corporation

Another option for the business structure of a club is a corporate entity. A **corporation** is a legal entity consisting of one or more people or entities that is separate from those people or entities. Although this structure is more complex than the other structures presented, it has many benefits. The most important is that it removes personal liability from the leaders of the corporation.

The **limited liability corporation (LLC)** is a popular corporate structure because it offers the owners of the corporation limited personal liability for the debts and actions of the LLC while also providing management with flexibility and the benefit of pass-through taxation. In the case of Bob Armstrong, he would file the paperwork to make Bob Armstrong Volleyball Club LLC. He would run his club as the owner and operator of the club and would not have any oversight in the form of a board of directors. At the end of the year the profit or loss of the club would be run through his personal income tax.

LLCs are a great option for people who organize teams. The structure provides a buffer between the person and her business actions in the case of financial issues or potential lawsuits, and it also provides tax benefits in the form of write-offs against the business activities.

limited liability corporation (LLC)—A corporate structure that offers the owners limited personal liability for the debts and actions of the LLC while also providing management with flexibility and the benefit of pass-through taxation.

501(c) Nonprofit Corporation

Organizations described under section **501(c)** of the Internal Revenue Code are referred to as charitable organizations. These entities operate for charitable, religious, educational, or scientific purposes. A sport club can be designed to meet one of these criteria. The purpose of this provision is to exclude charitable organizations from some federal income taxes. Once the entity is organized, it must develop organizing documents that state its purpose. These documents include a charter and a declaration of trust. Once an organization is considered tax exempt, the organization cannot make a profit to benefit anyone other than the organization itself.

501(c) corporation—A corporation that exists for charitable, religious, educational, or scientific purposes and thus is exempt from some federal income taxes.

A nonprofit corporation is overseen by a board of directors and guided by a set of **bylaws** crafted by the board and ratified by the home state of the corporation. The makeup of the board and the terms of each position on the board are outlined in the bylaws. The executive director of the club reports directly to the board of directors. Most boards meet monthly. At that time the executive director presents a monthly report to the board on the status of the club. Some of the advantages of the nonprofit structure are that the corporation is exempt from certain taxes, any donations to the organization are tax deductible for the donor, and a diverse board of directors offers oversight. A potential downside is that there is no true ownership of the club.

bylaws—Rules of governance created by the club leadership for the organization.

In the case of Bob Armstrong, he would file the appropriate paperwork to create a 501(c) corporation, he would enlist people to serve on his board, and he could either serve as a board member or take on the position of executive director. The upside is that the club would not have to pay certain taxes. The downside is that Bob would not have control of the club. If he served as executive director, he would serve at the discretion of the board. The original board may consist of Bob's friends, but over time that composition may change and Bob could lose his job or place on the board. He would be a founder of the club, but his involvement in the club would not be permanent.

Franchise

A **franchise** is a business structure in which an organization pays for the right to replicate an existing business plan including operating methods and trademarks. In return, the organization pays an initial fee as well as a percentage of the gross profits to the granter of the franchise. An entity contracts with a franchisor for the right to sell the franchisor's product or service at a specified location. Away from the sport club environment, popular franchises include McDonald's, Burger King, and Foot Locker.

The major advantage to a club of buying into a franchise is being able to use the franchisor's brand name, advertising, name recognition, and reputation. Along with those benefits, initial start-up time is relatively quick compared to starting a club from scratch. This is because club leaders can use existing operating procedures instead of having to develop them and can participate in existing training programs that will help them learn the business more quickly than they would if they had to figure it out on their own.

Franchises do have disadvantages. The main disadvantage is the loss of control: each franchise must follow the template set by the franchisor or risk losing the franchise. A franchised club must follow established rules, policies, and procedures and offer programs and schedule its facility in a manner specified by the franchisor. The franchised club may also have to buy a certain product at a higher cost, which would eat into its profits. A major expense of operating a franchise is the percentage of gross sales the franchisor requires the franchise to pay.

Club Governance

The governance structure of a sport club should be documented and followed. The role of the board and its committees should be clearly communicated and an organizational chart that communicates the lines of authority should be developed as well.

Articles of Incorporation

Articles of incorporation are the formal, legal description of a business. Also known as a certificate of incorporation or a corporate charter, articles of incorporation usually contain the following:

- Company name and structure type
- Name(s) of person(s) organizing the company
- Whether the business is a stock or nonstock corporation (if a stock organization, details on the amount and type of authorized share capital the company can issue)
- Purpose for formation
- Names of members of the board of directors
- Address of the company's registered office
- Accounting period the business will use for reporting purposes

The requirements for these articles vary from state to state. In the case of LLCs, the articles of incorporation are simple and can be completed in a manner of minutes and submitted online to the state board of incorporation.

Board of Directors

Clubs that are classified as 501(c) corporations or for-profit corporations are required by law to establish a board of directors. Sole proprietors, partnerships, and limited liability corporations are not required to do so. The board of directors is an important entity whose main function is to ensure that the club achieves its stated purpose. It can be said that the board sets the course for the club and the staff sails the ship. Nonprofit and for-profit boards both exist for this reason; they differ in that those on nonprofit boards are not compensated beyond expenses, whereas for-profit board members may be compensated.

The role of the board, the number of members, how one is placed on a board, grounds for dismissal, the term of board membership and officer position on the board, and the role of those positions should be clearly communicated in the organization's constitution. It is in the best interest of the club to have a diverse board. One member may be a former college player or a coach who understand the sport, and another may be a lawyer who brings legal expertise. An accountant can bring an understanding of the finances of the club, a person with Web design experience can bring that strength, and someone who has been involved in fund-raising or who has strong ties to the local business community can provide contacts and insights into these areas.

The National Center for Nonprofit Boards (1988) presented the following 10 responsibilities of an effective board:

- ▶ Determine and revisit the organization's mission and purpose
- ▶ Select the executive director
- ▶ Support the executive director and review his or her performance
- ▶ Ensure effective organizational planning
- ▶ Ensure adequate resources
- ▶ Manage resources effectively
- ▶ Determine and monitor the organization's programs and services
- ▶ Enhance the organization's public image
- ▶ Serve as a court of appeal
- ▶ Assess its own performance

A tool for evaluating a board's performance is provided in the sidebar on pages 16-17.

Committees

An effective board of directors establishes a **committee** structure to handle the specific aspects of the club and thus much of the board's work. These committees

committee—An entity created for the purpose of carrying out assigned responsibilities within a given area of a club.

Checklist for Evaluating Board Performance

Rating*	Indicator	Met	Needs work	N/A
E	1. The roles of the Board and the Executive Director are defined and respected, with the Executive Director delegated as the manager of the organization's operations and the board focused on policy and planning.			
R	2. The Executive Director is recruited, selected, and employed by the Board of Directors. The board provides clearly written expectations and qualifications for the position, as well as reasonable compensation.			
R	3. The Board of Directors acts as governing trustees of the organization on behalf of the community at large and contributors while carrying out the organization's mission and goals.			
R	4. The board's nominating process ensures that the board remains appropriately diverse with respect to gender, ethnicity, culture, economic status, disabilities, and skills and/or expertise.			
E	5. The board members receive regular training and information about their responsibilities.			
E	6. New board members are oriented to the organization, including the organization's mission, bylaws, policies, and programs, as well as to their roles and responsibilities as board members.			
A	7. Board organization is documented with a description of the board and board committee responsibilities.			
A	8. Each board has a board operations manual.			
E	9. If the organization has any related party transactions between board members or their families, they are disclosed to the Board of Directors, the Internal Revenue Service, and the auditor. (This is related to potential conflicts of interest.)			
E	10. The organization has at least the minimum number of members on the Board of Directors as required by its bylaws or state statute.			
R	11. If the organization has adopted bylaws, they conform to state statutes and have been reviewed by legal counsel.			
R	12. The bylaws should include (a) how and when notices for board meetings are made; (b) how members are elected/appointed by the board; (c) what the terms of office are for officers/members; (d) how board members are rotated; (e) how ineffective board members are removed from the board; (f) a stated number of board members to make up a quorum, which is required for all policy decisions.			
R	13. The Board of Directors reviews the bylaws.			
A	14. The board has a process for handling urgent matters between meetings.			

Rating*	Indicator	Met	Needs work	N/A
E	15. Board members serve without payment unless the agency has a policy identifying reimbursable out-of-pocket expenses.			
R	16. The organization maintains a conflict-of-interest policy and all board members and executive staff review and/or sign to acknowledge and comply with the policy.			
R	17. The board has an annual calendar of meetings. The board also has an attendance policy such as that a quorum of the organization's board meets at least quarterly.			
A	18. Meetings have written agendas and materials relating to significant decisions are given to the board in advance of the meeting.			
A	19. The board has a written policy prohibiting employees and members of employees' immediate families from serving as board chair or treasurer.			

Indicators ratings: E = essential; R = recommended; A = additional to strengthen organizational activities.
Greater Twin Cities United Way. http://www.managementhelp.org/org_eval/uw_brd.htm.

are often led or chaired by a board member and execute the responsibilities of the committee or oversee the execution of the responsibilities of the paid staff. The paid staff makes a report to the committee, which in turn reports back to the board at the planned meetings. The board approves the plans of a committee, hears reports on the activities and accomplishments of the area, and offers suggestions and insights. Based on what it deems most important, the board determines the number and kinds of committees it needs.

Board members should anticipate either chairing one or serving on several committees along with their other board responsibilities. Committees may include Fund-Raising/Sponsorship, New Membership, Strategic Planning, Public Relations, Budget, Facilities, Annual Tournament, and Government Relations. Again, each committee focuses on its specific area and reports back to the board on its activities and the staff achievement of goals established in each area.

Although board members are going to disagree from time to time, boards need an overall sense of cohesion and continuity in their decision making. The board is there to guide and lend support to the professional staff. It should not focus on micro decisions such as jersey colors and playing time, but rather on macro decisions that will make the club stronger in the future, such as developing a master plan for the development of a facility or initiating a capital campaign to pay for a new facility.

Organizational Structure

To achieve the stated goals of the organization, certain responsibilities and tasks must be accomplished. To be efficient and effective, a sport club must have a structure that assigns task to various units or personnel in the organization. A club operates efficiently when a situation arises and staff members know whether it is their responsibility based on the organizational structure. A call that comes into the club asking if a club team wants to participate in an upcoming tournament should be directed to the director of coaching, who oversees teams' tournament schedules. Task assignments are presented in job descriptions and are easily understood through the use of an organizational chart that shows the reporting lines for the organization and who is responsible for what.

The most effective way to structure a sport club is by function or task. Organizations can have either simple or complex organizational structures. A club with many full-time employees may give those employees specialized responsibilities. The key to an effective structure is grouping similar tasks and having employees performing those tasks report to a supervisor who oversees that area. For example, a club may separate its structure into sport and business. The sport function would include the recreational sport component, the competitive team component, league management, scheduling, tournament management, and the management and operations of the facility. The business side could include the accounting and budgeting, marketing and sales, and participant registration. One person or a department may handle each of those areas; a sport director may oversee the sport side of the club, and a business director may oversee the business side. An executive director would have the responsibility of overseeing both aspects of the club. To see the reporting lines and how similar tasks are grouped together, see figure 1.2.

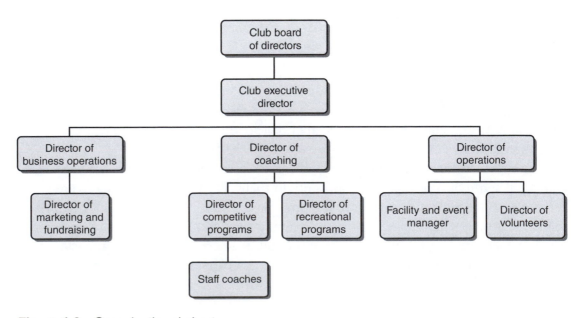

Figure 1.2 Organizational chart.

In the case of a club that has only one or a few full-time staff members, the organizational structure may be simple. A club director may have all of the responsibilities listed previously, or one person may handle either the sport aspect or business aspect, while the club director oversees the overall club plus that area. The reporting lines are very short in a simple organization. Figure 1.2 shows the organizational chart of a simple organization.

Clubs that rely on volunteers to carry out their operations need to develop an organizational structure for their volunteers. Some clubs' constitutions create volunteer positions such as fund-raising chair, recreation league commissioner, travel team coordinator, annual tournament chair, concessions chair, and membership chair. The upside of a volunteer workforce is that workers provide their services for free. The downside is that volunteers sometimes may not make their volunteer work a priority. Club leaders should make sure that a person taking on the responsibility of volunteer chair can make a commitment to executing the responsibilities.

In addition to deciding between a complex and simple organizational structure, club leaders must also determine whether the club is to be centralized or decentralized. In a **centralized** organizational style, all decisions are approved by the supervisor. If a call comes in about a tournament, the person assigned the task of scheduling tournaments has to clear her decision with the executive director of the club even if she knows the team is free and eligible to play in the tournament. A benefit of the centralized organizational style is that the executive director has the best interest of the club in mind and knows where each decision fits into the big picture. However, such a style slows down decision making, results in positions that are less autonomous, and hampers the professional development of employees, who are not given the opportunity to develop decision-making skills. Also, while waiting for a response from a supervisor, an opportunity may pass.

centralized—An organizational style that requires that all decisions be approved by club leadership.

Clubs that use a **decentralized** organizational style hire good people and let them do their jobs. Criteria may be established for when an employee has the autonomy to make a decision and when he must seek approval—for example, that every purchase over $500 must be approved by the executive director or that the executive director must approve decisions that affect other parts of the club.

decentralized—An organizational style in which employees have the autonomy to make decisions.

Summary

Many sport clubs start out with the same great intentions that Bob Armstrong had, but somehow get lost along the way. Club leaders must determine what the club is and what it wants to be by communicating its philosophy, its continuing purpose, and what the club will look like when it has reached its full potential. With this in mind a club needs a philosophy and mission and vision statements. These statements should be the bedrock of the club and should be publicized and communicated to everyone associated with the club. They also should be revisited and revised when appropriate.

Once they have established the club, club leaders also need to understand the range of services the club will offer. Will the club be everything to everybody or specialize in one area for one age group at one skill level? At this point club leaders should determine how they plan to attain the club goals within each subunit of the club and in the club as a whole. These goals communicate priorities to the club members, provide direction for employees, and provide performance measures for the club.

Club leaders also need to decide how the club will be organized: sole proprietorship, partnership, franchise, limited liability corporation, or nonprofit corporation. Each business structure has pros and cons to be considered. If a board is a part of the club structure, the makeup of the board, its role and power, and a way to evaluate the effectiveness of the board must be considered. Finally, club leaders must determine whether the club will be centralized, with all decisions made at the top, or decentralized, with employees being given the autonomy to make decisions.

The elements discussed in this chapter are the foundation for the creation or reorganization of a club. Skipping over them may lead to the club drifting away from what it had originally intended to be. An existing club can benefit from taking the time to revisit its philosophy, vision, and mission as well as the services it offers and its policies and procedures to determine whether it is still the club it set out to be. Successful clubs don't happen by accident.

———————————————— •●• ————————————————

Because Bob wanted to retain total control of his club and, more important, his dream, he opted to form an LLC so that he could be both owner and operator. Although he was aware of the tax benefits of forming a 501(c) corporation, he was not comfortable reporting to a board or risking being removed from the club he created. Bob secured loans and used the savings from his professional career to build an indoor and outdoor beach volleyball facility. He has four full-time employees, and more than 500 youths over multiple age groups and skill levels are training and playing for Armstrong Volleyball Club (AVC). Bob is living his dream.

———————————————— •●• ————————————————

By the end of the chapter, the sport club manager will be able to do the following:

▶ Explain the various management theories
▶ Acknowledge the importance of planning, organizing, leading, and evaluating
▶ List the three levels of management and the skills associated with each
▶ Evaluate leadership styles
▶ Describe the sources of individual and organizational power
▶ Distinguish among the general, task, and internal environments

2

Leading a Sport Club

Fifteen years ago the East Wilmington Lacrosse Club was created and Steve Goodwin was named the executive director by the club's board of directors. Steve had been an assistant executive director at a successful club in another state and has an undergraduate degree in management and a master's degree in sport management. Under Steve's leadership the club has consistently produced state championship teams, numerous players have earned college scholarships, and the club's facilities have expanded to include multiple fields (several of which are lighted) and an indoor complex.

Across town the West Wilmington Lacrosse Club started at approximately the same time as the East Wilmington club. West Wilmington has gone through a variety of executive directors who were not prepared for the responsibilities of the position. As a result, the club has not prospered. It has never won a state cup and its teams usually have losing records. Players often leave for other clubs, coaches and other employees leave because of the lack of leadership and direction, and the club has never moved beyond renting fields from the local high school.

What is the difference between the two clubs? Could it lie in leadership?

The club sport environment consists of thousands of sport organizations on several levels. Some clubs consist of one coach with a team of 12 basketball players competing in a local league; others are large organizations with 10 full-time staff members with several thousand participants of all ages. At all levels, some clubs are more successful than others. This chapter presents an overview of management and leadership theories and concepts that a club manager must understand, apply, evaluate, and synthesize to achieve the success Steve Goodwin achieved in the opening scenario. The chapter provides a theoretical base for understanding management and presents an overview of the functions and levels of management, sources of power, and the club sport environment.

Organizational and Management Theory

organizational theory—A theory that focuses on the nonhuman concepts of an organization such as goals, systems, organizational structure, policy, and procedures.

There are two ways to view a sport club—from an organizational theorist view or an organizational behaviorist view. **Organizational theory** focuses on the larger organization, whereas **organizational behavior** emphasizes the small group or individual within the organization (Slack, 1997). Organizational theorists explore concepts such as goals, systems, organizational structure, policy, and procedures. Organizational behaviorists focus on the individuals and small groups of people within the organization and study how their behavior affects the organization. Both must be studied to fully understand the forces affecting the management of a sport club. Chapter 1 addresses organizational theory in the form of the policies and procedures of operating the club. This chapter is steeped in organizational behavior, specifically examining the behavior of those who lead sport clubs.

organizational behavior—A theory that focuses on the individuals within the organization and how their behavior affects the organization.

management—The ability to get people to achieve organizational objectives through planning, organizing, implementing, controlling, and coordinating.

Management can be defined as the ability to get people to achieve organizational objectives through planning, organizing, implementing, controlling, and coordinating. Three major management theories can be applied to a sport club (figure 2.1). This section of the chapter examines the works and ideas of Freder-

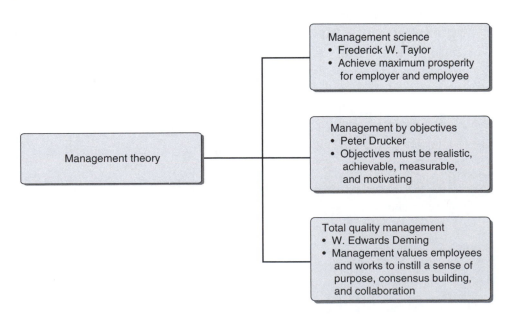

Figure 2.1 Management theories applicable to sport clubs.

ick W. Taylor, who was the first to view management as a science; Peter Drucker, who introduced management by objectives (MBO); and W. Edwards Deming, who devised the model of total quality management (TQM). Each theory is discussed briefly so that club managers can consider how they might apply it to their given situations.

Although this section briefly discusses the works of Taylor, Drucker, and Deming, entire books are devoted to these men and their theories. In addition to reading books on their respective sports, club managers should also read books on managing organizations so they have a sound theoretical understanding of the issues involved in managing their clubs or the subunits of their clubs.

Early Management Theory

The beginnings of management theory rest with Frederick Taylor, long considered the father of scientific management. Taylor (1911) stressed that management should work to secure maximum prosperity for the employer and employees. Taylor asserted that an organization cannot prosper unless the employees of the club prosper as well. To achieve maximum prosperity according to Taylor's system, managers should do the following:

1. *Develop a science for each element of a man's work.* The club environment includes coaches, administrators, directors of coaching, and directors of marketing and fund-raising.

2. *Scientifically select and then train, teach, and develop employees instead of requiring employees to chose their areas and train themselves.* Educational opportunities such as National Soccer Coaches Association of America (NSCAA) licensing courses prepare coaches and directors of coaching, and a sport management undergraduate degree can prepare a person to manage the facility, leagues, and programs.

3. *Heartily cooperate with employees to ensure that all work is completed according to the standards developed in the first point.* Club managers hire employees and then work with them to achieve the goals established for their positions, whether they entail winning state cups, developing players, or raising funds for the organization.

4. *Equally divide the responsibility between managers and employees so that managers focus on areas better suited to them and employees are not overextended.* Club managers take on responsibility and delegate the appropriate amount of responsibility to the other club employees.

Management by Objectives

Management by objectives, developed by Peter Drucker, is a management theory designed to encourage collaboration between management and employees to achieve success. According to Drucker (1954), objectives must be realistic, achievable, measurable, and motivating. Otherwise, they are meaningless. Drucker further postulated that objectives are inherently more realistic, achievable, measurable, and motivating when they are developed collaboratively with management and employees based on open discussion and mutual agreement. Individual and

management by objectives—A management theory designed to encourage collaboration between management and employees. Success is achieved by establishing objectives that are realistic, achievable, measurable, and motivating.

unit objectives must also align with the organization's overall objectives to achieve overall success.

Applying Drucker's theory to the sport club environment would entail the club leadership in collaboration with the board and the staff establishing goals and objectives for staff members, the units or departments of the club, and the overall club. These goals could apply to the number of participants recruited; the number of players selected for state teams or teams advancing to state, regional, and national championships; the revenue generated for the club; or the revenue generated through fund-raising, corporate sponsorship, or both.

Total Quality Management

total quality management—A management theory based on instilling a sense of purpose in the employees and focusing on continuous process improvement and the elimination of elements that don't promote quality.

Total quality management (TQM) is based on management instilling a sense of purpose in employees and developing a positive environment through consensus building and collaboration between management and employees. Managers using TQM focus on educating and training employees and understand that the process is cyclical (which means that TQM focuses on continuous process improvement and the elimination of elements that don't promote quality). A club manager who adheres to TQM believes that the club can always get better and listens to employees to learn how that can happen. TQM also emphasizes that the product should do what it is supposed to do. If a club is supposed to be producing elite players, then that is what it should be doing. Finally, TQM focuses on the customer having a positive experience with the product. TQM is about promoting quality throughout the organization so that in the end the club member is satisfied.

Functions of Management

Chelladurai (2001) mentioned that the functions of management have evolved from the original list of five (planning, organizing, commanding, coordinating, and controlling) presented by Fayol (1949). While recognizing Fayol's (1949) original list, Chelladurai (2001) asserted that the functions that are most applicable to the sport environment are planning, organizing, leading, and evaluating (figure 2.2).

planning—Setting goals for the organization and its members and specifying the activities or programs through which to achieve those goals.

Planning may be the most important process within the function of management. The old saying is, "Organizations don't plan to fail; they fail to plan!" Chelladurai (2001) defined planning as "setting goals for the organization and its members and specifying the activities or programs through which to achieve those goals" (p. 95). In planning, the club manager must identify the desired outcome, understand what environmental constraints are present, and establish activities that will lead to the desired outcome. What steps must be taken for a club to win a state or national championship? What must be done to increase participation levels for in-house recreation leagues? What is needed to increase ancillary revenues for a club? These are questions for the planning process.

Successful planning involves all elements of the club. An effective way to plan is to hold an annual retreat to develop objectives and plans for achieving those objectives. Once plans are made, however, the club manager must also recognize the need to be flexible to adjust to real-life situations that arise that were not foreseen in the original planning.

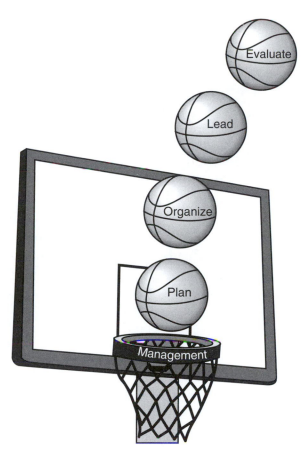

Figure 2.2   An understanding of these functions of management is important to being an effective manager in the sport world.

Chelladurai (2001) described **organizing** as the process of breaking down the jobs that must be completed to achieve the organizational goals and defining the relationships between the jobs and the people in the organization. Organizing requires a club manager to be able to see the big picture while also assigning the smaller tasks to the people within the organization who execute the day-to-day operations.

To see Taylor's principle in action, let's consider the scenario of a club manager hiring a director of coaching. The manager must be able to recognize that the person has the skill, experience, and temperament to be the director of coaching. The club manager needs to communicate that the responsibility of the director of coaching is to oversee and develop the coaches who work with the athletes. The club manager also needs to communicate that coaches should be training and developing athletes to meet the club's goal to develop elite national-level players. (Job descriptions are discussed in chapter 3.)

Leading is another important function of management. Chelladurai (2001) recognized that planning and organizing "set the stage for work activities" (p. 97) and stated that leading deals with influencing or motivating the employees to execute the responsibilities assigned in the organizing step to reach the goals developed in the planning process. A leader may have a good plan and have organized the employees well, but if she cannot influence the members of the organization to

organizing—Breaking down the jobs that must be completed to achieve the organizational goals and defining the relationships between the jobs and the people in the organization.

leading—Influencing or motivating employees to execute the responsibilities assigned in the organizing step to reach the goals developed in the planning process.

perform, the organization is doomed to failure. Some people are uncomfortable leading. They would rather be told what to do than to direct others. Whether the club achieves its goals and objectives will depend greatly on the ability of the club to influence others to work toward achieving its goals. The leadership styles and sources of power that enable leaders to influence the members of an organization are discussed later in the chapter.

evaluating—Measuring performance and comparing that performance to the standards set in the planning process.

Chelladurai (2001) defined **evaluating** as measuring performance and comparing that performance to standards set in the planning process. A manager must evaluate many aspects of the organization ranging from processes to personnel and evaluate feedback to determine whether the process or the behavior of those in the organization is working or in need of corrective action. Evaluating is a major part of TQM because it helps managers know when a modification to a process or personnel issue is necessary. What is the club's player selection process? What should be done if a player who is cut from a team leaves the club and excels on a rival club's team? Does this indicate a breakdown in the system? Is the facility schedule always incorrect, do games start late, and is the facility not up to the club's standards of excellence? Does the club need to find a new facility manager?

These four functions are the foundation of managing an organization. Club managers who practice these functions increase their club's chances of success. Planning, organizing, leading, and evaluating are important as independent functions, but they also affect one another. A sport leader must be conscious of the functions and strive to master them to succeed.

Levels of Management

Within a sport club there are three levels of management: top-level, midlevel, and first-level. The responsibilities of each level vary in terms of context as well as importance, and at each level a different managerial skill is of a greatest importance. In smaller organizations a manager may operate at all three levels; larger clubs may have three distinct levels.

technical skills—A leader's knowledge of operations, activities, processes, inventory, and the mechanics of performing particular tasks.

The general skills used throughout the levels of management are technical, human, and conceptual (figure 2.3). Bridges and Roquemore (1996) defined **technical skills** as "knowledge of operations, activities, processes, inventory and the mechanics of performing particular job tasks" (p. 37). In a sport club this could include coaching; facility management; league, camp, and tournament management; and travel and sponsorship sales. Katz (1974) saw these technical skills as being specialized to a given organization or area within an organization.

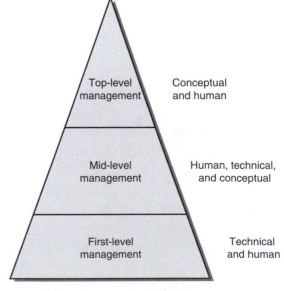

Figure 2.3   Management skills needed at each level of management.

Katz (1974) defined **human skills** as "the leader's ability to work effectively as a group member and to build a cooperative effort within the teams he or she leads" (p. 91). Human skills enable a sport club leader to motivate people to achieve their goals, to get volunteers to work on a weekend to host a tournament, or to get a coach to improve a team that won only one game the year before.

Bridges and Roquemore (1996) believed that **conceptual skills** are the rarest of all skills. Katz defined these skills as "the ability to see the organization as a whole, [including] recognizing how the various functions of the organization depend on one another and how changes in any one part affect all the others" (p. 93). The club manager with conceptual skills can see the existing club that borrows fields and whose teams are coached by unskilled volunteers 10 years out with a new facility, top coaches, and teams that compete with the best clubs in the country. Such a manager also has the know-how to get there.

First-Level Manager

First-level managers focus on technical aspects and may have some responsibility for overseeing others. An example of this would be a staff coach. His main responsibility is to train teams. He plans practice sessions and implements those plans. To assist him with these responsibilities, he may have volunteer coaches. Although he has subordinates, he is still very involved in the technical aspects of the position and may be working side-by-side with his subordinates to ensure that sessions run as planned. The staff coach may not have a great deal of say in how the overall club is run, but he will do his part in achieving the overall goals of the organization by making sure the participants are having positive experiences in training sessions and over the course of a season.

human skills—A leader's ability to work effectively as a group member and to build a cooperative effort within the teams led.

conceptual skills—A leader's ability to see the club as a whole and how the various functions of the organization depend on one another and how changes in any one part affect all the others.

first-level manager—A leader who mostly uses technical skills but also human skills.

Courtesy of the Brandywine Youth Club

As a first-level manager, this coach's responsibilities include training his athletes, overseeing their practice, and ultimately helping them improve their skills.

Midlevel Manager

A **midlevel manager** is more involved with the management of staff while also participating in the conceptual aspects of leading an organization. The technical aspect is not as significant at this level as it is at the first level. A person in this position is usually promoted from a first-level management position. In a sport club, the midlevel manager could be the director of coaching (DOC), who oversees five staff coaches. This person may have been promoted from the ranks of staff coach or gained experience at another club. The DOC oversees the five staff coaches and works with them to achieve the goals established for each coach. During a given day she may review practice plans with a staff coach, discuss problems a staff coach is having, select the tournaments in which teams will participate, and evaluate a staff coach's training session.

Another midlevel manager is the business manager. A person in this position oversees the administrative staff, the business operations staff, and the marketing and fund-raising personnel. Like the DOC, the business manager works with first-level managers to achieve the subunit goals that are tied to the overall success of the club.

Along with motivating those under her charge, a midlevel manager must understand the role of her department in the overall achievement of the club's goals. For example, the club executive director may communicate that a certain amount of revenue must be generated to cover the expenses of the club and for club teams to be successful. A DOC must think in a broader organizational context. Knowing that participant registration is a significant source of revenue for the club, the DOC must play her part in recruiting and retaining participants. In addition to thinking in terms of the sport, the DOC must appreciate the fact that revenue generation is an integral part in maintaining and growing the sport.

Top-Level Manager

The **top-level manager** sets the vision for the club. He needs to see the big picture and how all of the units interact to achieve organizational goals. Again, considering the scenario in the first-level section, the former staff coach who rose to director of coaching has now become the executive director of the club. As a top-level manager, he must understand not only the sport but also the business side of the club. If the business manager rose to the top of the club, she would have to have a grasp of the sport side of the club.

The executive director or club president has a vision of the club's elite teams competing for state, regional, and national championships; he wants athletes from the club to earn athletic and academic scholarships to high schools and colleges; he would like to see a 10 percent growth in in-house recreation league participation; he would like to generate 30 percent of the operating budget from corporate sponsorship and fund-raising efforts; and he would like to see an all-weather surface field with lights constructed within five years. Having set this vision for the club, the executive director needs to have midlevel managers buy in to his vision, and he needs to motivate them to do their part in realizing it.

Centerville United Soccer Association

In January of 2009 the Centerville United Soccer Association (CUSA) hired Brett Thompson as the club's first executive director. Thompson came to the club as one of the most influential and well-respected people in Ohio South, Region 2, of the United States Soccer Federation, and nationally. Previously, Thompson was the director of coaching and education for the Ohio South Youth Soccer Association (OSYSA), a position he had held since 2002.

The CUSA organization consists of four programs: CUSA Recreational; CUSA Courage (youth competitive program: U8–U14); Ohio Galaxies Futbol Club (high school program: U15–U18); and the Mead Cup Tournament (youth program).

The leaders of CUSA hired Thompson because they wanted the club to be one of the top clubs not only in Ohio South but also in all of Region 2 and for it to be known regionally and nationally as a club that focuses on a quality soccer education and experience for the children and families who are members of the organization.

In his new position Thompson works closely with all four CUSA programs and oversees the day-to-day operations while charting the long-term course for the club. He also supervises three full-time directors of coaching and reports to the CUSA executive board, which has equal representation from all four programs.

When Thompson was hired, Dean Burgess, president of CUSA's executive board, stated, "We couldn't be more excited as a Club to bring a person with the all around qualities and experience that Brett has to lead our Club into the future. Brett's passion and desire to 'make a difference' and to help children develop is critical to our Club's vision and future. His diverse communication skills allow him to work with a 5-year-old on a soccer field one minute, and present topics such as 'Player Empowerment' and 'How to build a Model Soccer club' at the National Youth Soccer Workshop the next minute. These characteristics make Brett a very unique individual and we are thrilled he has joined the CUSA family. We believe the addition of Brett Thompson will bring even greater opportunities and experiences to the people we serve which are the children and families that participate in our great organization."

It appears CUSA has hired a proven leader who is prepared for the responsibilities assigned to him, and that the club's best days are ahead.

Information from www.cusasoccer.org/

The executive director may realize that the club is behind in player development. He communicates to his middle manager, the DOC, the need to enhance the training of the club's athletes by adopting a long-term athlete development (LTAD) philosophy (see chapter 9). The DOC works with the executive director to learn more about LTAD and implementing it across the club. The DOC then communicates the LTAD plan to the first-level managers and the staff coaches, who go about implementing the new initiatives when working with the athletes.

A successful organization clearly delineates the levels of management. All three play an integral part in achieving the club's goals. Top-level managers rise from the ranks of midlevel and first-level managers. Skills needed at all three levels are important, and managers must understand how to use them at the various levels.

Leadership Styles

Those in management positions must develop a leadership style. The selection of the style is contingent on the leader's personal traits, the people she will lead,

McGregor's theory X—A theory that contends that employees inherently dislike work and therefore must be coerced into doing it; they avoid responsibility, prefer to be directed, have little ambition, and value personal security above all else.

McGregor's theory Y—A theory that contends that employees view work as a source of satisfaction, are committed to achieving organizational objectives, are self-motivated and self-directed and accept responsibility, and find work as natural as play.

autocratic leaders—A leadership style in which the leader tells subordinates what to do and expects them to do it.

and the nature of the activity. Ultimately, the leader has to select a style that will be most effective for the situation at hand.

Mondy, Shaplin, and Premeaux (1991) identified four general leadership styles: autocratic, democratic, participative, and laissez-faire (table 2.1). Each is discussed here within the context of **McGregor's theories X and Y**. (The sidebar on page 33 can help you determine if you and your employees are a theory X or a theory Y.) McGregor (1960) contended that people manage others based on two theories of employee motivation. Managers who subscribe to theory Y believe that employees view work as a source of satisfaction, are committed to achieving organizational objectives, are self-motivated and self-directed and accept responsibility, and find work as natural as play. An exemplar of theory Y would be a club staff member who looks to create new initiatives and is the first in the office in the morning and the last to leave at night. He asks for the responsibility of developing a coaching course for volunteer coaches or runs an individual training session for an athlete who wants to work on a particular skill.

Managers who subscribe to theory X believe that employees inherently dislike work and therefore must be coerced into doing it; they avoid responsibility, prefer to be directed, have little ambition, and value personal security above all else. An exemplar of this theory would be a staff member who shows up on time and leaves on time. She does only what she is asked or told to do and just wants a weekly paycheck and the guarantee of a job. Theory X workers do what they are told; they don't seek responsibility.

Autocratic leaders tend to tells subordinates what to do and expect them to do it. The subordinates of an autocratic leader are not involved in decision making and have little if any autonomy. The autocratic leadership style is commonly practiced by people who view their employees as having a theory X orientation and in situations in which tasks are simple and repetitive (Mondy et al., 1991). Autocratic leaders tend to believe that subordinates would provide input that would lead to less work or responsibility for them rather than to achieving organizational goals.

Table 2.1   Pros and Cons of Leadership Styles

Style	Pros	Cons
Autocratic	• Effective for theory X workers • Gives leader control over decisions	• Loses effectiveness over time • Theory Y workers may not respond • Does not develop future leaders
Democratic	• Results in high employee morale • Motivates theory Y workers	• Leader gives up decision-making responsibility • Leader has to abide by a vote
Participative	• Results in high employee morale • Grows future leaders	• Theory X workers may not give input that is in the best interest of the club
Laissez-faire	• Results in high employee morale • Grows future leaders	• If a worker is unqualified, the club may suffer

Employee X or Y?

Are you a theory X or a theory Y employee? What is the orientation of the other employees at your club?

Theory Y

- Experiences work as a source of satisfaction
- Is committed to organizational success
- Is self-directed and self-motivated
- Likes responsibility

Theory X

- Sees work as just a job
- Is committed to personal security
- Does what is directed to do
- Avoids responsibility

Autocratic leadership may be effective with employees with a theory X orientation, but any success may be short term. Motivated subordinates with a theory Y orientation eventually tire of the lack of autonomy and leave to look for positions with more autonomy. The autocratic DOC who tells the coaches what to do in practice, when to practice, and how to manage a game may lose motivated coaches who want the autonomy to make those decisions themselves. Also, clubs that use an autocratic leadership style do not cultivate future leaders because employees are not given the opportunity to make even minor decisions.

Democratic leaders seek input from subordinates and do what the majority of subordinates want. Some argue that a democratic leader is more of a facilitator than a leader. A person who selects this leadership style views his employees as having more of a theory Y orientation. This type of leader trusts that subordinates will make decisions that will enable the club to attain its goals. For this to happen, the subordinates need to be highly motivated employees who are looking out for the best interests of the organization. This style can lead to high employee morale because employees feel a part of the decision-making process and in turn buy in to the vision of the organization.

democratic leader—A leadership style in which the leader seeks input from subordinates and will do what the majority of subordinates want.

Some leaders have difficulty adopting a democratic style because they believe that doing so would force them to give up ultimate control. This can be especially difficult because ultimately the leader will be judged on the success or failure of his decision. An example of this would be an executive director who holds a staff meeting in which the staff puts forth ideas on what tournaments teams should attend for the coming year and what capital projects should be addressed. The staff votes on the actions to implement for the upcoming year. The executive director may not agree with the majority, but he has to live with and ultimately implement the initiatives.

Participative leaders tend to involve subordinates in leadership activities and decision making, but ultimately they retain final authority. Like democratic leaders, participative leaders view their subordinates as having a theory Y orientation. They differ from democratic leaders in that even though they seek input, they make the final decisions. Like the democratic style, the participative style helps develop future leaders and leads to high morale among employees, who feel a part of leading the

participative leaders—A leadership style in which the leader involves subordinates in leadership activities and decision making, but ultimately the leader retains final authority.

organization. An added benefit is that the leader is getting input from those with expertise in given areas. Consider a club's executive director who needs to make a decision related to marketing. Her background prior to becoming the executive director was in coaching. She consults her business director about the situation. She may decide to use all or some of the input, or she may disregard the business director's input altogether. Ultimately, the decision is hers.

A **laissez-faire leader** takes a hands-off approach to leadership, allowing subordinates to make decisions. The mantra of a laissez-faire leader is "Hire good people and get out of their way." The laissez-faire leader defers to the person he has selected for a given position to provide the leadership in that area. This type of leader offers incredible autonomy to subordinates—so much so that it can be argued that it goes beyond a theory Y orientation.

The most important aspect of the laissez-faire leadership style is the recruitment and hiring of qualified people. If an executive director of a club comes from the ranks of the marketing side of a club, she should look to hire the best person possible to run the sport side of the club because she will be turning those decisions over to that person. She chooses someone who knows how to select good coaches, knows how to train players, is a master in game strategy, and relates well with parents and athletes. The executive director then steps back and lets this person work his magic for the benefit of the club. The executive director's role, then, is to support that person and give him what he needs to be successful and to achieve the club's goals.

Adopting an autocratic, democratic, participative, or laissez-faire style of leadership is contingent on the personal traits of the leader, the people being led, and the nature of the activity. Each style has a track record of success, so leaders must carefully consider them all before adopting one of them.

laissez-faire leaders—A leadership style in which the leaders takes a hands-off approach and allow subordinates to make decisions.

Power

Power can be defined as the ability to get people to do things they would not ordinarily do. Those who lead sport clubs use power to achieve the club's goals. They must understand the individual and organizational sources of power and determine which powers they can use.

power—The ability to get people to do things they would not ordinarily do.

Individual Power

French and Raven (1959) cited five forms of power a leader can use to influence others to do things that they may not normally do. It is the use of these powers that motives the subordinates to do what they are asked to do.

▶ **Legitimate power** is power that is inherent in the position. Subordinates respond because the person is in a position to tell them to do something. A coach does what a director of coaching tells her to do because he is the DOC and coaches are supposed to listen to and follow those directives. The DOC derives his power from the title. Parents often refer to this form of power when their children ask why they have to do something and they respond, "because I told you so and I am the parent!"

legitimate power—Power that is inherent in a position.

▶ **Reward power** is derived from the leader's ability to provide rewards to those who do what is asked of them. These rewards can come in the form of raises, promotions, recommendations, and perks. An employee responsible for selling sponsorship for the club does what the executive director asks because he knows the executive director makes decisions on raises and bonuses, and the employee would like a bonus for the upcoming year.

reward power—Power that is derived from the ability to provide rewards to those who do what is asked of them.

▶ **Coercive power** is based on the leader being able to punish those who do not do what is asked of them. A coach responds to an order from the DOC because she fears the wrath of the DOC if she does not follow the order. The punishment can come in the form of a demotion, the removal of certain responsibilities, suspension, or firing. Coercive power motives, but as with the autocratic leadership style, it eventually loses its effectiveness. Theory Y workers do not respond well to coercive power. They do not have to be threatened into action; they act on their own accord.

coercive power—Power based on the leader's ability to punish those who do not do what is asked of them.

▶ **Referent power** refers to the force of the leader's personality. Subordinates respond to the personal qualities of a leader with referent power. The personality traits of a leader with referent power can vary, and certain people respond to certain qualities. The term often associated with referent power is *charisma*. A coach who works under a DOC with referent power may come in on his off day to help plan an upcoming tournament because he likes the DOC and wants to help him.

referent power—Power that comes from subordinates responding to the personal qualities of a leader.

▶ A leader who relies on **expert power** is one who has knowledge or expertise to which a subordinate wants access. A coach may want to work for a respected director of coaching or executive director to learn from the expert. A young swimming coach or aspiring club manager may want to work under Bob Bowman, coach of Olympic champion Michael Phelps, to learn about training world-class athletes and running a very successful swim club.

expert power—Power that comes from the knowledge or expertise of the leader, to which a subordinate wants access.

Organizational Power

Along with determining the source of their individual power, club leaders also need to assess and understand the degree of power of the organizational subunits and their leaders. Slack (1997) identified five sources of **organizational power.** The first source Slack (1997) identified was acquisition of resources. A subunit that has the ability to secure the recourses needed by the organization has more power than one that does not. For example, a club leader who, because of her reputation, is able to attract top talent as well as a lot of players to the club would have more power within the club than a coach who, although qualified, does not have the ability to attract players to the club. On the business side of the club, the marketing director who is able to generate significant revenue for the club through the sale of sponsorships and fund-raising efforts would wield more power than the administrator who organizes the leagues. Again, the marketing department wields the power because it generates revenue that is essential to the club's success.

organizational power—The power of organizational subunits to get others to do what they otherwise may not do.

The second source of organizational power is the ability to cope with uncertainty. The club sport environment changes quickly, and uncertainty is associated with change. Hickson, Hinings, Lee, Schneck, and Pennings (1971) cited three ways to address uncertainty: acquiring information about future trends, taking action after the fact, and prevention. Subunits and their leaders who are able to address or prevent uncertainty have more power than those that do not have the ability to respond. Consider a club that leases its facility and is told by the landlord that it must vacate the premise within one month due to a violation of the lease. The club business manager knows the terms of the lease and also knows the legal system and so can get a temporary restraining order to prevent the landlord from evicting the club from the facility until the courts can determine who is right in the case. Addressing the uncertainty through knowledge prevents the club from losing its facility and in essence shutting down.

The third source focuses on centrality. The more central a subunit is to the primary focus of a sport organization, the more power that subunit will have based on centrality. The central purpose of a sport club is to offer participation opportunities. With this in mind, it can be argued that coaches have more power within the organization than those who hold positions that are less central (e.g., marketing directors, facility managers, office managers). In essence, there would be no need for these positions if there were not participants there to be coached. Using this rationale, the coach is closer to the core purpose of the club than the others, and thus the coaching department has greater power within the organization.

The fourth source is the level of non-substitutability. A subunit and its leader who are viewed as irreplaceable would have more power than those that could be replaced. Again, the successful coach who wins and is able to attract players based on her reputation would be harder to replace than the person who organizes the in-house recreation leagues. If that coach left, the club may not be able to replace her with someone who would be as successful. So in this case, the team and coach would have more power within the organization than a person and a subunit that provides a service that, although important, can be done by someone else. Clubs vary in terms of who or what subunit would be the hardest to replace.

The final source of organizational power is the control over the decision making process. Subunits of the club engage in decision making, and Slack (1997) stated that those subunits "that influence what decisions are made, when decisions are made, who is involved in the decision process and what alternatives are presented have power" (p. 184). A business director who oversees the fund-raising and marketing efforts may be consulted about the feasibility of embarking on a capital campaign to renovate the club facilities. He would provide guidance on when the campaign should begin and suggest donors and corporations that could purchase naming rights. The fact the business director is consulted demonstrates the power the business unit and its director have within the club.

Sport club managers need to determine the source of their individual power and assess the level of organizational power of the various subunits. Individual power gets people to do what they may not want to do. Understanding the sources of organizational powers and recognizing the degree of that power within an organization is important for a sport leader as well.

Understanding the Environment

Sport clubs do not operate in vacuums. A number of factors outside and inside the organization can either contribute to or detract from the club achieving its goals (figure 2.4). A leader not cognizant of these environmental factors is doomed to failure.

The **external environment** consists of the general and task environments. Slack (1997) defined the **general environment** as those sectors that may not have a direct impact on the operations of a sport organization but can and sometimes do influence decisions made by the organization. In other words, aspects of the general environment may affect other aspects of society of which the sport club is a part. Slack (1997) listed the elements of the general environment as political, economic, demographic, sociocultural, legal, environmental, and technological.

In terms of politics, a local government entity promises a sport club the lease of a piece of land for $1 a year so the club can build a new facility. However, the politician who has viewed the club favorably and made the promise is not reelected and the new politician has other plans for that land. There goes the facility. This demonstrates the impact of politics on a club's achieving its goals.

external environment— Factors outside the club that affect the club's ability to achieve its goals.

general environment— Factors that may not have a direct impact on the operations of a sport club but can influence decisions made by the club.

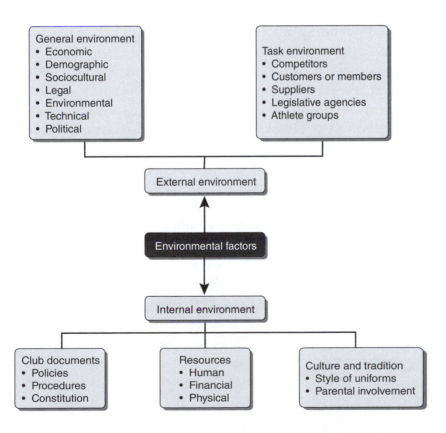

Figure 2.4   Internal and external environmental factors that affect club success.

In 2008 the price of gas increased significantly, causing an increase in the cost of other goods. Also, Americans became increasingly less likely to drive or fly. A club that had counted on attracting a number of teams to its tournament lost participants from outside of the area because the cost of traveling had increased dramatically. Demographics weigh heavy in the pricing of a club. Pricing, as discussed in chapter 6, is partly based on what customers can afford. Club leaders must keep this in mind when setting the price structure. Mistakes include pricing the club out of the market and charging too little, creating a negative impression of the quality of the club.

As presented in chapter 5, a club must know laws, statutes, and standards established by governments, precedent cases, and sport governing bodies and adhere to them. In terms of environmental factors, sport leaders can't fool mother nature. Sport clubs must have contingency plans for weather conditions such as rain, snow, lightning, and heat. For example, if a club relies on a summer outdoor tournament as a significant revenue source, it may want to purchase an insurance policy for the event in case it has to be cancelled because of weather and entry fees have to be refunded.

Finally, an effective sport leader must keep abreast of technological advances. The Internet, e-mail databases, scheduling software, and operating systems have become standards, and leaders must keep abreast of changes in these technologies. Clubs that do not adapt are at a competitive disadvantage. For example, online registration is very convenient for parents of participants. A club that does not provide the convenience of online registration may lose participants to another club that does.

task environment—
Factors that directly affect the club and whether it achieves its organizational goals.

Slack (1997) defined the **task environment** as more directly tied to the sport organization than the general environment. The elements of the task environment directly affect the club and whether it achieves its organizational goals. Competitors, customers, members, fans, suppliers, legislative agencies, and athlete groups are all aspects of the task environment. In terms of competitors, an aspect of sport that is unique is that two clubs may compete on the court or field, but away from it they may cooperate. For example, a basketball club in New York may share ideas on sponsorship or player retention strategies with a club in Los Angeles. They may compete at the national championships, but the sharing of ideas makes each a stronger club.

The leader of any organization must be conscious of the customer. This can be best summed up with the cliché "The customer is always right." A sport club that has a $100,000 corporate partner had better understand the concept of "under-promise and overdeliver" to keep that partner satisfied and willing to renew when the contract expires. This is also true about club participants. They are customers that have joined the club for a particular reason or as a result of a unique selling point. The club needs to deliver on that promise. If the club promised that an athlete would improve, coaches need to do everything in their power to work with the athlete to make that happen.

In terms of legislative agencies, it is safe to say that every sport organization must follow guidelines and rules established by a governing agency. For example, clubs must adhere to rules established by state and national sport associations. These regulations can include age requirements, club transfer policies, the number of contests, the number of guest players, and coaching credentials. Each sport has its own set of guidelines that clubs are required to follow. The actions of a sport organization and its members are limited by the guidelines and rules established by the agency. Not following those rules can lead to the suspensions of athletes and punishment of the clubs.

Besides external factors, clubs must also recognize the factors from within that affect what they do. These factors constitute the **internal environment.** Club managers must be cognizant of any official club documents that lay out the guidelines and policies and procedures for how the club is to be run. For example, a club should have a constitution and bylaws that serve as a framework for how the club will operate and be governed. These documents may address such issues as board composition and requirements for employment with the club. Club leaders must adhere to these documents.

internal environment— Factors within the club that affect the club.

The club should also have a policies and procedures manual that spells out how to do things. Policies are the rules that staff and members of the club must follow. Policies take away the need for decision making by spelling out how to act. A policy may be that a staff employee may not generate sport-related outside income. If the staff member asks the club's executive director if he can do personal training of athletes on the side, the executive director need only refer to the policy that has been established. If the staff member decides to do so anyway, there are grounds for punishment or termination. Procedures are the steps staff and participants need to take to act on policy. If the club has a policy that all parent volunteers must participate in a preseason training session, the procedure to enforce the policy is that parents sign up online, sign an attendance sheet at the start of the session, attend the session, take the exam, and confirm attendance by submitting the exam. Policies and procedures are extensions of the mission and vision of the club and provide the framework for it. These documents ensure that all involved with the club understand how it runs and ensure consistency in decision making and action.

Along with being familiar with the documents that create the framework for the club, leaders must also be conscious of the resources at their disposal. The three common forms of resources are human, financial, and physical. A club manager may want the club to be successful, but can that be accomplished with an all-volunteer coaching staff and no marketing director to sell sponsorships or generate revenue in other ways? These limited **human resources** will prevent the club manager from achieving her goals of developing players and winning state cups and generating the necessary revenue to grow the club.

human resources—The employees that a club has access to, to achieve its stated goals.

Limited **financial resources** is the most common complaint of club leaders. Clubs are often described as being either large or small. The larger clubs may get that designation based on the revenue generated from a large number of participants. The manager of a small club with few participants is contending with this internal environmental factor when trying to hire staff, offer programs, and maintain facilities. The revenue is not present to grow the club.

financial resources— Capital that a club has to achieve its stated goals.

physical resources—The space and facilities that a club has access to, to achieve its stated goals.

Finally, club managers must be conscious of their **physical resources.** In recent years many clubs have built or renovated facilities. The rationale was often that the current facilities did not meet the training and competition needs of the club. Many clubs offering outdoor sports have either installed all-weather terrain or built indoor facilities. Some have built knowing that they could generate revenue from the facility and contribute to the local economy by hosting events that would draw visitors from outside the area. Chapter 6 addresses the importance of the facility in the marketing of the club. It can either attract new club members or deter them from joining.

A club leader must also be conscious of the culture of the club and the traditions that have been established. Ignoring the culture and those traditions can be detrimental. For example, participants in a club may have worn a particular style of uniform or had a pregame ritual for decades. Changing or eliminating those elements of culture could cause an adverse reaction among the club staff and members who consider them vital to the club's identity.

Certain aspects of a club's culture may be negative and need to be eliminated. A new club manager, for instance, may adopt a policy that parents may not coach their children because favoritism had prevented the best players from being selected for teams. Changing the culture in this case may be for the best, but the club manager should expect resistance. Managers walk a thin line of recognizing which aspects of the culture cannot be changed and which need to be changed for the good of the club.

Environmental factors affect a manager's ability to lead the club. Recognizing, understanding the significance of, and adapting to the aspects of the general, task, and internal environments are vital to a manager's, and ultimately the club's, success.

Summary

It is not an accident that certain sport clubs are more successful than others. An appreciation of both organizational theory (the policies and procedures and organizational structure) and organizational behavior (leadership styles, sources of power, and understanding the environment) is essential to implementing the vision and mission presented in chapter 1.

Best practices and theories are associated with managing and leading a sport club, and those hired to lead the club should understand them and be well versed in them whether through formal education (e.g., a business administration or sport management degree) or through outside reading or professional development courses. Taylor was the first to communicate that it is best to take a scientific approach to leading an organization. The principles he put forth almost a century ago still ring true today for those leading sport clubs. Drucker's ideas of clearly defining the objectives and outcomes for a club help provide direction regarding motivating employees. A club that adheres to total quality management (TQM) always looks to improve and listens to its employees to find better ways to run the club and to eliminate anything that negatively affects the club's quality.

Along with understanding these theories, club leaders must also recognize the functions associated with managing and leading a club. According to Chelladurai (2001), the management functions most applicable to the sport environment are planning, organizing, leading, and evaluating. The size of the club determines how many levels of management are needed and the skills that are required at each level. First-level managers use technical skills and some human skills, whereas midlevel managers use human skills, technical skills, and some conceptual skills. Top-level managers use conceptual skills and some human skills. Leaders of small clubs may have to develop and use all of these skills.

While executing the previously stated functions and skills, a club leader must come to terms with his leadership style, determining which one fits his personality as well as that of the people he will be leading. McGregor's X and Y theories are helpful in determining which leadership style would be best for a given situation. In some instances, an autocratic approach is most appropriate; in others, a democratic or participative approach may be best, whereas others may take a laissez-faire approach. Again, the choice of style depends on the leader and the people he will be leading.

In addition to leadership style, club leaders need to appreciate the sources of individual and organizational power and use them to their benefit. As with leadership style, choosing these requires self-analysis and organizational analysis. Power enables leaders to get people to do what they want them to do. Finally, club leaders need to understand the environment and the constraints and opportunities presented in that environment that will either enhance or hinder their ability to lead.

The pace of the pack is set by the leader. Clubs that hire and retain good leaders reap the benefits of those leaders' abilities. Ultimately, it is the athletes in the club who benefit.

● ● ●

The West Wilmington Lacrosse Club board of directors finally wised up about hiring an executive director. In the past they had considered factors such as whether the person was a good player, was friends with a board member, or was looking for a change in career rather than his leadership ability, his understanding of the environment, his past experiences in leading and motivating people, and his long-term vision for the club. The most recent hire has those traits, and the club is headed in a different direction. It is now a true rival to the East Wilmington club.

● ● ●

By the end of the chapter, the sport club manager will be able to do the following:

► List the elements of human resources management.

► List the steps in the recruitment and hiring process that will lead to hiring the right people for the right positions.

► Design jobs that are challenging and rewarding to employees.

► Write effective job descriptions.

► Describe the components of an effective employee training program.

► Appreciate the importance of evaluation in professional development.

► Explain what should be evaluated in the evaluation process.

► Appreciate the importance of empowering staff members.

► Describe methods of enriching a position for a staff member.

► Recognize how pay, promotion, coworkers, the supervisor, the work itself, and the job in general affect the employee satisfaction.

► Appreciate the role of a rewards system in motivating employees.

3

Human Resources Management and Development

• • •

Rachel Anderson is the manager of a midsize multisport club in the midwestern United States. The club has teams in soccer, basketball, volleyball, lacrosse, and field hockey. The club board approved the funding for three full-time positions for the club and wants a proposal from Rachel defining the positions, the responsibilities, the compensation package, desired qualifications, and a plan for recruiting talented candidates for the positions. The board is also interested in seeing an evaluation plan to ensure that new hires are executing their responsibilities as well as growing professionally. In the past the club has primarily offered recreational sport opportunities, but it wants to expand into elite player development. The board also would like to see more revenue generated from selling sponsorships and renting its facilities to outside groups. The board has not been pleased with several past hires, and there has been a lot of turnover in staff over the past several years. The board would like to see that changed. Where does Rachel start the process, and how will she proceed?

• • •

The opening scenario addresses the issue of staffing a club. Club managers need to decide who to hire and then ensure that the new hire works for the betterment of the club. Too often the hiring process is not formalized and no evaluation plan or reward system is in place for employees of the club. This can lead to the hiring of unqualified personnel and club managers not knowing whether those hired are doing what they were hired to do.

human resources management—Having the right people in the right place at the right time who are capable of completing the tasks that help an organization achieve its continuing purpose.

Human resources management has been defined as ensuring that an organization has the right people in the right place at the right time who are capable of efficiently completing the tasks that help an organization achieve its goals (Robbins & Stuart-Kotze, 1990). Human resources management in the sport club environment entails understanding the club and its priorities and needs; recruiting and hiring the right staff for the right positions at the right time; developing job descriptions that accurately communicate the expectations of the position; and designing challenging, rewarding, and fulfilling positions. Club managers need to create evaluation systems that promote professional development and reward systems that motivate employees and promote job satisfaction by understanding how pay, promotion opportunities, supervisors, coworkers, and the work itself affect job satisfaction.

Effective human resources management is essential to the success of a club. The club's staff dictates whether the club achieves success because it touches every aspect of the club. Staff members coach the athletes, sell sponsorships, and do the bookkeeping. As discussed in chapter 5, the club will be held liable for the actions of its employees and for not supervising a staff member. Finally, staff members have the most direct contact with club participants and customers. They provide the services, and how they do so can determine whether a participant remains with the club. Thus, understanding the importance of human resources management should be a priority.

Human Resources Management

The composition of a club's staff makes a statement about its priorities. Sport clubs must allocate financial resources to support human resources to achieve their goals. Hiring full-time coaches instead of asking for parent volunteer coaches makes a statement that the training of elite athletes is a priority. Clubs that understand why they exist and are striving to achieve both short- and long-term goals communicate this in their strategic plans. Staff evaluations are also tied to the strategic plans and goals documents. If a staff member contributes to meeting the club's goals by achieving his individual goals, he should receive a positive evaluation and be justly rewarded. If he does not, the club should help him improve and develop. Not growing and failing to meet established goals are grounds for dismissal. It should be evident that human resources management is closely tied to achieving the goals in all aspects of the club.

In addition to hiring staff to achieve their stated goals, clubs also hire staff to generate revenue through sponsorships and fund-raising. To justify hiring personnel in such positions, club leaders should see a return on their investment. The funding of a position should be based on generating revenue that is greater than the salary of the person in the position. If the revenue generated is less than the salary, club leaders should reconsider the position or replace the person in the position with someone who can generate the required revenue.

As the club grows and evolves, its human resources needs may change. More coaches may be needed if there is an increase in participants; a facility supervisor may be needed if the club builds or enlarges its facility. Newly created positions should be related to the purpose of the club and the goals it establishes. The staff is responsible for making the club's goals a reality.

Job Description

Developing a **job description** is an important task. A well-written job description addresses the priorities and needs of the organization and communicates the responsibilities, work schedule, and performance standards of the position. Developing comprehensive job descriptions ensures that all club employees know their areas of responsibility and for what they will be evaluated and compensated. A well-written job description also enables the club to attract qualified applicants for a position. A candidate should be able to determine from a job description whether he is qualified, underqualified, or overqualified for the position; whether he is interested in the responsibilities, work schedule, and performance standards associated with the position; and whether he would like to work for the person to whom he would report (e.g., does he report directly to the executive director or to a middle manager). A candidate may read a job description and decide that the position is of no interest because it would be a step back in terms of responsibilities; another candidate may view the same job description and recognize an opportunity to grow as a professional and to focus on responsibilities that interest her. An effective job description, therefore, attracts qualified and interested applicants while discouraging those who are not.

The job description also allows the club management to screen candidates for a position. As much as the individual looks at the club and its position, the club needs to look at the individual. The job description assists the club in identifying those who are worthy candidates and those who are not qualified for the position. This is discussed later in the chapter.

Finally, the job description plays an important role in the evaluation of an employee by laying out the responsibilities of the position. The employee's level of execution of those responsibilities is the foundation of an annual evaluation. The evaluation process is discussed in more detail later in the chapter. Two sample job descriptions are presented in the sidebar on page 46.

job description—A document that communicates the responsibilities, work schedule, and performance standards of a position.

Elements of a Job Description

A job description includes the following elements:

▶ *Title.* The title of a position should communicate the level and function of the position. Titles such as executive director, director of coaching, assistant director of coaching, director of marketing, facility manager, and administrative assistant all achieve this goal. The remaining elements of a job description provide the details of the position.

Sample Job Descriptions

Assistant Director of Coaching

The assistant director of coaching will report directly to the director of coaching and will focus on the growth of the in-house recreation league, club tournaments, and summer camps. The individual will plan and manage all aspects of the already established in-house recreation program including scheduling games, practices, and referees; initiating annual fund-raising efforts; creating and managing the four annual indoor and outdoor tournaments for the club; and creating and administering the summer camp program. All league and camp workers and volunteers will report to the assistant director of coaching, and the assistant director of coaching will work closely with the director of coaching as well as members of the club's board of directors to achieve club goals. The position entails evening and weekend hours throughout the year. Job performance will be based on increased participation in recreation leagues, tournaments, and camps as well as meeting annual fund-raising goals. Candidates must have a bachelor's degree in a related field (master's degree preferred) and five years of club coaching experience, administrative experience, or both.

Club Technical Director

The club technical director will report directly to the club director of coaching and will be responsible for the training of volunteer coaches and players within the club through preseason and in-season training sessions in addition to supervising full-time staff coaches and serving as a liaison with the state association. The technical director will report directly to the director of coaching and will work with the assistant director of coaching and the board of directors and club members in achieving club goals. Job performance will be based on attracting and developing players and the success of the club's teams in the state cup. Candidates must have a bachelor's degree in a related field (master's degree preferred); an NSCAA advanced national diploma; and five years of club coaching experience, administrative experience, or both. The job entails working evenings and weekends throughout the year.

▶ *Supervisor.* The job description should communicate to whom the employee will report and who will ultimately direct and evaluate the employee. In complex organizations with multiple levels, it is not a given that an employee will report directly to the club manager or executive director or to the board of directors. In clubs with a simple organization structure, all employees may report to the club manager or to the board.

▶ *Purpose of the position.* Like a mission statement, the purpose of the position communicates why the position exists and what the person in the position will accomplish for the organization. This is often communicated in conceptual terms, as seen in the sample job descriptions, providing a general understanding of why the person in this position is employed by the club.

▶ *Specific responsibilities.* The specific responsibilities define the tasks associated with the position and are tied to the purpose of the position. If the purpose of the position is to train and develop elite athletes, the specific responsibilities would include developing training sessions and arranging for participation in national tournaments and events. The specific responsibility component is very important to recruiting for the position. If a person is interested in working for a sport club as a coach and sees a job description that includes marketing and fund-raising responsibilities, she may not apply if she is not qualified or interested in having those responsibilities.

▶ *Supervisees, if applicable.* If a position entails supervision, the job description should communicate which and how many employees will be supervised. As discussed in chapter 2, some people want to focus only on a task and do not want managerial responsibilities. This element of the job description helps eliminate candidates who are not interested in supervising others.

▶ *Qualifications.* Qualifications communicate the work experiences, years of experience, education level, certifications, and skills needed for executing the responsibilities of the position. Qualifications are related to the specific responsibilities sections. If the club is hiring a director of coaching, should that person have the highest coaching certification level in the sport? Is a college degree important? How many years of coaching experience are desired? Has the person overseen a coaching staff before? Has the person arranged for overseas team travel? These questions are asked because the person in that position will be required to train elite athletes, oversee a staff of seven coaches, and take teams to international tournaments on an annual basis. This section also plays an important part in the screening of candidates. The club must determine which qualifications are needed, which are of the highest priority, and whether not having a particular qualification eliminates a candidate from consideration.

▶ *Work schedule.* The work schedule communicates the expected working hours. Because most sport club positions entail evening and weekend hours, that should be documented so it is not a surprise. On the other hand, some positions may have a more traditional 9 to 5 schedule, such as an administrative assistant position. The work schedule, like the other elements, assists in defining the position.

▶ *Performance standards.* Performance standards communicate expectations. The purpose states why the position exists, the specific responsibilities section explains what the person will be doing, and the performance standards section communicates the desired outcomes. These standards relate to the purpose—if the position is about increasing club membership, the employee will be judged on whether the number of participants has increased. Performance standards also relate to the specific responsibilities—if one of the responsibilities of the position is to run a coaching clinic for volunteer coaches and that clinic is not run, the person in that position has not met a standard. Employees must know the rules of engagement, and the club must adhere to the established performance standards. The importance of this is discussed in more detail in the evaluation section of the chapter.

▶ *Critical working relationships.* An employee has to interact with others both inside and outside the club who are neither supervisors nor subordinates. The relationships with these people are crucial to the execution of the responsibilities of a position. A club manager may have to interact with representatives of sporting goods manufacturers when ordering equipment, or with the city manager if the club leases fields from the municipality. In a multisport club, the director of basketball may have to communicate with the director of volleyball because they share the same gym space. Defining these relationships assists in defining the overall position.

Job Design

A position within a club is based on the needs of the organization, but as Chelladurai (2001) pointed out, the needs of the employee should be considered as well. Hackman and Oldham (1980) stated that skill variety, task identity, task significance, autonomy, and job feedback are the foundations of job design. The club in the opening scenario wants to develop elite players and generate revenue for the club. Rachel Anderson needs responsibilities that fit her skills and an opportunity to be challenged as a professional to feel enriched and stay motivated. Several variables need to be considered in designing a position to achieve both of these purposes. When a job is designed well, the employee is motivated based on feelings of meaningfulness, responsibility, and knowledge of the results of his efforts. (See the sidebar at the bottom of this page for a sample job design.) From this come the benefits of internal motivation, job satisfaction, work effectiveness, and growth satisfaction (Hackman & Oldham, 1980). All the while the club is achieving its purpose through the efforts of the employee.

Skill Variety

In designing a job, the club must consider the needs it plans to address with the position and create a balance so that the person is not overworked or underused and the responsibilities are neither overly specialized nor too complex. Often,

Job Design for a Director of Coaching

- Hire qualified coaches and trainers for club program.
- Develop a sound direction and foundation for both competitive and recreational soccer components.
- Assist with training and developing training sessions for staff and coaches.
- Develop curriculums.
- Facilitate coaching education opportunities.
- Promote player development.
- Attend games and tournaments to evaluate coaches.
- Conduct game analyses with coaches.
- Organize player clinics and camps.
- Give exposure to college-bound players.
- Serve as a liaison with college coaches to help players gain soccer scholarships.
- Initiate public relations efforts with internal and external constituents.
- Communicate with parents.
- Serve as the liaison with the club's board of directors.

positions are created because another position had too many responsibilities. A good example is a club manager who oversees both the sport and business sides of a club. As members and services increase, one person cannot handle all of the responsibilities without compromising the quality of the services. A business manager position can be created to handle the accounting, budgeting, marketing, facility scheduling, and fund-raising tasks so the club manager can focus on the competition and coaching tasks. The design decision is based on limiting the number and variety of tasks.

In a small, simple organizational structure, one person commonly has many tasks and is able to handle them. As the organization becomes more complex, the number and variety of tasks may be reduced. The ideal job strikes a balance between challenging and routine tasks. If there is not enough to do, the person is not being used and may become bored or complacent and may look for a more challenging position in another organization. If there is too much to do, the person may become overworked and burned out and look for a position that is not as demanding.

Along with the number of tasks, those designing jobs should consider the variety of those tasks. There needs to be a balance between specialization and generalization. In simple organizations, one person may have a lot of tasks that vary dramatically. On a given day a club manager may be lining a field for competition, meeting a potential corporate partner, paying the club bills, writing a press release for an upcoming event, and training a team. The person in that position has marketing, public relations, accounting, and coaching responsibilities. However, in a larger and more complex organization, those responsibilities may be divided among three positions.

Task variety refers to the day-to-day responsibilities of the job as well as the unique experiences that may be planned or unplanned. A club may decide to host a regional or national championship tournament every five years. The club submits a bid and has the responsibility of organizing the event for that given year. Another example would be a capital fund-raising campaign, which is discussed in further detail in chapter 7. In this case a campaign is initiated to meet a predetermined goal in a predetermined time for a project such as a new indoor facility or the addition of a strength and conditioning room. These unique situations offer a new challenge to the employee and may enrich the position, but if the employee is currently overworked, they can actually lead to high levels of dissatisfaction.

Task Identity

Hackman and Oldham (1980) defined **task identity** as the degree to which the completion of a piece of work requires an employee to work from start to finish. A director of in-house recreation leagues who oversees participant registration, schedules the facility and games, trains the coaches, and organizes the end-of-season ceremony has high task identity because she is associated with this aspect of the club. This is also true of the person who oversees the sponsorships for the club and the person who trains the elite teams or athletes. Employees can take pride in being identified with certain aspects of the club and are identified by

task identity—The degree to which completion of a piece of work requires an employee to work from start to finish.

participants and other employees according to the tasks they oversee. A person can experience a high level of motivation as a result of being identified with particular tasks. Titles of positions with high task identity include marketing director, director of coaching, recreation league coordinator, and general manager.

Task Significance

task significance—The degree to which a piece of work is essential to the club achieving its mission and goals.

Employees like to know that what they do makes a difference and affects others. **Task significance** is essential to helping a club achieve its mission and goals. Every job should be designed so that the person in that job plays a part in achieving the mission and goals of the club and executing the strategic plan and therefore is viewed as important. A club cannot achieve excellence unless the facility manager ensures the upkeep of the facility. The club also cannot grow and expand unless the marketing director increases membership and sells sponsorships. Club leaders may have great ideas, but they cannot achieve them without funding. A club needs all employees to believe that what they do is essential to the club and that they are all equal in contributing to its success.

Task Autonomy

task autonomy—The degree of freedom and independence that employees feel in relation to their work and the control they have over when and how they do the work.

Task autonomy refers to the degree of freedom and independence employees feel in relation to their work and the control they have over when and how they do the work. Self-motivated people desire this autonomy and thrive when given it. Those who are not, on the other hand, may not be able to handle the freedom; they perform better when there is less autonomy and they are told what to do.

Task Feedback

Jobs that are effectively designed have measurable outcomes and means for evaluation. Club managers need to communicate performance standards to employees, supervise them to be sure they understand the standards, and evaluate them to let them know whether they have met those standards. People desire feedback on their efforts. Feedback can be an informal "Great job" to the person who organized a 32-team tournament that went off without a hitch, or a formal year-end review. In year-end reviews, employees may be told they have met and exceeded all of the goals set for the year and will earn a bonus. Others may learn that they did not meet the standards for the second year in a row and must follow the professional development plan and meet their goals for the next year or risk termination.

Hiring Process

Of all the responsibilities of a club manager, the hiring of employees is one of the most important. A good hire can benefit the club for many years; on the other hand, a bad hire can damage the club's reputation and keep the club from achieving its purpose and goals. The process of hiring a new employee should not be taken lightly, and club leaders should develop a process to ensure that they are hiring the right people for the right jobs. The hiring process includes selecting the leader or decision maker for the search, recruiting candidates, screening applicants, interviewing, and hiring.

Choosing the Decision Maker

A person within the club, whether it be the manager or a member of the board of directors, should be appointed to lead the search process. This person will be the primary contact for applicants and organize the overall search. This person may be granted the authority to make the selection or may make a recommendation to the board, which then votes on the recommendation. How the decision is made should be predetermined, and the club may even want to establish a policy that appears in the club policy manual.

It is common for the decision maker to chair a **search committee** that could include employees of the club with whom the person hired will interact (as supervisors or supervisees), club members, and board members. Members of a search committee can provide valuable input by offering perspectives on the areas they are representing. The role of the committee should be defined as well—the search committee can make a recommendation or make the final decision. Whatever model is chosen, it should be determined in advance, but one person should serve as the primary contact for applicants.

search committee—An entity charged with recruiting and hiring a new employee. The committee may include employees of the club with whom the person hired will interact (as supervisors or subordinates), club members, and board members.

Recruiting

After the decision to hire someone has been made, the next step is to gather a qualified pool of candidates; this is known as **recruitment**. A club can choose among several recruitment methods depending on the position. The most common recruitment methods are advertising the position, consulting with peers, contacting potential candidates, and promoting from within. Clubs may use one, some, or all of these methods to develop a deep pool of qualified candidates.

recruitment—The gathering of a pool of qualified candidates for a position.

Advertising

Advertising a position is the most effective way to secure a large applicant pool for a position. The process entails developing a job announcement based on the existing job description or one that has been developed for this process. The job announcement should also include a request for a cover letter, resume, and list of references; a deadline for when applications are due; the name of the contact person; and an address to which applicants can send their information. Three weeks to one month is a standard amount of time from initial announcement to the deadline for applications. If a position is open because an employee has left, there may be a time constraint if the responsibilities are essential to the club. If the job responsibilities must be executed while the position is vacant, an interim person can be selected from within the club or the responsibilities can be shared among the staff until a person is hired.

The club should identify the media through which potential applicants can read the announcement based on the position. A budget for advertising should be determined in advance for media that involve a cost. Ads in local, regional, and national newspapers cost money, as do ads on employment Web sites. Some professional organizations charge a fee for running an ad, whereas others offer such ads as a service to members. Other cost-effective strategies are sending an

advertising—The most effective way to secure a large applicant pool for a position through purchasing ads in related media outlets or posting the position on appropriate Web sites.

e-mail blast with the announcement to similar organizations around the area or country and posting electronic mailing lists to which potential candidates may belong. The purpose is to make potential candidates aware of the opportunity.

Consulting With Peers

Another method of identifying qualified candidates is consulting with associates in the field. The executive director of another club may have an assistant director of coaching who is looking for the opportunity to serve as director of coaching. The executive director can recommend the assistant director of coaching, and the club can reach out to that person to gauge her interest in the opportunity and to encourage her to apply. A recommendation from a trusted associate can carry a great deal of weight.

Contacting People of Interest

A leader of a large sport organization said that he keeps a drawer full of "potentials"— people he has observed or with whom he has come in contact or worked. When a position opens in his organization, he goes to his file and shares the job announcement with those he believes would be a good fit.

Another approach is contacting someone who has contributed greatly to another organization and asking whether she has an interest. There are ethical issues associated with this method, because it can be viewed as tampering or stealing. There may be legal issues if the person is under contract with her current employer. The club could be sued for interference with a contract. Safe options are to ask for permission to speak to the potential candidate or to wait for the person's contract to end before making contact. If the club can offer better pay, more responsibility, or greater decision-making opportunities than the person has in her current situation, she may welcome the opportunity to grow.

Promoting From Within

Sometimes the best candidate is already with the club. Often, clubs do not benefit from the training they give young employees, because they then leave the club to advance their careers elsewhere. When a position opens in the club, leaders should determine whether a current employee is prepared for the position and, if so, encourage him to apply. Often, an assistant is doing much of the work of the director and needs only a change of title. Promoting from within rewards loyalty and hard work and can serve as incentive for others to work hard for the club because they see the potential payoff.

Screening Candidates

Once a job opening is announced, applicants forward the requested information to the leader of the search. At this time the screening process begins. The first step is reviewing the resumes of candidates to determine their fit with the club in terms of meeting the requirements and qualifications for the position and understanding the club sport environment. This is done by those directly involved in the hiring process. Qualifying standards should be established for those reviewing the resumes, and the club should determine the degree to which screeners must adhere to those standards in the screening process.

If the job announcement states that five years of coaching experience in the club environment and a masters' degree are required, should a candidate who has coached five years in a high school and has only a bachelor's degree be automatically eliminated from consideration? Some clubs are stringent about their qualifications, whereas others are willing to be flexible if they believe that a candidate who does not meet all of the qualifications is still an attractive candidate. Ultimately, the search committee is looking for a good fit for the position and the club.

At this point some candidates may stand out by having all of the qualifications and experiences desired, steady career progressions, and recognized and credible references. On the other hand, red flags may emerge on some candidates. Stops and starts with positions in various career orientations, gaps in the resume, and past employers not being listed as references should raise concerns. Contacting references, past employers, or people who may have interacted with the person in the past can confirm or dispel these concerns.

SUCCESSFUL STRATEGY

Importance of Background Checks

The circumstances surrounding the 2009 arrest of a male youth swim coach in California underscores the importance of a sport club doing its due diligence in the hiring process. Executing the required background check is not enough to determine whether someone is the right person for a position with a club. Although this example might not show a *successful* strategy, it does show why having successful strategies in place are so important.

The coach in question had the reputation of being a strong youth swim coach with several clubs on the West Coast of the United States, and there was no concrete proof or evidence of inappropriate or illegal behavior. Required background checks identify criminal behavior, but they do not address incidents that may call into question the character of a coach.

In April 2009, when he was a coach at the San Jose Aquatics Club, the coach in question was arrested on suspicion of molesting a young swimmer. Club officials stated that they relied on the background checks performed by USA Swimming when they hired him, but it was not determined whether any other type of reference check was done on his character or past behavior. As it turned out, a pattern of behavior from the coach's past that did not appear in a background check would have raised concerns if it had been revealed. For example, the coach had a policy that parents were not permitted at the pool during practice. If parents did show up, the coach would drop their child from the team. With no parental observations during practice, the coach would ask a girl and a boy to kiss each other in front of the rest of the team on the high board while he timed it. A complaint about abusive behavior and the "kissing ritual" in 2002 had been filed with the West Coast Division of USA Swimming, but no action was taken and the complaint has since been lost.

Yes, the law requires a background check, but a club owes it to its members to conduct reference checks to learn about a candidate's character before deciding whether the person is the right fit for the club.

Information from Goldston, L. (2009). Screening coaches: Are background checks protecting kids in youth sports? *San Jose Mercury News*, July 6, 2009.

The goal of the initial review of the resumes is for each member of the committee to develop a list of potentials to bring to a meeting of the committee. Figure 3.1 shows a matrix that can be used to evaluate candidates based on required and preferred qualifications. The hiring matrix enables the committee members to quantify why one person is a better candidate than another based on the qualifications.

Committee members can be asked to present their top picks depending on the applicant pool size. If the pool is in the hundreds, they may bring the top 10; if it is smaller, perhaps the top 5. Those candidates who are on all the lists should make the first cut. Discussion should follow about those who are on some lists and not others. Committee members should make the case for why a particular candidate should make the cut as opposed to another based on the criteria presented in the matrix. Those discussions should lead to a group of between 5 and 10 candidates who can participate in a phone interview either with the chair of the search committee or the entire committee.

The phone interview is a cost-effective way to determine whether a person is seriously interested in the position and to get a feel for the person. (See the sidebar on page 55 for some sample interview questions.) It also allows the candidate to ask questions to decide whether she is interested in going further with the process. A salary range can be presented during the phone interview. A candidate may remove herself from consideration based on this variable. The phone interview can also avoid a situation in which a person says during the final interview that

	Professional experience	Education	Meets job description	Years of experience	Leadership experience	Professional reputation	Supervisory experience	Technical ability	Required certifications	Subtotal	References	Total points	Comments
Point total	**10**	**10**	**10**	**10**	**10**	**10**	**10**	**10**	**10**	**90**	**10**	**100**	
Candidate 1	9	9	10	10	10	9	8	9	10	84	9	93	
Candidate 2	8	8	8	8	8	8	9	9	9	75	9	84	
Candidate 3	8	7	8	8	7	8	8	9	9	72	9	81	
Candidate 4	9	7	8	8	8	8	8	8	9	73	9	82	
Candidate 5	10	8	9	9	8	7	6	7	9	73	9	82	
Candidate 6	6	8	6	7	8	7	8	9	9	68	7	75	
Candidate 7	6	5	8	7	7	8	5	7	9	62	8	70	
Candidate 8	8	7	8	8	8	8	9	8	9	73	7	80	
Candidate 9	7	8	8	8	7	7	9	7	9	70	8	78	
Candidate 10	9	8	7	7	7	7	8	7	9	69	8	77	

Figure 3.1 A club can develop a hiring matrix in an Excel spreadsheet. The hiring matrix shown here uses criteria that can be judged.

Sample Interview Questions

The following questions can be asked during either the phone interview or the final interview.

- In two minutes or less, tell me about yourself.
- What do you know about our club?
- What aspects of the job intrigue or interest you the most?
- What aspects of the job are you least interested in?
- Why should we hire you?
- What can you do for us that someone else can't?
- What do you look for in a job?
- How long would it take for you to make a meaningful contribution?
- How does this position fit into your overall career plan?
- Describe your management or leadership style.
- What do you believe is the most difficult part of being a supervisor?
- What are your core values?
- Give an example from your past in which you demonstrated these core values.
- How would your colleagues describe you?
- How would your past supervisor describe you?
- How would you describe yourself?

her spouse does not want to relocate, the salary is not right, the job would be a lateral move, or she was using the club to get a raise out of her current club. The goal of this step is to identify between two and four finalists for the position who will be invited to the club for in-person interviews and if offered the position are prepared to accept. Candidates who participate in phone interviews but are not selected as finalists may still be considered if the finalist who is offered the position does not accept it.

The Final Interview

The final interview is an opportunity for the club to learn about the employee and the employee to learn about the club. A full-day interview is ideal, or a two-day interview for candidates outside the geographic area. The interview should include both formal meetings and interviews and informal situations that allow the person to interact with the constituents of the club. A schedule should be developed for the day and sent to the candidate in advance. A sample interview schedule is provided in the sidebar on page 56.

Dinners are also commonly held the night before the interview with the candidate and selected club leaders. This is especially the case if a candidate comes from out of town. The candidate can arrive early in the day, receive a tour of the surrounding area, and then meet for dinner before the next day's schedule.

Sample Interview Schedule for a Director of Coaching Candidate

9:00	Arrive at the club and meet with the executive director or the chair of the search committee
9:30	Interview with the search committee
11:00	Tour the club facilities with either the chair or an employee
12:00	Have lunch with the search committee
1:00	Meet with club employees
2:00	Meet with club parents, participants, or both
3:00	Meet with the board president
4:00	Have an exit interview with the executive director
4:30	Depart

In the opening meeting, the agenda for the day can be discussed and any questions the candidate may have about the day, the club, or the process can be answered. A format should be set for the interview with the search committee. Following is a common interview format:

▶ The search committee chair convenes the meeting and introduces the candidate.

▶ The search committee members introduce themselves and explain their roles with the club.

▶ The candidate presents an overview of herself and explains why she is interested in the position.

▶ The search committee members ask questions of the candidate. The questions should be developed in advance by the committee, and certain committee members may be assigned certain questions. Committee members may also ask questions related to their specific areas of expertise. The committee should have an understanding of what type of answer they are looking for from candidates. Questions should relate to philosophies, influences, vision for the club and the position, how the candidate would handle given situations and responsibilities, examples from the candidate's past that will help the club understand who she is, past successes and failures, and future aspirations. Discussions with the candidate's references may provide insight for questions to ask. A reference may bring up a past success or failure, and the candidate can be asked to explain.

▶ The committee should allow the candidate to ask questions about the position, the club, or both.

If the committee is interested in formal presentations from candidates, they should let them know and offer the same opportunity to all candidates. Some candidates may indicate their preparation and seriousness about the position by bringing portfolios of past accomplishments or plans for the position. Candidates who make specific references about aspects of the club or ask specific questions show that they have researched the club.

The search committee should view the entire day as one interview. They can learn as much from a candidate by interacting in informal situations as they can in the formal interview setting. How the candidate talks and what he says over dinner can be as revealing as his answers to a question. How the candidate treats an administrative assistant who is escorting him through the club says as much about him, if not more, as how he answers a question about motivating and communicating with subordinates. At some point a candidate may let his guard down to reveal the real person. That real person may or may not be a good fit for the club.

The successful interview is also based on honesty. If the candidate is honest about her background and what she plans to accomplish and the club is honest in presenting the vision for the position and the club, both parties will be satisfied. If the candidate is dishonest and the club is honest, the club will be disappointed with a hire who becomes a liability. A candidate may overpromise on what she can do and then not deliver on the job. If the club is dishonest and the candidate is honest, the candidate will be dissatisfied with the position, which will lead to turnover. Many times, a candidate accepts a position based on promises that are not delivered. If both parties are dishonest, in the long run everyone is hurt, especially the members of the club.

Hiring

Hiring has four parts: the decision, the offer, the acceptance, and ending the search. At the end of the interviews, the committee should rank the final candidates. It should also develop a rubric for the final interview candidates to quantify the process and ensure that all committee members are evaluating the same criteria. (See a sample rubric in the sidebar on page 58.) This rubric may include more qualitative aspects. For example, a committee member who gives a candidate a 3 out of 5 on the interview, should explain the score based on the candidate's responses in the interview, body language, personal philosophy, and so on. This provides a framework for a discussion of the candidates and a basis for the decision on whom to hire.

The search committee must then decide what to do if the first person offered the job does not accept it. Are committee members willing to offer the position to the second or third candidate, do they go back to the candidates who participated in the phone interviews, or do they call it a failed search? The decision may have been very close among the final three candidates, and if one does not accept, the others may be acceptable. If, on the other hand, the committee members determined in the interviews that one or both of the other candidates were not suitable, they may go back to the original pool or initiate a new search.

Once approved, the offer should be made to the candidate. The offer should address salary, benefits, length of contract, and fringe benefits. The candidate may want to negotiate, and it is up to the search committee members to determine to what degree they are willing to do so. If the candidate accepts, a contract can be signed. At that point, it is a common courtesy to notify the other final candidates

Sample Rubric: Applicant Evaluation

Applicant's name _____

Open position _____

Rate the applicant on the following criteria based on the applicant's resume, references, phone interview, and on-site interview and compare your ratings with the requirements listed in the job description.

5 = Excellent;   4 = Good;   3 = Average;   2 = Poor;   1 = Very poor

Education	5	4	3	2	1
Relevant job experience	5	4	3	2	1
Supervisory experience	5	4	3	2	1
Technical skills	5	4	3	2	1
Interpersonal skills	5	4	3	2	1
Motivation	5	4	3	2	1
Enthusiasm for the position	5	4	3	2	1
Knowledge of the club	5	4	3	2	1
Knowledge of the industry	5	4	3	2	1
Verbal communication skills	5	4	3	2	1
Initiative	5	4	3	2	1
Ability to speak about self	5	4	3	2	1
Ability to answer questions	5	4	3	2	1
Ability to articulate thoughts	5	4	3	2	1
Applicant questions	5	4	3	2	1
Informal interaction	5	4	3	2	1
Overall interview	5	4	3	2	1

Comments: _____
_____
_____
_____

Salary expectations: _____

Interviewer: _____

Date of interview: _____

From M.J. Robinson, 2010, *Sport Club Management* (Champaign, IL: Human Kinetics).

by phone or in person that they have not been selected. A letter is appropriate for those who applied but did not make the final cut.

The hiring process is time intensive, but it is worth it if the club does its due diligence and hires the right person for the position. The club that makes a commitment to the process will reap the rewards tenfold.

New Employee Orientation

Newly hired employees need an understanding of the overall organization as well as the position. This can be accomplished through an orientation program. In planning a **new employee orientation,** club leaders should ask themselves what the new employee needs to know about the club to succeed in the position—that is, the who, what, when, where, how, and why. (See the sidebar at the bottom of this page for items that should be covered in a new employee orientation.) The answers to those questions are the foundation of an effective orientation program.

The *who* involves having the new employee meet coworkers, customers, external parties, board members, supervisors, and subordinates. The new employee needs to start developing relationships with these people and understand their roles and importance to the club as well as their personalities, work habits, and interests. She may need to know who to ask to use the club van, or that a coworker likes to have forms completed two days in advance of the deadline. Meeting board members enables the new employee to engage them in conversation if she passes them on the street or on the court, pool deck, or field.

The *what* involves educating the new employee on the club, its mission, its culture, and its purpose. He needs to know what the club stands for, the ethics and beliefs of its leaders, its vision for the future, its traditions, the stories and heroes from the past, and why it exists.

The *when* involves educating the new employee on how time affects the position. She needs to know the deadlines for reports or important communications; times and days of daily, weekly, monthly, and annual meetings; when paydays are; how vacations are scheduled; and about important club events such as the annual retreat, the club banquet, or the golf tournament fund-raiser.

The *where* involves introducing the employee to his work space, whether it be an office or a cubicle, as well as giving him a tour of the entire facility. If he is new to the geographic region, a tour of the local area can also be beneficial. Explaining where he can go for lunch and showing him the local bank, a dry cleaner, a competitor's facility, or a route for a lunchtime run is useful in familiarizing him with the overall position.

new employee orientation—A human resources tool that acquaints new employees with the policies, procedures, and culture of the organization; their job responsibilities; fellow employees; and the overall operations of the club.

New Employee Orientation

Who: Coworkers, customers, external parties, board members, supervisors, subordinates

What: The club and its mission, culture, and purpose

When: Deadlines for reports, times of meetings, paydays, vacations, important club events

Where: Employee's work space, tour of the facility, tour of the local area

How: Policies and procedures

Why: The meaning behind what is done, such as explaining the club's traditions

The *how* involves explaining the club's policies and procedures. The new employee should become familiar with these as soon as possible so that she is working in accordance with the framework of the club. What is the procedure to make a purchase, get reimbursed for mileage, schedule a practice for the indoor facility, and complete an accident report? Are forms completed online or on paper? This is the most technical part of the orientation.

Finally, the *why* entails sharing the meaning behind what is done. It may involve explaining a club tradition or why receipts must be turned in with a reimbursement request. A new employee may make reference to how he did something in a former job, so an explanation of why it is done the way it is done at the current club is useful.

See the sidebar at the bottom of this page for other tips for developing a new employee orientation schedule.

Finally, orientation is important in setting the tone for the person's work experience. If the club is formal and policy driven, the orientation experience should reflect that; on the other hand, if the club is more informal, the orientation may be less structured but still informative. The orientation should provide the new employee with the information or training for job responsibilities, explain the club's organization and culture, and introduce the person to coworkers and participants or customers. The sooner the new employee is comfortable in the new surroundings, the sooner he will begin to make a contribution to the club.

Helpful Hints for Developing a New Employee Orientation

- Prepare a schedule in advance and share it with the new employee prior to her arrival.
- Have all necessary human resources forms and information available (e.g., health insurance, direct deposit forms, information about the 410(k) plan and opening an e-mail account).
- Prepare an orientation packet with items such as a policy manual, important forms (e.g., travel reimbursement forms, time sheets, accident reporting forms), and pictures and names of coworkers or VIPs in the club, such as board members and longtime members.
- Review the job description, responsibilities, and expectations.
- Notify coworkers of the start date of the new employee so they can be available to meet the person and introduce themselves.
- Focus on orienting the new employee before assigning new or major tasks. Make sure she is comfortable with the surroundings before doing so.
- Arrange a social gathering for the new employee to interact with coworkers, club members, and others.
- Assign a mentor who will meet monthly for the first year with the new employee.

Enriching the Employee Experience

Club leadership can initiate a number of activities that will enrich employees' experiences within the club. These enrichment activities can promote personal, professional, and organizational growth, and in the end the club as a whole will benefit.

Retreats

An annual **retreat** gives employees the opportunity to take a break from the normal routine to focus on the broader picture of the organization. The retreat can be used as a year-end event or to launch the coming year. This will depend on the club. Ideally, the retreat should occur away from the work space. It can take place in a meeting room at a local hotel or a vacation-type area a few hours from the club. That decision will depend on finances, but the club should view the expense as an investment in the development and enrichment of its staff and the overall organization. The retreat should be something employees look forward to attending as opposed to feeling like a burden.

retreat—An opportunity for employees to take a break from the normal routine to focus on the broader picture of the organization; it is usually held at the beginning or end of the year.

The retreat should have formal and informal components. Suggestions for formal sessions include revisiting and potentially revising the club's mission, establishing a long-term or annual strategic plan, listening to presentations from speakers on topics of benefit to the staff, taking part in brainstorming sessions about future projects and initiatives, and evaluating the staff's past-year successes and failures and discussing ways to improve. The informal activities can be team-building exercises such as competitions (e.g., volleyball or a golf outing), excursions (e.g., whitewater rafting), sightseeing, meals, or socials.

The ultimate goal of the retreat is for the staff to leave refreshed and focused and optimistic about the upcoming year.

Professional Development Opportunities

The club should encourage its employees to grow as professionals and should support their efforts to do so. The club's mantras for its staff should be "If you are not getting better, you are getting worse" and "The day you know everything is the day you should get out of what you are doing."

During the course of a year professional organizations hold weekend seminars, workshops, licensing courses, and conventions to benefit employees. Such professional development opportunities provide club employees with new information and give them the chance to network and share ideas with peers in their area and establish important contacts for the growth of the club. In some instances attendance and passing a course may be required to perform the responsibilities at a club.

Attendance at professional development programs should be included in employees' performance goals. A director of coaching for a soccer club should attend the National Soccer Coaches Association annual convention or one of its licensing courses. A marketing director may want to attend a sales seminar on improving promotional strategies for the club. The key to effective professional development opportunities is for the employee to present a proposal for why she wants to attend and the intended outcomes of attending; she should justify why she is attending and what she expects to get from the training. She should then present an action plan explaining how she plans to use the information she learns for the benefit of the club.

Because club leaders should want to invest in the club's human resources, they should budget money for and encourage employees to attend professional development events. The club can establish a policy for funding such as providing a set amount for each person and paying travel and lodging expenses and registration fees. The level of financial support will depend on the club.

Visits to Similar Organizations

A less expensive but sometime just as effective means of professional development is to have staff members visit other organizations and their leaders. This is a common practice in the coaching world. A program that has had success with a particular strategy or system will host coaches from other programs, who spend a day or a week observing and sitting in on meetings with the staff to learn about the system. The same can be done for other areas of the club. Granted, clubs that are in direct competition may not be willing to offer such opportunities, but those that are not in close proximity may.

After learning how another club runs the entire club or certain aspects of it, employees can compare that club to the club they are working for. Based on these comparisons, they can determine whether changes or modifications are needed or whether their club is operating in the best way. Clubs that use this strategy for professional development should extend the same professional courtesy to other clubs and individuals who would like to visit them.

Publications and Information

Staff should be encouraged to subscribe to publications related to their areas of expertise and have them delivered to the office. After reading them, staff members can donate them to the club library for others to review as well. Staff should also have funds to purchase instructional books and videos. They should also bookmark Web sites that provide useful information about executing the responsibilities of the club.

Related Professional Activities

Staff members should also be encouraged to remain active professionally outside the club. This may come in the form of serving as an officer in a professional organization; teaching education courses if they have the certification; serving on an editorial board for a publication; or coaching a state, regional, or national-level team. In so doing, the person can grow professionally for the benefit of himself and the club.

Some employees bring prestige to the club. If a staff member is elected president of a professional organization or asked to coach a regional team at a national competition, both the person and the club she works for are recognized. Staff members can also establish important relationships that can benefit the club while also making a positive contribution to their profession. In all cases, they should make the club aware of the opportunity to determine whether there is any conflict of interest or whether the commitment would interfere with their responsibility to the club.

Individual and Program Performance Evaluation

Club leaders understand well the importance of evaluating team and player performance, but they also must understand the importance of evaluating club coaches and other personnel. This evaluation process critiques not just the employee, but also the entire club. At the heart of the evaluation process are two questions: How can the club achieve its fullest potential? and, How can employees excel at what they do? Answering these questions enables clubs to succeed both on the field and off.

Employee evaluations are essential to enabling people to excel at what they do. They are conducted by employees' supervisors and serve administrative and developmental purposes. In both cases the organization benefits from the process. Many employees view performance evaluation in a negative sense, believing that the supervisor is looking for what is wrong with their performance. Supervisors need to communicate to employees that the process is a positive one aimed at recognizing their contributions to the club and developing them as professionals in addition to improving their performance. Both supervisors and employees need to buy into the process for it to be successful.

In terms of an administrative purpose, the evaluation process provides feedback to employees about where they stand. Are they meeting, not meeting, or exceeding goals and expectations? This information gives the club documentation and data for raises and promotion, but it also can provide justification for withholding a raise or promotion or for dismissal from a position.

In our current litigious society, employers need justification and documentation before terminating an employee, because it is common for former employees to file wrongful termination suits. An employee who receives five straight years of positive performance evaluations and then is fired for incompetence may seek remedy in the form of a civil suit.

The performance evaluation can also be used to discuss areas of concern that need to be improved. Also, during the process the supervisor and employee can discuss career ambitions or the employee's desire to take on additional responsibilities or change the nature of her responsibilities. The performance evaluation can enable the supervisor to recognize the employee's accomplishments and offer suggestions for improvement.

Employee evaluations are also used for developmental purposes. For this to occur, the supervisor and employee must establish measurable goals related to the job description, establish an action plan related to the goals, meet to discuss progression toward attaining the goals over the course of the year, and conduct a year-end evaluation to assess goal attainment and develop a plan for the upcoming year.

The developmental approach to evaluation is time intensive because it may mean more meetings over the course of the year to closely monitor the progress of the employee in meeting the goals, but it is an investment in a valuable human resource in the form of mentoring. The supervisor can provide input on how to better attain the desired goals, and the year-end meeting may be easier because the supervisor is more informed of the employee's progress. Once an employee has grown professionally, the developmental model may still be used but the need for ongoing meetings may decrease. In that case the supervisor has done his job.

The Process

The evaluation process involves the supervisor completing an evaluation instrument on the employee, and the employee conducting a self-evaluation using the same instrument. (The sidebar on page 65 shows a sample performance appraisal record.) The two then meet to discuss the evaluations form and compare, contrast, and discuss their responses on the form. This gives the supervisor the opportunity to praise the employee's accomplishments and to point out areas of concern. This is also the time to begin to discuss goals and steps for professional development for the next year. The attainment of these goals will serve as the foundation for the coming year's performance appraisal.

Criteria for Evaluation

The criteria for evaluation can include a number of topics and questions that can be answered either on a Likert scale or in an open-ended way. The criteria can be directly related to the employee's responsibilities or simply about the overall success of the club. Areas to consider for evaluation include commitment—which is related to the employee's dedication, dependability, and willingness to be a team player—and skills, which are related to the employee's ability to execute the responsibilities of the position. This portion of the instrument will vary based on the job description. An evaluation of leadership skills addresses an employee's initiative, independence, creativity, and human resources management abilities. Lastly, intangibles such as sense of humor, positive attitude, leadership in informal groups, effort, communication skills, relations with coworkers, conscientiousness, punctuality, courtesy, and altruistic contributions to the local community can also be evaluated.

Rewards Systems

It is important for a club to develop a structured rewards system for its employees. This system should offer both intrinsic and extrinsic rewards that meet the psychological, life, and financial needs of the employees. A rewards system often makes a position attractive to a candidate and ensures that quality employees remain with club.

Sample Performance Appraisal

Name: _____

Position: _____

5 = Exceptional
4 = Exceeds expectations
3 = Meets expectations
2 = Does not meet expectations
1 = Needs improvement

Criteria	Score	Comments
Quality of work: Completes high-quality work in areas specified in the job description		
Desire for improvement: Continually explores new ways to improve and promote excellence		
Job knowledge: Possesses and uses the technical skills required to execute the job at a high standard		
Communication: Organizes thoughts and expresses them in an appropriate manner		
Interpersonal skills: Is sensitive to the needs of others, both subordinates and supervisors		
Ability to work with others: Works within a group to achieve organizational goals		
Ethics: Maintains a high level of ethical standards and promotes the club's code of ethics		
Customer service: Understands the importance of satisfying customers' needs and knows that the customer is always right		
Initiative: Seeks ways to improve personally and professionally and takes on projects voluntarily		

From M.J. Robinson, 2010, *Sport Club Management* (Champaign, IL: Human Kinetics).

Intrinsic rewards are tied to the job design, which was covered earlier in the chapter. An employee can be rewarded for his contribution to the club by being assigned a position that is interesting, has a great deal of responsibility and recognition, and makes a significant contribution to the success of the club. A person who has excelled in overseeing the volunteer coaching staff may be promoted to director of coaching, which oversees the paid coaching staff. This position has more responsibility and recognition and is more challenging professionally.

Extrinsic rewards can come in both financial and nonfinancial forms. Financial rewards include direct compensation, merit pay, and bonuses that are negotiated and stipulated in a contract. They also include indirect compensation such as pensions, health insurance, health plans, vacation time, and paid leave time. Some benefits are not financial in nature but valuable to employees. These may include social awards such as a title, office location, parking spot, company car, or work schedule. These are very effective when a club does not have the financial ability to reward employees. There may not be funds to provide a raise, but a new title, if deserved, can be very motivating.

The allocation of rewards is one of the most important tasks of a club manager and will lead to very difficult decisions. Who is deserving of a raise or a promotion? How should merit pay be allocated? Distributive justice, which is discussed in chapter 10, can help a club manager address the rewards system within the club.

Job Satisfaction of Employees

job satisfaction—The emotional state resulting from the appraisal of one's job or job experience.

The leadership of a sport club should understand the importance of job satisfaction of employees and have a vested interested in promoting it. Locke (1976) defined **job satisfaction** as "the emotional state resulting from the appraisal of one's job or job experience" (p. 1300). Locke (1976) also proposed that a job is not an entity but rather an interrelationship of tasks, roles, responsibilities, interactions, incentives, and rewards, and that, to understand job satisfaction, people must consider the parts instead of the whole. By developing a comprehensive human resources program that develops staff and promotes two-way communication, club leaders have a greater chance of promoting job satisfaction among employees. Employees with lower job satisfaction have a greater tendency to demonstrate behavior detrimental to the growth of the club (e.g., absenteeism, missed meetings, stealing, wasting time, and looking to change jobs). On the other hand, satisfied employees are more productive.

Five elements that are associated with job satisfaction are pay, promotion, coworkers, supervisors, and the work itself (Smith, Kendall, & Hulin, 1969). Research has indicated that if an employee considers an element important and her needs are met in that area, she will be satisfied; whereas if the opposite occurs, she will be dissatisfied. For example, a director of coaching enjoys his fellow staff members, has a great relationship with the executive director, and likes his responsibilities, but he is not happy with his pay or opportunity to move up in the club. Because he considers pay and opportunity to move up important, he is dissatisfied and may begin to demonstrate behavior detrimental to the club, which could affect his satisfaction with the other elements of his job. Understanding employees' values and priorities is important in developing them as employees. If an employee's main focus is pay and the club will never be able to compensate her at the level she wishes, it may be a time for her to move on because she will remain dissatisfied.

Job design, which was discussed earlier in the chapter, has an impact on job satisfaction as well. Siegrist (1996) found that an imbalance between effort and reward can lead to dissatisfaction. If an employee feels he is giving great effort to the club (e.g., working every weekend, taking on extra responsibilities) but sees no reward (e.g., a raise, a promotion, an increase in budget), he can become dissatisfied. Gardell (1982) found that job control and autonomy also affect job satisfaction. Club leaders should consider these issues when designing positions for the organization. Also, they should ask questions related to satisfaction during evaluation interviews. A person who was once satisfied in her position but has become dissatisfied can become a liability. She should be given the opportunity to offer her views during the annual review meeting. If she is valued, the club should consider what to do to keep her satisfied and thus productive.

Summary

Rachel Anderson should view the opportunity presented to her positively because she has the opportunity to make the club better through human resources management. Rachel needs to find the right people for the right job and then implement a plan to ensure that they grow as employees and become the best they can be while making the club better. The key to doing this is developing effective job descriptions that clearly articulate the responsibilities of the positions, and designing the positions with appropriate titles, significant and varied responsibilities, and appropriate degrees of autonomy.

Just as important are the steps the selection committee needs to take to recruit qualified people for positions and do its due diligence when interviewing and selecting a candidate. Once a new employee is hired, club leaders need to orientate the person to the position and the club. A new employee orientation includes elements that range from explaining how the copier works to orienting the person to the culture of the club. Club leaders should also offer opportunities for the employee to be enriched and empowered on a regular basis.

Along with all of this, the club should have an evaluation plan in place for administrative as well as professional development purposes. Finally, club leaders should assess employees' job satisfaction. They should appreciate the elements of the job that are important to the employee and try to satisfy those needs. In the end the club can have qualified, motivated, empowered, and satisfied employees who contribute to the club's achieving its purpose and overall excellence on a daily basis.

● ● ●

Recognizing an incredible opportunity to grow and improve the club, Rachel took her task seriously. She developed job descriptions based on the needs of the club for each of the three positions. She understood the qualifications and experiences that she desired in the people who would fill the positions and communicated them in the job announcements that she placed in the appropriate media where they would be seen by the right candidates. The screening process of those who applied and who Rachel recruited to apply led to a pool of talented candidates. The interview process enabled Rachel and the club leadership to select three candidates who were prepared for the positions for which they were hired, and the club is now headed in the direction of achieving its full potential as a first-class multisport club.

● ● ●

By the end of the chapter, the sport club manager will be able to do the following:

▶ Embrace the importance of collaboration among coaches, clubs, and parents.

▶ Engage in behaviors designed to build a shared understanding with parents.

▶ Recognize the reciprocal influences between parents and coaches and athletes.

▶ Describe strategies for maintaining or improving coach–parent relationships.

▶ Take steps to increase positive interactions and reduce the potential points of conflict in coach–parent relationships.

4

Effective Coach–Parent Relationships

Dena A. Deglau, PhD

The executive director of the Kerry Lacrosse Club spent most of the day returning phone calls from parents of the under-10 team. The calls related to concerns about the coach. Parents complained that the team was not winning enough and that the best players (their children) were not on the field the entire game. Two parents suggested that the coach's decision to play several of the weaker players at the end of the first half cost the team the win, and as a result they might consider leaving the club at the end of the season for the crosstown rivals. The parents believed their highly skilled children would get a more quality experience somewhere else. Upon talking with the coach, the executive director discovered the coach provided all children equal playing time because of an underlying belief that the focus ought to be on player development and fostering a love for the game at this young age. Further, the coach was frustrated with parents who coached from the sidelines and who applied continual pressure to play only the best players. The coach believes the parents are the problem and their behavior is highly disruptive both during and after the games as they continue to plead their case while leaving the facility. As a result of many uncomfortable interactions, the coach has avoided talking to the parents.

Coaches today have an enormous responsibility. In addition to meeting the needs of their athletes, coaches must meet the expectations of the clubs they represent. They must also engage with and answer to parents, who come with their own expectations and desire to be involved. Some parents want to be highly involved, others wish to be minimally involved, and a number can become overly involved. Coaches who have experienced parents who yell at their children to perform, try to coach from the sidelines, or consistently question coaching decisions understand how difficult it can be to deal with parents, particularly the most difficult ones who behave poorly during games. Accounts of parents engaging in inappropriate behaviors ranging from verbal to physical assaults on other parents, coaches, and referees appear frequently in the media. Sport club leaders who have experienced parental complaints about coaches understand how difficult it can be to bridge the gap between the needs of the parents and the coach's need for a certain degree of autonomy.

Given the central role of parents in club sports (particularly when dealing with young participants who cannot drive), coaches and sport club administrators must be prepared to deal with parents on a regular and ongoing basis and to respond to their needs. This chapter is grounded in a philosophy that embraces parents as in important part of the club sport experience. Rather than casting them as peripheral to the sport experience, club leaders and coaches should consider parents valuable resources who deserve to feel valued, respected, and central. Research has shown that parents, along with coaches, peers, and siblings, play an important role in athletes' prolonged sport participation (Cote, Baker, & Abernethy, 2003; Cote & Fraser-Thomas, 2007).

This philosophical approach departs from the "my way or the highway" model of coaching in which the coach is considered the expert and parents are expected to accept coaching and club decisions without question or explanation. Instead, the relationship between coach and parent is seen as a process of social negotiation that enhances the experience of the child. A study of junior tennis players revealed that 59 percent of coaches believed that parents contributed to the success of their children (Gould, Lauer, Rolo, Jannes, & Penniski, 2006).

Finally, this philosophical approach accepts that parents have the best interests of their children at heart regardless of their level of involvement or their motivations for enrolling their children in the sport. Too often, coaches and others assume that parents who don't come to practices and games are not interested in their children's sporting experiences, or that parents who are over-involved pressure their unwilling children. These negative assumptions must be suspended and replaced with one that assumes parents have the best intentions, not the worst.

Embracing Collaboration

The first step in embracing parent collaboration is to accept that parents have a right to understand and be informed about all aspects of their children's experiences. Too often, parents are left to learn about the experiences of their children by listening to their comments or by observing their children, the coach, and their interactions during games and practices. Although both of these are important and valid ways to learn about the experiences of their children, this two-dimensional view does not allow the parent to fully understand how and why the coach and child interact the way they do, nor the reasons the coach has made the decisions she has.

For parents to fully understand the complex learning environment and specific cultural context that is unique to each team within the club, they need to be considered part of a **communication triad** that includes the child, the parent, and the coach (figure 4.1). Within this triad the parent and the coach work collaboratively to help the child learn (improve skills) and have a successful experience as an athlete. In the process, both coach and parent also learn—about themselves, about each other, and about the child. They are bound together because they both have the best interest of the child at heart while each holding beliefs and expectations (sometimes similar and sometimes different) about the child's sporting experience.

Each member of the communication triad comes to the team experience with different knowledge, skills, and dispositions that underlie their temperaments and guide their behaviors. Children come with knowledge and skills learned through participation in physical education class and on other sport teams, extra coaching from their parents, or informal pick-up experiences with friends and family. No player arrives devoid of knowledge and skills, but each arrives with differing levels grounded in their own personal experiences.

Parents come with intimate knowledge of their children and parenting skills necessary to deal with them. They also come with variety of strengths that may include varying degrees of knowledge and expertise about the sport, an understanding of the developmental needs of a particular group of students, or skills in managing the athletes. An elementary teacher, for example, would have a great deal of knowledge about age-appropriate behaviors and complimentary pedagogies that a coach may not have.

Coaches arrive with varying degrees of sport-specific knowledge, skills, and pedagogies. Although paid coaches may have a higher level of experience and knowledge than volunteer coaches, all arrive with a well-intentioned willingness to teach the athletes.

Importantly, parents and coaches also come with parenting and coaching philosophies that underlie their dispositions and guide their decisions and behaviors These philosophies are grounded in their beliefs about a myriad of aspects that affect the child's experience as an athlete. These include beliefs about discipline, work ethic, winning, determinants of playing time, what constitutes commitment and skill improvement, and even the role of the coach (figure 4.2).

communication triad—A triad that consists of parents, coaches, and children working collaboratively to ensure that children have successful experiences as athletes and improve their skills over the season.

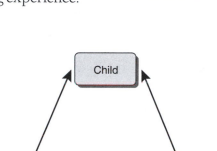

Figure 4.1   Communication triad.

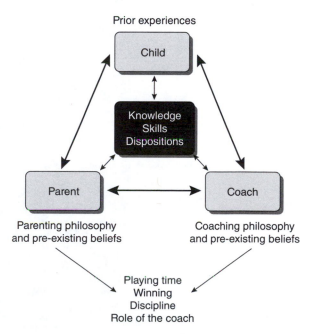

Figure 4.2   Reciprocal influences within the communication triad.

Developing a Shared Understanding

By recognizing and acknowledging the reciprocal and sometimes competing influences of coaches and parents, the club and its coaches can work toward **developing a shared understanding with parents.** This is different from working to change the beliefs of parents. We know that beliefs are strongly resistant to change (Pajares, 1992), sometimes regardless of new experiences. As such, the club's focus should not be on changing beliefs but rather on being explicit and straightforward about what parents might expect of the coach. A change in fundamental beliefs may happen, but ensuring appropriate interactions and behaviors is the ultimate goal.

For example, parental coaching from the sidelines is not only disruptive and inappropriate, but has also been shown to influence the dropout rates of adolescent swimmers' sport participation (Fraser-Thomas, Cote, & Deakin, 2008). To reduce or eliminate these behaviors, a coach must explicitly state his expectations about parental behavior at games and practices. Simply put, he must communicate that parental coaching from the sidelines is unwelcome because it distracts the players from focusing, and further, that parents who continue to do so will not be welcome at practices or games. The parents may continue to believe that coaching from the sidelines is appropriate and beneficial to their children, but they may choose to reduce or stop their behaviors at the behest of the coach.

Developing a shared understanding in the coaching context is also different from negotiating and consensus building. Not everything is negotiable, and coach–parent consensus is not always required. Sideline coaching is one example; another might be playing time (who gets it and under what conditions). Coach–parent

Parents and coaches need to come to a shared understanding about the parents' role during competition.

Courtesy of the Brandywine Youth Club

consensus about playing time is not the desired outcome, nor should parents be allowed to negotiate on behalf of their child for more of it. Instead, a shared understanding is achieved when parents understand exactly how players are granted playing time and the coach understands that she will be held accountable for applying playing time rules equitably.

Developing a shared understanding does not happen by accident or default. Rather, it is a multidimensional process that begins with self-reflection and ends with a commitment to building relationships with parents that extend beyond the coaching context. The remainder of this chapter outlines four ways coaches can intentionally work to develop a shared understanding with parents to ensure positive interactions and a successful and enjoyable experience for the athletes: (1) being transparent about one's coaching philosophy, (2) engaging in appropriate and ongoing communication, (3) collecting data to guide decisions and assess athletes' progress (and select athletes for the team), and (4) providing social opportunities outside of the coaching context.

SUCCESSFUL STRATEGY

Effective Parents

The ideal situation for any club is to have supportive parents who have a healthy and realistic perspective in regards to their child's abilities, are supportive in a constructive manner, and who know how and when to interact with club personnel and coaches. However, it is well documented that this ideal scenario is not always the case. Parents threatening coaches, causing scenes that embarrass all involved, and in some instances, driving athletes and coaches from a sport and activity that they truly love, are too often the norm and not the exception.

The sport club can and should take steps to ensure that its coaches follow the strategies presented in this chapter (e.g., holding pre-season meetings, creating clear communication, assigning parent responsibilities, etc.). Additionally, the club can go one step further to ensure a positive parent–athlete–coach triangle by making parents aware of materials that are available to help them understand a parent's role in creating a positive experience for their child, the coach, the club, and even themselves.

To assist parents, Liberty Mutual, in partnership with Positive Coaching Alliance, US Youth Soccer, and USA Football, launched an online resource site dedicated to fostering positive sporting experiences in the youth sport environment. Found at www.responsiblesports.com, the site provides parents with advice, toolkits, and best practices in being involved with their child's sport participation, as well as with the coach and the club.

Topics covered in the Responsible Sport Parenting Toolkit section of the site are key safety measures, mastery approach tools, how to fill the emotional tanks of players, how to provide responsible criticism and engage in empowering conversations, teaching children to honor the game, and parent and coach intervention tools. The information is available for download if the club wants to share it with all parents at a meeting or to parents who inquire.

The key is that the sport club does not have to reinvent the wheel in order to promote better relations with parents. Clubs can rely on best practices that are provided by a reputable organization like the Positive Coaching Alliance (www.positivecoach.org), who receive input from an established sport governing body such as US Youth Soccer. The strategies presented have a proven track record of success over the years. In the long run, making parents aware of these resources will enable them to better understand their role and will ultimately benefit everyone involved with the club.

Being Transparent About One's Coaching Philosophy

A coach who shares an articulate and reflective coaching philosophy with parents (both verbally and in writing) has taken an important first step in helping parents understand her behavior. The philosophy statement should articulate what the coach (and club) values and believes. It provides a window into the experiences the coach is committed to providing the athletes during the season. The philosophy statement is also informed by the club philosophy. Where possible, a coach's personal philosophy should be congruent with that of the club in order to avoid surprises and conflicts later in the relationship. A discussion of coaching philosophy should be a part of the hiring process, and both parties should fully understand any points of difference.

The creation of a coaching philosophy is an important precursor to communicating openly and consistently with parents. A coaching philosophy is an honest reflection about what the coach and club value. It helps parents fully understand what they can expect from the coach so they are able to clearly see similarities and question important differences. If, for example, parents value equal playing time and the coach's philosophy is that every team should experience the thrill of winning regardless of the fact that some children may not play, then a discussion with the parents will be required. The difference in philosophies may not be reconcilable and the child may be moved to a different level of competition or team, but ultimately that decision may be in the best interest of all concerned.

When crafting a coaching philosophy, coaches must be truly honest and reflective because the goal is to ensure that their coaching behaviors reflect and align with their philosophies. (See the sidebar on page 75 for an exercise that will help you craft a coaching philosophy.) They might begin by asking themselves what they value as a coach, such as hard work, winning, teamwork, effort, knowing their athletes and how to motivate them, being a positive role model, or providing athletes with a certain degree of autonomy. There are no correct responses, just honest ones.

Next, coaches should consider whether their coaching behaviors actually align with their values. A coach who says he values hard work should reward it. He needs to ask himself how he currently encourages and rewards hard work in practices and games. Does he allocate playing time based on an athletes' ability to work hard in practice, regardless of their technical or tactical ability, or does he play only the more highly skilled athletes who he thinks might help the team win? Does allocating playing time truly reward hard work? Are there other ways he might consider rewarding hard work in practice?

By reflecting on their behaviors and how those behaviors align with their philosophies, coaches are also forced to answer the fundamental questions that link the two: How will I know hard work when I see it, and how will my players know I am valuing their hard work? and, What can I do to be a positive role model, and how will my players know I am being a positive role model? Answering these questions is an important part of the reflection process and will assist with effective communication with the athletes and parents. A coach might decide, for example, that being a good role model requires refraining from yelling at officials and setting a rule that requires athletes and parents to do the same.

Crafting Your Coaching Philosophy

To help you determine whether your values and behaviors are congruent, try the following exercise.

1. List five things you value as a coach.

   1. Being supportive and motivating my athletes

   2. _____

   3. _____

   4. _____

   5. _____

2. List five slogans or statements that you use as a coach on a regular basis.

   1. This isn't Burger King; you can't have it your way.

   2. _____

   3. _____

   4. _____

   5. _____

3. Do the coaching statements you listed in question 2 reflect what you value in question 1? If there are differences in what you're saying and what you truly believe you value, then you might want to modify your core values or choose phrases that better reflect your values.

4. Once you have identified or modified your core values, write about them in a philosophy statement that outlines what you value and believe about coaching.

My philosophy statement is . . .

_____

_____

_____

_____

From M.J. Robinson, 2010, *Sport Club Management* (Champaign, IL: Human Kinetics).

Engaging in Appropriate and Ongoing Communication

A second way to develop a shared understanding with parents is to engage in **appropriate and ongoing communication** with both parents and athletes. A coach who communicates well with athletes makes a lasting impression on both athletes who continue in sport and those who drop out (Fraser-Thomas, Cote, & Deakin, 2008). Strong communication also helps to reduce parent–coach conflicts that often arise as the season progresses.

appropriate and ongoing communication—The extent to which parents are kept fully informed about all aspects of their children's experiences and continue to feel comfortable with the frequency and nature of the communications.

Appropriate and ongoing communication can be achieved to the extent that parents are kept fully informed about all aspects of their children's experiences and continue to feel comfortable with the frequency and nature of the communications. To set the tone from the beginning of the season, the coach should send each parent an initial welcome letter. This should be followed by an information meeting with parents and players in which the coach hands out and discusses an information package. As well, the coach should create a parents' forum with regular meetings and a specific agenda, hold ongoing information meetings with all parents, and conduct an exit meeting with all parents at the end of the season. These strategies are addressed in detail in the following sections.

Welcome Letter

The purpose of the welcome letter is to introduce the coach, welcome parents to the new season, and invite them to an information session on a specified evening or weekend. This letter (sent by either mail or e-mail) should include a brief introduction (e.g., previous coaching experience, coaching philosophy), contact information, and details about the information meeting. Rather than include this letter with the information package, it is sent as a stand-alone to encourage par-

Sample Welcome Letter

Dear Parent,

I would like to welcome you to the 2010 season of lacrosse. I am very excited about the upcoming season, and I hope you share in that excitement.

Allow me to introduce myself for those of you who don't know me. My name is Jane Smith, and this is my second year coaching the 12- to 13-year-old county lacrosse team. Prior to coaching this team, I spent three seasons coaching the under-10 team. I believe that [add coaching philosophy here].

I would like to take this opportunity to welcome you to a team meeting on Saturday, March 6, 2010. The meeting will take place from 2:00 to 300 p.m. at the Kerry Parks and Recreation Building located at 11 Dingleway Road in Kerry. All parents and children are welcome to attend.

During the meeting you will receive an information package that provides all of the details about the upcoming season. In addition to providing details about the team functioning and schedule, the meeting will give you an important opportunity to ask me any questions you might have and meet some of the other parents and players.

Your attendance at the meeting would be greatly appreciated because it will also give me a chance to meet you in person. If, however, your schedule does not permit your attendance, please contact me at 555-5555 and I will send you the information package.

I am delighted to be back and look forward to seeing you on Saturday, March 6.

Best regards,
Jane Smith

ents to attend the information meeting. The sidebar on page 76 shows a sample welcome letter to parents.

Information Package

The information package should include the club leaders' and coach's contact information, policies, rules, expectations of the athletes, expectations of the parents, and the practice and game schedules. The intent is to provide a complete set of guidelines so that both the athletes and parents know what to expect.

To create the information package, the coach must reflect on his philosophy and consider the club standards, rules, and regulations prior to developing the package. Once again, there must be a connection between the rules and expectations and what those would look like in terms of behaviors. For example, a coach might expect athletes to treat each other with respect. To understand what this means, athletes and parents will need an explanation—what does showing respect look like? Perhaps it means refraining from teasing, taunting, or bullying; encouraging each other in practices and games; or helping other players who do not understand a drill.

The club can assist in the process of creating the information package, but the coach must have a central role in its preparation because it is the document that guides his behavior The creation of this package can be time consuming and difficult and will require reflection and introspection, but the benefits outweigh the cost. This document allows each member of the triad to begin the season with a full understanding of the expectations. A sample information package is presented in the sidebar on page 78.

Parents' Forum

A **parents' forum** is an organization run by parents that helps the coach by shouldering some of the administrative responsibilities of the team, such as organizing transportation to and from games and tournaments, providing refreshments at tournaments, recording game data, and helping to choose uniforms. (Additional parents' forum roles are listed in the sidebar on this page.) Parents involved in the forum must be self directed. They schedule their own meetings and assume roles based on the team's needs and their own individual areas of expertise or interest. The list of responsibilities of the parents' forum should be generated by the coach and the parents. In order to ensure ongoing communication with this group, the coach should have meetings with one or two representatives of the group periodically throughout the season. Not every parent is expected to join the forum, but all should have the opportunity to provide input or join at any time. E-mail and electronic mailing lists allow for ongoing communication.

Parent Forum Roles

Activate a phone tree in the event of an emergency or the cancellation of a practice or game.

Provide transportation to and from games and tournaments.

Sell refreshments at games and tournaments.

Keep statistics.

Raise funds.

Organize a family day.

parents' forum—An opportunity for parents to take on roles within their children's team to keep them involved in areas they may be interested in and also to help the coach shoulder the administrative responsibilities of the team.

Dear Parent,

This information package is designed to provide you with the information you will need this season. It includes the following:

1. Contacting the coach(es)
2. Expectations of athletes
3. Expectations of parents
4. Policies and rules
5. Practice schedule
6. Game schedule
7. Facility contact information and directions

1. Contacting the Coach

Head coach: Jane Smith

Home phone: 555-5555 (after 5:00 p.m. and weekends)

Cell phone: 666-6666 (anytime—leave a message)

E-mail address: jsmith@kerry.edu

Please feel free to phone me at either of these numbers. I will not be able to chat with you during the business day, but if you leave a message on my cell phone, I will be happy to get back with you at my earliest convenience. Similarly, I will respond to e-mail messages as soon as I am able.

2. Expectations of Athletes

- Athletes are expected to give maximum effort at all practices. This includes hustling to retrieve balls and when transitioning to new drills and maintaining a focus on completing all drills.
- Athletes are expected to treat each other with respect. This includes refraining from teasing, taunting, or bullying another athlete; assisting when peers need help; and encouraging teammates in games and practices.

3. Expectations of Parents

- Parents are expected to help their children arrive on time to practices and games.
- Parents are expected to show respect for other parents, coaches, and referees by refraining from yelling negative comments. Encouragement is always welcome.

4. Policies and Rules

- *Attendance:* Athletes are expected to be at all practices and to be ready to participate when practice begins. Athletes who need a change in equipment before practice should arrive early. If your child cannot make a practice, please let me know in advance if possible because I may need to adjust my practice plan as a result.
- *Playing time:* Athletes who attend all practices during the week of a game will get equal playing time during games. Athletes who have missed one or more practices will get limited playing time during the game.
- *Water bottles:* All athletes are required to bring their own water and bottles.
- *Parent disruptions:* Parents are welcome to attend practices and games but are not allowed to coach from the sidelines. Parents who yell at, heckle, or verbally attack coaches, players, referees, or other parents will be asked to leave and will no longer be welcome.

5. Practice Schedule

[Provide the practice schedule for the entire season in calendar or table format.]

6. Game Schedule

[Provide the game schedule for the entire season in calendar or table format.]

7. Facility Contact Information and Directions

[Provide contact information for the facility—address and phone numbers—as well as directions in written form or as a link to a Web site such as Mapquest.]

Regular Parent Information Meetings

Parent information meetings can be scheduled two or three times during the season depending on the length of the season. These meetings provide an opportunity to revisit the team goals and answer any questions that might have arisen. Providing these regularly scheduled meetings can prevent a barrage of individual meetings because parents who wish to discuss an issue with the coach know they will have an upcoming opportunity to do so. These meeting are separate from parents' forum meetings because not all parents will be interested in joining the forum and because both serve different functions. Having one or two parents present an update of the forum's work at the general information meetings will keep all parents informed.

Exit (End-of-Season) Meeting

The purpose of the exit meeting is to find out what the parents liked or didn't like about the season in general and to communicate with the coach specifically. Parents are also asked to provide suggestions for improvement. An anonymous parent questionnaire distributed at the exit meeting can provide important feedback for the coach to assist in planning for the next season. The sidebar below lists some questions coaches might want to ask parents at an exit meeting.

Questions for the Exit Meeting

Communication

1. Did the coach communicate with you effectively throughout the season?

   If yes, please provide examples:

   If no, please provide examples and suggestions for improvement:

2. How can the coach improve communication with you next season (in addition to those mentioned above)?

3. Did the coach communicate with your child effectively throughout the season?

   If yes, please provide examples:

   If no, please provide examples and suggestions for improvement:

4. How can the coach improve communication with your child next year (in addition to those mentioned above)?

Policies and Procedures

1. Were the policies and procedures effective this season?

   If yes, please provide examples of the ones that were most effective:

   If no, please provide examples and suggestions for improvement:

2. How can the coach improve the policies and procedures next season?

Collecting Data to Guide Decisions and Assess Progress

A third way a coach can create a shared understanding with parents is to ensure that parents understand how she makes coaching decisions relative to each athlete. The coach is expected to make decisions with regard to positions (i.e., goalie versus midfielder) in addition to determining who gets to play and for how long. In order to demonstrate to parents and athletes that her decision and allocation process is fair, the coach needs to base her decisions on data she has collected.

Parents have the right to hold coaches (and clubs) accountable for their decisions, and coaches have a duty to apply the same criteria to all athletes regardless of their ability or likeability. Collecting and recording data is one strategy coaches can use not only to ensure that they are being fair, but also to prepare themselves to respond to parents who ask why their children are not getting enough playing time. The playing time discussion occurs frequently because parents compare the performance of their children to that of others as the season progresses. A coach needs to be prepared with facts and figures related to her decisions in order to help parents understand and accept them.

Data should be collected throughout the season and should extend beyond game statistics. It is helpful to know who is scoring points and how many turnovers a team has, but it is also important to know the strengths and weaknesses of each player in a number of areas. These data also assist in motivating athletes and focusing on improvement rather than on the team's win–loss record.

Although many data collection sheets or instruments are available from sport governing bodies, many decisions must be made prior to deciding which instruments to use or what to include in one's own data collection instrument. The first step in considering strengths and weakness, for example, is to decide what dimensions to measure and what criteria to use to determine athletes' relative strengths and weaknesses. Coaches can compare these data to age-appropriate norms or simply rank-order the performances within the team. The following examples each have a specific performance measure, criteria used to assess that performance, and a ranking system that will help compare each athletes performance:

Speed (as measured by a timed sprint): poor, fair, good, excellent

Agility (timed agility score): poor, fair, good, excellent

Jump (height from standing): poor, fair, good, excellent

Coaches and clubs are strongly encouraged to be creative and extend the data collection to aspects of the game that are meaningful in terms of an athletes' ability to actually play the game or other areas identified in the club's or coach's philosophy. For example, speed, strength, and agility do not directly measure strengths or weaknesses relative to game performance; nor does the ability to pass back and forth to a partner. Instead, the focus should be on measuring the specific behaviors that make athletes successful in games and practices. These may include the following:

Knowledge of the Game

- ▶ Offense (ability to pass to the open player in a scrimmage): poor, fair, good, excellent
- ▶ Defense (ability to stay between the opponent and the goal): poor, fair, good, excellent

Hustling

- ▶ Runs to get the ball: always, sometimes, never
- ▶ Focuses on task rather than chatting with friends: always, sometimes, never

Too often, coaches rely on general terms to explain differences in playing time to parents, making statements such as "Latoya needs to work on her defense" or "Shaun doesn't understand the game." The type of data collection described previously allows coaches to move away from these generic and vague responses. Instead they are able to provide specific data that indicate the strengths and weaknesses of each player along each dimension measured. Because these data are sport specific and must be developmentally appropriate for a particular age group of the children, coaches and clubs should consider creating these data collection sheets prior to the beginning of the season.

As the season continues, it makes sense to reassess these measures periodically and interpret them within the data collected during games. For example, if a player has a very high number of turnovers in a game, he might not be seeing the open player when passing. This would therefore become an area for improvement and a point of discussion with a parent who is upset over her child's lack of playing time. Having data to support decisions will show the parent that decisions are not subjective but grounded in ongoing and continuing data collection and assessment.

An additional benefit of collecting this type of data is that it provides information that might assist with planning practices and improving the technical and tactical ability of every player on the team. If turnover rates are consistently high across the team, then practices must be planned to help the athletes learn to recognize the open player when trying to make a pass.

Providing Social Opportunities Outside of the Coaching Context

Beyond being explicit about what parents can expect of the coach within the practice and game contexts, clubs should also encourage coaches to build relationships outside of the coaching context. During practices and games coaches have very little time to socialize informally with parents and siblings and therefore miss important opportunities to get to know them and understand the athletes within the context of their families and friends. Additional opportunities for social interactions must therefore be planned and scheduled in advance of the season.

One very effective way of fostering these relationships is to organize a family day. It could take place at a state or local park where coaches, athletes, and families gather for a cookout and pick-up games. Another option is meeting at a local bowling alley. Alternatively, asking parents for ideas might help them feel valued in the process, and the organization of the event might become the responsibility of the parents' forum.

Summary

This chapter presents a model for understanding and building collaboration between coaches and parents to help children have successful sporting experiences in their local clubs. The coach, parent, and child are each part of a communication triad, with each bringing different knowledge, skills, and dispositions that guide their behaviors and decisions.

Accepting similarities while valuing and respecting differences within each of these domains requires an intentional focus on building a shared understanding between coaches and parents. Four strategies for building a shared understanding are (1) being transparent about one's coaching philosophy, (2) engaging in appropriate and ongoing communication, (3) collecting data to guide decisions and assess athletes' progress, and (4) providing social opportunities outside of the coaching context. These strategies will help the coach and the club successfully communicate with parents, thereby reducing potential points of conflict and misunderstandings that may arise during the season.

By embracing collaboration and using strategies that help build a shared understanding, coaches can reduce the conflict and confrontation that can characterize coach–parent interactions. By having a transparent and articulated philosophy, a communication plan, accurate data reflecting athletes' strengths and weaknesses, and a commitment to developing a relationship with parents, coaches can avoid many situations in which parent–coach tensions can arise.

The executive director of the Kerry Lacrosse Club recognized the problem as a lack of communication between the coach and the parents. Even though the season was underway, the director helped the coach understand the central role of the parents and the need to develop a shared understanding to communicate effectively with them. The coach was asked to create a coaching philosophy and write down her expectations of both parents and athletes. Once she had done this, the executive director called a parent meeting. During the meeting the coach had the opportunity to outline her philosophy and the parents had the opportunity to share some of their concerns. Following the extensive meeting, the majority of the parents agreed with the coach's decisions and were supportive of the decision to play everyone even if it resulted in a loss. The parents who did not agree understood that no amount of berating would change the amount of playing time their children received this season and that they would need to make a decision about moving to another club next year. Following the meeting, the executive director decided to prevent these problems from occurring next season by creating a shared understanding among coaches, parents, and athletes at the start of the season.

iStockphoto/dswebb

By the end of the chapter, the sport club manager will be able to do the following:

▶ Define the terms associated with the legal aspects of the sport environment.

▶ List the elements of negligence and explain the difference between negligence and intentional torts.

▶ Control the inherent dangers associated with the supervision of the athletic programs through risk management procedures.

▶ Use risk management procedures to develop a comprehensive risk management plan.

▶ Develop a professional perspective on the legal issues sport managers face in the professional setting.

5

Legal Aspects of Club Management

• • •

The swim club that Rick Burleson runs has five full-time coaches. One of his coaches is his best friend of 10 years. He is also the top coach at the club and has coached many regional, state, and national championship swimmers over the years and has led teams to eight state championships in 10 years. Rick has evidence that his friend is having an inappropriate relationship with one of the swimmers, who is a minor. Rick had suspicions in the past but no evidence, and when he confronted the friend, the friend denied having a relationship. Now, instead of confronting his friend with the new evidence or reporting the behavior to the authorities, Rick is considering ignoring it. What is Rick's legal responsibility in this situation? Can he or the club be held liable for his lack of action? Have any statutes been violated? What is his legal responsibility to the swimmer?

• • •

The opening scenario is fraught with legal issues, including liability, criminal law, and basic morality. Rick owes the participants a standard of care in his supervision of employees. If he does not meet that standard of care, he is demonstrating deliberate indifference to the violation of the minor's civil rights. If the activity is discovered, the club could be sued for Rick's nonfeasance. The coach will face criminal charges on statutory rape. Finally, Rick's placing his concern about the consequences of losing a top coach over the concern of the minor can be viewed as immoral and unethical by society and by his profession. Rick's professional reputation as well as the reputation of the club will be permanently damaged.

A club manager must know about situations for which he or the club can be held liable, but he must also accept the moral responsibility to make decisions in the best interest of the club and, more important, its participants. This is an important issue because most sport clubs cater to kids so they have a moral and legal responsibility to offer their participants the highest standard of care. If the actions of staff members fall below that standard, the club has not met its moral or legal responsibility. In the latter case, the person involved or the club can be sued and the person could be fined or even go to prison.

Of all of the chapters in the book, this may be the most important in terms of the negative ramifications related to a lack of knowledge in this area. When it comes to the law, ignorance is not an excuse. The club manager must know the established standard of care and legal principles that are applicable in the situation. Therefore, this chapter addresses the legal principles club leaders need to be aware of, risk management, and defenses a club can use if they are sued.

Legal Principles

Laws were created because the rightness of an action is open to debate. If a club manager is not aware of or does not meet her legal responsibilities, she can face civil lawsuits if she caused harm to another, or criminal charges for unlawful action against the state. The club is ultimately accountable for the well-being of participants, visitors, and spectators and can also be held accountable for the actions of the club's coaches, participants, and administrators.

This chapter addresses a number of legal principles with which a club manager should be familiar. The areas of concern include liability, intentional torts and product liability, contracts and breach of contracts, hiring, evaluation and termination of employees, breach of fiduciary duty, risk management, and adherence to statutes and regulations.

Doctrine of Respondeat Superior

doctrine of respondeat superior—A legal doctrine that states that an employer is liable in certain cases for the negligent acts of an employee if the act is done within the scope of that employee's responsibilities.

The **doctrine of respondeat superior** is an important legal concept that applies to the club sport environment. Under the doctrine, the employer is liable in certain cases for the negligent acts of an employee within the scope of that employee's responsibilities (Cotton, 2007b). The employee is not sued by the plaintiff; rather, his employer is. In the opening case study, the club could be sued by the parents of the minor for the non-action of Rick.

If the club manager or an employee of the club does something that is outside the realm of that person's responsibilities within the club, that can be considered an **ultra vires act**, and the person can be held liable and not the club (Cotton, 2007a). This approach is often taken by a club if the act is viewed as a malfeasance. This could be the case in the situation of the coach in the case study. The club could argue that the actions of the employee were outside the realm of the coach's responsibility and that meetings occurred away from the club. In this case, the employee could be sued and not the club.

ultra vires act—An act by an employee of the club that is outside the realm of the person's responsibilities within the club, thus freeing the club from liability for the action.

Torts

Black's Law Dictionary defines a **tort** as a civil wrong ("Tort," 1991). A club or club manager who has committed a tort will not face criminal charges from the state (and therefore not face a fine or jail time); rather, the club will be asked to compensate the person who was harmed. Three types of torts have an impact on club sport: negligence, intentional tort, and product liability. (See the sidebar below for an overview of each type of tort.) Of the three, the club manager will encounter potential negligence most frequently. Potential negligence can be avoided by creating a proactive risk management plan; this will be discussed in more detail later in the chapter.

tort—A civil wrong.

Three Types of Torts

- *Negligence:* Someone sustains personal injury, but there was no intent to cause injury.
- *Intentional tort:* Someone sustains personal injury, and there was an intent to do that person harm.
- *Product liability:* Someone sustains injury from a consumer product.

Negligence

Negligence can be defined as a failure to exercise care in the way a normal person would under the circumstances. On a spring evening, a lightning storm moves into the area. Would a normal person serving as a club manager order all youth lacrosse teams practicing at an outdoor complex to go into a covered shelter area, or allow the teams to remain on the open fields? Clearly, a normal person would not put the youths at risk by having them stay out in the storm.

A negligent act can be an action of omission, in that the person did not do something she should have or failed to comply with a legal standard, or an act of commission, in that the person did something she should not have done or did something incorrectly (van der Smissen, 2007).

What is interesting about negligence is that the behavior that ultimately led to harm was unintentional. The club manager who allows the teams to stay out in the storm does not do it with the hope that a player will be struck by lightning,

negligence—A failure to exercise care in the way a normal person would under the circumstances.

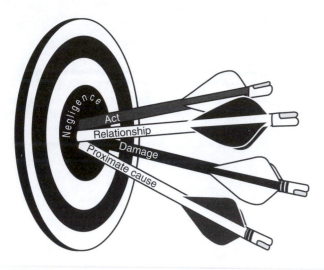

Figure 5.1 All four elements of negligence must be proven before negligence can exist.

invitee—A person who has been asked, or invited, and may have paid the defendant to participate.

but because he doesn't think anyone would be struck by lightning. The fact that the club manager didn't intend for a lightning strike to happen is not a defense against negligence.

van der Smissen (2007) stated that precedent cases have determined that four elements must be present for an act to be deemed negligent: the relationship, the act, proximate cause, and damage (figure 5.1). Knowing these elements will make club managers aware of their responsibility and hopefully influence how they act.

The Relationship For negligence to be proven, there must be a relationship between the plaintiff (the harmed party) and the defendant (the club). If a relationship exists, then the club can be liable. The court will determine whether a relationship exists and the strength of that relationship. The club owes the highest standard of care to an **invitee.** This is a person who has been asked or invited and may have paid the defendant to participate (van der Smissen, 2007).

SUCCESSFUL STRATEGY

Preventing Liability

In the spring of 2009, a jury in Santa Barbara, California, awarded the parents of deceased Yoni Gottesman $16.3 million in compensatory and punitive damages related to the drowning of four-year-old Yoni in 2005. The case demonstrates the importance of hiring responsible and qualified staff; developing, implementing, and monitoring a supervisory plan; and understanding the abilities of participants. If not done, the entity will be held liable for its actions.

The Gottesmans paid for Yoni to attend a day camp at Cathedral Oaks Athletic Club. Therefore, Yoni was classified as an invitee and was owed the highest standard of care. Yoni was permitted in part of a pool that was one inch higher in depth than his body height, and Yoni had only barely passed a swim test earlier in the day. In addition, a surveillance video showed a counselor throwing Yoni into the pool. Yoni's body was later discovered in the pool facedown. It was estimated that the body was there for eight minutes before it was discovered by the athletic club's staff. A staff member administered CPR, but Yoni did not revive.

The jury determined the cause of the drowning to be the inattentiveness of the club and its employees. Some staff members were milling about the pool deck, and a lifeguard had gone to purchase a soda during the time Yoni was in the pool. The jury found the defendants in the case to have acted with willful misconduct and determined that to be the proximate cause of death.

The club is responsible for $2.3 million in punitive damages, and all 11 defendants in the case are responsible for the remaining damages. Along with this, the club lacked the appropriate state permits to provide child care, and it is possible that the club's liability insurance will not pay for the damages.

This case doesn't show a *successful* strategy; rather, it underscores the importance of understanding the risks associated with operating a sport club and taking steps to ensure the safety of all participants. It is also worth noting that before a club ventures into a new activity (e.g., care and after care, strength and conditioning training), it should make sure that its current liability insurance covers that activity.

A **licensee** is a person who was not invited but was not asked to leave (van der Smissen, 2007). A good example of a licensee is a father who comes to a facility to watch his child participate in an activity. The club did not invite him to come, but the club did not tell him to leave once he was there. If the club does not offer a safe environment, it can be held liable if the father is injured while at the facility.

The last relationship is the weakest, and that is the relationship with a **trespasser.** If someone enters the club facility without the consent of the club and that person is harmed, in most cases the club will not be held liable. The only way the club could be held liable is if the facility were made unsafe and the trespasser was harmed by that modification. The club must also address what are known as attractive nuisances, such as a pool or a piece of equipment. The club must take steps to deter potential trespassers from being attracted to the nuisances through fencing and warning signs. If those steps are not taken, the club could be liable even though the defendant was a trespasser.

The Act   The second part of proving negligence is the act itself. This act can be one of either commission or omission. In terms of omission, the legal term is **nonfeasance.** Acts of nonfeasance by a club manager include not instructing, not inspecting, not fixing, not supervising, and not having the appropriate certification. In terms of commission, doing something incorrectly would be classified as a **misfeasance.** This would entail instructing incorrectly, not meeting professional accepted standards, or addressing an emergency situation incorrectly. **Malfeasance** is an act that should not be done. Using dangerous games in a training session, offering alcohol to minors, and having a relationship with a minor are categorized as malfeasant behavior.

A court considering whether an action was negligent refers to two legal concepts to assist with the decision. The first is the **reasonable man doctrine.** Did the defendant act as a reasonable person would in the given situation? Did the club manager who told teams to stay on field during a lightning storm act as a reasonable person? The **doctrine of foreseeability** is about projecting what could happen based on an act of omission or commission. The gym in which a club basketball team practices has a leaking ceiling. The club manager sees the puddle on one of the courts, but instead of foreseeing a player running into the area and slipping, the club manager decides that the puddle is in the corner of the court and not much action will occur in that area. A player going for a loose balls slips in the puddle and hits his head on the wood floor and has a serious head injury. Could the club manager have foreseen that happening?

Proximate Cause   **Proximate cause** involves demonstrating that there is a relationship between the act and the harm to the plaintiff (van der Smissen, 2007). Actions may be taken that would be viewed as either a nonfeasance or malfeasance, but unless someone is harmed, the act is not negligent. For example, a coach of a club instructs a swimmer to dive into the shallow end of a pool. Although this is bad advice given the potential danger to the swimmer, there is no negligence if the swimmer is not harmed. The role of the plaintiff's attorney is to prove that what the defendant did caused the injury.

licensee—A person who was not invited but was not asked to leave.

trespasser—A person who enters the club facility without the consent of the club.

nonfeasance—An act of omission by a club professional that leads to an injury.

misfeasance—An act done incorrectly by a club professional that leads to an injury.

malfeasance—An act that should not have been done by a club professional that leads to an injury.

reasonable man doctrine—A doctrine that determines whether the actions of a club professional were consistent with what a reasonable person would do.

doctrine of foreseeability—A determination of whether a club professional should have been able to foresee a potentially dangerous situation.

proximate cause—The demonstration of a relationship between the act and the harm to the plaintiff.

damage—The harm caused by a negligent act that can be categorized as economic loss, physical pain and suffering, emotional distress, or physical impairment.

Damage   The final element necessary for proving negligence is **damage**. (See the sidebar at the bottom of this page for a table summarizing the four elements of negligence.) The plaintiff's attorney will try to demonstrate that there was a relationship between the defendant and the plaintiff and that the defendant either did something or did not do something that was directly related to the harm caused to the plaintiff. van der Smissen (2007) categorized that harm as economic loss, physical pain and suffering, emotional distress, or physical impairment.

Consider an athlete who is injured as a result of the action of one of the club's coaches. This athlete was being recruited by universities and would have received a full athletic scholarship. The college scholarship can be valued in the hundreds of thousands of dollars. This would constitute economic loss. Also, the injury itself was very painful and the athlete had to go through several months of painful rehabilitation. This would constitute pain and suffering. The athlete has the memory of the injury and remains distressed over the fact that her athletic career is now over. This constitutes emotional distress. Finally, the athlete will never again be able to perform certain physical activities or day-to-day activities that she was able to do prior to the injury, and special accommodations will have to be made for the rest of her life. This constitutes physical impairment. These are the factors that are considered when a court awards a financial judgment to a plaintiff.

Again, it is important to note that negligent acts are not intentional. They are usually committed because of a lack of knowledge of standards, a lack of judgment or common sense, laziness, or the belief that "it will not happen to me." Club managers should encourage all coaches and employees to foresee what could happen based on their actions and to use good judgment and common sense to ensure the safety of participants.

Elements of Negligence in a Sport Club Setting

Element	What it means	How it applies to a sport club
The Relationship	A relationship exists between the person harmed and the one causing the injury.	Clubs need to take steps to ensure that anyone who comes into contact with the club is safe—this includes participants, spectators, and uninvited visitors.
The Act	The injury was caused by an act of commission or an act of omission.	Clubs need to make sure that employees' actions do not fall below the established professionally accepted standard of care.
Proximate cause	A relationship exists between the act and the injury sustained.	Club leaders and employees need to provide logical guidance to participants, making sure they are not exposed to potential danger.
Damage	Injury or harm has occurred.	Clubs need to make sure that all employees behave in a way that keeps participants safe.

Intentional Torts

Intentional torts differ from liability in that they are civil wrongs with the intent to cause harm to the defendant. As with negligence, the defendant must prove damages, which can come in the form of physical or emotional damage or damage to the person's reputation. This can occur through libel or slander, assault or battery, misappropriation of an image, deliberate interference with a contract, or breach of fiduciary duty (see the sidebar at the bottom of this page for a quick summary of each). In each of these cases, a person has been harmed by the intentional actions of another.

Libel and Slander   **Libel** and **slander** pertain to false statements either stated (slander) or written (libel) about another person or entity. If damage to the person or entity can be proven, the person who made or wrote those statements can be found liable. For example, a club manager tells the families of potential players that a rival club physically abuses athletes and requires them to take performance-enhancing drugs. If none of these statements are true, and these false accusations lead to players not joining or leaving the rival club resulting in the director of that club losing his position, that club and the former director can seek legal recourse based on damage to the reputation that has injured the person's career and the club's reputation.

Assault and Battery   Assault and battery pertain to the threat of harming someone through physical touch. Within the sport environment physical confrontations can occur between parents and between parents and coaches, parents and officials, coaches and officials, players and players, players and coaches, and players and parents. Again, the key to civil claims being made is the proof of damages. Assault is the threat of harm, and battery is the actual touching (Hums, 2007).

If a parent yells to a game official: "You stink and I'm going to knock your head off!" that is a threat. To prove that an assault has occurred, the official must believe that there is intent to cause harm, and there must be a lack of consent. Battery is the use of force. If after making the threat, the parent leaves the stands and attacks

intentional tort—A deliberate attempt to harm someone either physically, financially, or reputationally.

libel—False statements written about another person or entity.

slander—false statements stated about another person or entity.

Types of Intentional Torts

- *Defamation (libel and slander):* Untrue and harmful statements that are written (libel) or spoken (slander).
- *Assault and battery:* The threat of a harmful act (assault) or the actual harmful act (battery) that involves touching another person.
- *Misappropriation of image:* Using someone else's image or likeness without that person's permission.
- *Deliberate interference with a contract:* Purposely interfering with a contractual promise.
- *Breach of fiduciary duty:* Not putting self-interests aside for the betterment of the whole.

the official, battery is present. Clubs must give coaches clear directions about what they cannot do to players and provide an environment that deters violent behavior on the part of all involved. In the previous example, the club could be party in a suit for not taking action to prevent the official from being attacked by the parent.

Misappropriation of Image   Misappropriation of image entails a club's using a likeness or image without the consent of the entity or person that owns it (Rushing, 2007). If a soccer club in Middletown, Delaware, USA, would like to call its club Middletown United and be known as MU and develops a crest very similar to the crest of the Manchester United Football Club without that club's consent, that is a case of misappropriation of image. Before using a logo or developing a name, clubs need to take the time to discover if any entity owns the rights to the name or logo. In the case of Middletown United, Manchester United could seek legal recourse to prevent the use of the logo and seek damages for the confusion created because of the logo or name being used by the club.

In terms of likeness use, a club must have the approval of anyone whose image they wish to use to promote the club. A basketball club cannot use photos of Lebron James, Kobe Bryant, or Yao Ming on its promotional materials without the consent of those people. Using their likenesses implies that they are affiliated with the club when they are not. The club may attract members who think that these players are affiliated with the club or will appear at club functions. That is very misleading and the club may gain financially from the use of the images, but Lebron, Kobe, and Yao would not.

Using the images of participants for the promotion of the club can also be an issue. A club that wants to use photos of athletes playing on its Web site or a brochure for a summer camp program must first receive permission from the athletes to use their likeness for that purpose. This can be solved rather easily by providing a place on the registration form for participants to agree to the club's use of their images to promote the club.

Deliberate Interference With a Contract   Clubs and club managers enter into a variety of contracts. The types of contracts are discussed in more detail later in the chapter. A contract is a promise between two parties. If a third party interferes with that promise, that party can be found liable (Rushing, 2007). This may occur if a club manager is interested in hiring a coach or staff member from another club. If the club manager talks that person into leaving without the consent of the other club, it can be viewed as interference in the contract between the coach or staff person and the rival club. The appropriate action in this situation would be to ask permission of the rival club to speak to that coach or to wait until the contract expires before approaching the person about employment.

Breach of Fiduciary Duty   A club executive director has an obligation to act in the interest of the club and put personal interests aside. Not doing so is a breach of fiduciary duty. Consider a club director who enters into a contract with a service provider in exchange for being hired as a consultant on future projects even though the service provider will charge the club more than another provider would. The executive director convinces the board to approve the contract and does not inform them of the consulting contract. In this case the executive director acted in her best interest and not the club's. She will make more money, and the club will pay more for the services provided.

Product Liability

Sport involves the use of equipment, whether it is the bats and balls needed for playing or the protective gear worn by athletes. The club can be found liable in relation to the equipment the club staff either provides, assembles, or endorses for its members to use. If a club distributes equipment, participants will assume that the equipment will do what it is intended to do. Therefore, club employees should only purchase and distribute equipment that they believe is safe and will fulfill its intended purpose.

Risk Management

Risk can be defined as an uncertainty. Thus, **risk management** is about managing uncertainty, reducing exposure to risk, and limiting loss. Clubs can manage the many uncertain aspects of the environment by taking proactive measures to eliminate, transfer, or reduce risk.

risk management—The process of managing the unknown and taking steps to reduce exposure to risk and limit loss.

Some clubs neglect risk management because they believe they will not see the financial return on reducing risk. For example, a risk assessment may identify that a facility has a structural flaw that makes a playing area unsafe. Altering the structure will require a significant expenditure. The club may decide that there is a one-in-a-million chance that someone will be hurt and will play the odds and not address the risk. Another club may not see a potential risk or may not be aware of the professionally accepted standard. Some clubs rely on the insurance they carry to compensate anyone who is harmed. Ignorance is not an excuse, however, and a lawyer for a defendant will have a trained eye to see what the common eye may not see. To determine the risks associated with its operations, a club should conduct a risk management assessment to analyze the current practices of the club and determine what can be done to manage the uncertainties that may be present.

The DIM process is an anticipatory technique to address risk management. The process involves developing, implementing, and managing a risk management plan (Ammon & Brown, 2007). The development stage entails identifying risk, classifying it, and selecting the appropriate method of treatment (Ammon & Brown, 2007). Each facility, sport, or event has unique risks, and they need to be identified. After identifying a risk, the organization should classify its presence on a continuum from very frequent to not frequent at all, and the harm it could potentially cause from mild to very severe (Ammon & Brown, 2007).

After identifying a risk, the club can transfer the risk, reduce the risk, or eliminate the risk. There is uncertainty in every activity. The most effective measure is to eliminate the risk. For example, if coaches in the club use a game in the training of participants that is dangerous, eliminating the risk would entail not allowing the coaches to use the game in training. Coaches who continue to use the game would be terminated to eliminate the risk.

Reducing the risk entails recognizing it and taking steps to reduce it. For example, if a club manager recognizes that a post in a gym is very close to the playing area, he could reduce the risk by adding protective materials around the post so that participants who run into it would hit the padding. He could also rearrange the playing area to move the post farther from the playing surface.

Transferring risk involves recognizing a risk and passing it on to a third party. The best way to do this is to buy insurance. If something does happen and the club is sued, the club's insurance company, rather than the club, pays for the damages. The doctrine of respondeat superior, in which the action of the employee is passed on to the club, was presented earlier in the chapter. In the case of transferring risk, the club can hire an independent contractor rather than an employee to provide a service. A club can hire a coach to coach only one team as an independent contractor. If the club manager has done her due diligence in checking on the coach's background and is not aware of any problems or concerns about this coach's past, then the club is not liable for that coach's actions. The risk has been transferred to the independent contractor. Clubs can also transfer risk to professional transportation companies. In the case of an accident, the transportation company is held liable, and not the club.

Implementing a risk management plan requires effective communication of the plan to all employees and volunteers of the club as well as participants. This is accomplished by presenting the plan verbally as well as by spelling it out in documents such as policy manuals and risk management plans.

Managing the plan is primarily a human resources role. The risk manager should be a full-time employee who is assisted by a risk management committee made up of staff and volunteers. Ammon and Brown (2007) suggested that risk managers be given the authority to implement the plan. Lastly, Ammon and Brown (2007) cited the importance of continued input from all involved with the club to revise and improve the plan to address new risks.

The harming of a participant either physically or emotionally can ultimately affect the bottom line as the club pays legal fees associated with a lawsuit or experiences a rise in insurance premiums. Also worth noting is that although the injured party may be compensated by the insurance company, the person is still suffering from the injury and may even be physically impaired for life. A proactive risk management program makes the uncertain more certain. The club manager looking to manage risk must consider the competence of personnel and volunteers, the management of services, participants, equipment and facilities, policies and procedures, environmental conditions, warnings, standards, and public relations.

Competence of Personnel and Volunteers

Risk management ultimately falls to the employees and volunteers of the club. The club itself can be held accountable for their actions.

Personnel Hiring, evaluating, retaining, and terminating employees is an important and even vital part of a club manager's position. In addition to meeting the requirements laid out in the job description as discussed in chapter 3, a candidate must meet the legal standard for the position. Because club sports inherently deal with youth, clubs must execute appropriate background checks on any candidate who would have contact with participants. If the background check is not done and the employee acts inappropriately or harmfully, the club is liable for negligent hiring. Club managers should research background check procedures to ensure that they perform comprehensive checks for local, national, and international incidents in which a prospective employee may have been involved.

Due diligence is not just in the hiring process. A club manager who discovers something about a newly hired employee via a background check or another source has the legal responsibility to act on that information. If the club decides to continue to employ that person because no problems have occurred and then the person acts harmfully, the club would be liable for negligent retention. Finally, if the club manager knows that an employee is doing something harmful and does not address the problem, the club manager is liable for negligent supervision.

In the opening case study, the club manager knew that a coach was having a sexual relationship with a minor who was a participant in the club and did not stop the relationship and terminate the coach. The club could be found liable for **deliberate indifference** on the part of the club manager. Coaches and club managers who know that hazing is occurring among participants and look the other way can be found liable for deliberate indifference. Looking the other way is not an option for a club manager when the well-being of participants is at stake.

> **deliberate indifference**—A case in which a club professional knows of a tortious situation and does not take action to discontinue or prevent it.

It is incumbent on the club manager to do the due diligence in the hiring process from a moral and legal perspective. A coach may have all of the skills and experience desired for the position, but if an action from his past or something in his character suggests that his hiring could place club participants in danger, the club manager has the legal and moral responsibility to first consider the well-being of the participants and not hire or retain that person.

Volunteers   Volunteers are a valuable resource for a sport club. They can provide services and support the efforts of the full-time staff in a number of ways from coaching to running a concession stand or serving on a board. Volunteers should also be subjected to background checks to make sure there are no incidents from their past that suggest that they could pose a danger to participants. Volunteers and the club in most instances are protected from lawsuits based on **volunteer immunity.** It is important to note that once a person is paid for services, that person loses the volunteer immunity. To be granted that immunity, the following criteria must be met: The volunteer acts in good faith and within the scope of his or her duties within a specified position; the volunteer went through an approved training program related to the position; and the volunteer was supervised appropriately.

> **volunteer immunity**— Immunity extended to unpaid workers in an organization.

The club is responsible for making sure all volunteers meet the requirements for volunteer immunity. For example, if volunteers are used to coach teams in an in-house recreation league, all coaches should be required to participate in a coaches education program, the league should be supervised by a paid professional, and any volunteer coach acting in a manner that is not appropriate or that would put participants in danger should be terminated. If any of the requirements are not met, or if the volunteer does something that can be viewed as grossly negligent, the club and the volunteer may be sued for those actions.

Management of Services

As stated earlier, there are risks associated with every activity, but how clubs manage the risks associated with the services they provide depends on the services themselves. Standards of care that state the minimum requirements for providing a safe experience have been developed for most activities. Table 5.1 lists organizations that have established safety standards in relation to various aspects of sport participation.

A club manager must be aware of the standards established by professional organizations as well as legal cases that have established precedence. Clubs that do not recognize these standards and precedents are not meeting their legal or moral obligations and may be liable if someone is injured. In all of the preceding areas, standards have been established.

Participants

Risk management associated with participants primarily has to do with the type of supervision provided, the ratio of participants to supervisors, and the nature of the activity. The less skilled the participants are and the higher the danger associated with an activity, the more supervision is required. Twenty 6-year-olds on ice skates for the first time will require more supervision than 20 college-aged participants playing volleyball.

Another issue that arises with participants is **mismatching**. The most common way to match participants equally is by chronological age, but that is not a foolproof method because of differences in developmental age and maturity level. There may be bigger kids in one group and smaller kids in another, although all are the same age. Because mismatches can cause harm to one or more participants, coaches must use common sense when matching participants by age, size, skill, and gender to ensure the safety of everyone.

mismatching—Assigning participants to an activity in such as way as to create a clear disadvantage for some participants in terms of size, age, or skill level.

Table 5.1 Safety Issue and Risk Implementation Sources

Safety issue	Organization	Abbreviation	Home page
Sports equipment	American Academy of Orthopaedic Surgeons	AAOS	www.aaos.org
Child-protective equipment	American Academy of Pediatrics	AAP	www.aap.org
Aquatics	American Red Cross	ARC	www.redcross.org
Emergency policy for health and fitness	American College of Sports Medicine	ACSM	www.acsm.org
Sports equipment and facilities	American Society for Testing and Materials	ASTM	www.astm.org
Soccer goals	U.S. Consumer Product Safety Commission	CPSC	www.cpsc.gov
Lightning	National Athletic Trainers' Association	NATA	www.nata.org
College athletics	National Collegiate Athletic Association	NCAA	www.ncaa.org
Crisis planning for schools	U.S. Department of Education	USDOE	www.ed.gov

Reprinted from J.O. Spengler et al., 2009, *Introduction to sport law* (Champaign, IL: Human Kinetics), 57.

Equipment and Facilities

The appropriate use, construction, maintenance, and cleaning of facilities and equipment must be a priority for sport clubs. Facilities should be inspected on a daily, weekly, monthly, and annual basis to ensure that they are structurally sound and safe for use. Equipment should also be constructed and used the way it was designed to be used. Earlier in the chapter the concept of product liability was discussed. The club can be held liable for the equipment it uses or endorses. Because manufacturers named in lawsuits often argue that the participant did not use the equipment the way it was intended to be used or did not assemble it correctly, the club should have the manufacturer assemble the equipment to negate that defense and ensure the safety of participants. Finally, all areas of the facility (e.g., playing surfaces, locker rooms, bathrooms) and all equipment should be kept clean so as not to spread infections among members.

The club should provide the appropriate supervision to ensure that movable equipment is anchored while in use and stored in a manner that will prevent it from being used without supervision. Leaving open a storage room where mini-trampolines are kept can tempt participants to use them for unintended purposes such as dunking basketballs. Portable soccer goals should have sand bags to keep them stationary during games, and they should be locked up when not in use. Weight rooms and pools should be locked when not in use and have supervisors on site; in the case of a pool, certified lifeguards should be on duty. If any of these risk management practices are not implemented and a participant is harmed, the club can be held liable.

Environmental Conditions

Many club activities occur outdoors. Consideration must be made for environmental conditions to ensure the safety and well-being of participants. Excessive heat or cold, rain, and lightning are all conditions with which a club must contend. Clubs are liable if they ignore the conditions and participants are harmed in some way. The Internet has made weather service information more accessible than ever before. Club managers should monitor weather conditions throughout the day and practice good judgment. They need to be prepared to cancel or reschedule games or practices to ensure the safety of participants and spectators.

Transportation

Some of a club's activities may occur away from the club. Whether it is a league game across town or a weekend tournament out of state, the club takes on added liability when participants travel to participate in club activities. A very common method of transferring the risk of transportation is requiring participants to make their own travel plans. In this case, the participants accept the risks associated with traveling to events.

If the club decides to take on the responsibility of transporting its participants, the most effective way to manage this risk is to transfer it to a professional transportation company. This is the most expensive way to transfer this risk, but poses the least amount of risk for the club and is the safest. The second way to transfer transportation risk is to have a club employee drive a professional carrier's vehicle.

If an accident related to the maintenance of the vehicle occurs, the independent contractor is liable; if the accident is the fault of the driver, the club is liable. Another option is to have a club employee drive a club vehicle. In this case the club is accepting the risk of the vehicle and the driver, but the risk can be managed by keeping the vehicle in good working order and ensuring that the club employee is a safe driver.

A risky proposition is when the club passes the responsibility of transporting participants to volunteers who use their own vehicles. Background checks of volunteers' driving records can reduce this risk. The club manager should also consider the types and conditions of volunteers' vehicles. If a volunteer transporting participants to a club event has an accident, she may be protected under voluntary immunity if the accident was not the result of gross negligence such as speeding or driving under the influence of alcohol.

Clubs that take on the responsibility of transporting their participants must take the appropriate steps to make the situation as safe as possible for everyone involved by eliminating, reducing, or transferring the risk.

Warnings

Clubs must alert participants of the dangers associated with activities or the facilities. When a club takes the appropriate measures to warn and a person is harmed, the club can argue that the person was warned and thus assumed the risk associated with the activity. Warnings can come in the forms of signs posted throughout a facility communicating that certain activities should not be conducted without a supervisor present, that strength training requires a spotter, or that participants swim at their own risk when no lifeguard is on duty. Warnings also come in the form of agreements to participate that communicate the risks associated with activities. People who sign these documents indicate that they have been warned of the dangers and are choosing to participate in the activity anyway.

Public Relations

A sport club must communicate that it has done everything in its power to make its facilities and experience as safe as possible. If it does, then the first thought of someone injured at the facility or participating in a club activity may not be that the injury was the club's fault. If the club has taken every possible precaution, and if those efforts are visible and communicated to its members, the injured party may be more likely to view the accident as the result of the activity rather than the fault of the club. How club leaders act after an incident also influences how the injured person responds. They should demonstrate care and understanding and follow up with the injured. Those types of actions send the message that the club cares.

Policies and Procedures

Chapter 1 discusses the importance of policies and procedures in club management. To be effective, of course, policies and procedures must be followed, particularly those related to risk management. Policies for reporting accidents, submitting medical forms, having participants sign waivers and agreements, supervising appropriately, using the DIM risk management approach, and using facilities and equipment safely must be known by all employees of the club, and they must be put into action. If a policy is not followed and a participant is harmed as a result, the club can be liable.

Defenses

Once a club is aware of its legal responsibilities, it needs to consider what defenses it has against liability claims. (Table 5.2 provides a summary of the defenses that are discussed in the following sections.) Anyone believing he has been harmed has the right to file a lawsuit against the club, but the club may not be liable based on some the following concepts.

Contributory Negligence

The **contributory negligence** defense is based on the belief that the plaintiff contributed to the harm or injuries he sustained (Cotton, 2007a). For example, if a club has posted warning signs, has verbally warned participants about not doing a particular activity, and had adequate supervision on site, but the participant still did the unsafe act and was injured, it can be argued that the participant contributed to the harm. A great example of this is the use of spotters in a strength and conditioning area or athletes not using required protective gear such as a mouthpiece or shin guard. The club must prove that the plaintiff had a duty to follow a standard, that the plaintiff's actions were below that standard, and that the plaintiff's actions were the cause of the harm.

contributory negligence—A defense based on the belief that the plaintiff contributed to the harm or injuries sustained.

Table 5.2 Summary of Defenses Against Liability

Defense	Defined	Example
Contributory negligence	The defendant contributed to the accident.	Athlete does not wear protective equipment to compete even though he has been instructed to on numerous occasions.
Inherent risk	The injury to a participant occurred as part of the game.	A basketball player's nose is broken when she blocks a shot by a defender.
Assumption of risk	Participant is aware of risks and voluntarily exposes themselves to the risks.	Participant agreeing to play football exposes themselves to being tackled during the course of a game, practice, and season.
Ultra vires act	A club employee does something she should not have done or something outside of her job description.	An athlete is injured during a dangerous activity that was organized by a coach but had been deemed unsafe and was prohibited by the club leadership.
Procedural noncompliance	A club employee does not follow statutes.	A defendant files a lawsuit after the statute of limitations or in the wrong jurisdiction.
Immunity	A volunteer is free from liability based on his classification.	A volunteer coach's actions were not willful or wanton, and he had been properly trained and supervised.
Waiver	A participant waives the right to sue the sport club.	A participant signs the waiver when joining and cannot sue after he sprains an ankle during an adult league game.
Agreement to participate	A participant acknowledges the risks associated with an activity.	A participant is knocked down during a basketball game. She cannot sue because she assumed the risk when signing the agreement to participate.

comparative negligence—A defense that assesses the degree to which the plaintiff and the defendant are at fault.

What if the both the club and the plaintiff were at fault? **Comparative negligence** assesses the degree to which each party is at fault. If an athlete, the plaintiff, has been told to use some type of equipment on numerous occasions, but disregarded the requirement during play, she may be found to be 60 percent at fault. The defendant, the club, would be 40 percent at fault, because the supervisory staff should have seen that the person was not using the equipment as required.

Comparative negligence has an impact on the award from the court. In pure comparative negligence cases the award is based on the percentage of blame. So, in the preceding case, if the court determined damages to be $100,000, the plaintiff would get only $40,000 because she was 60 percent responsible for what occurred. In other forms of comparative negligence, if the plaintiff is determined to be over half responsible, she does not receive any award. Comparative negligence standards vary from state to state in the United States and from country to country around the world. Clubs should investigate the standard that applies to them.

Inherent Risk

inherent risk—Any aspect of a sport that, if removed, would fundamentally change the nature of the sport.

Risks are associated with participation in sport because people come into contact with one another. Inherent in the activity is the chance for injury. Thus, inherent risk is a legitimate defense. An **inherent risk** can be defined as any aspect of a sport that, if removed, would fundamentally change the nature of the sport

Every sport contains some element of risk. Athletes assume that risk when they agree to participate.

Courtesy of the South Orange County Wildcats

(Cotton, 2007a). Can you imagine American football or European soccer without tackling, or baseball without sliding? The games would not be what they are. So, if a plaintiff is injured in what is deemed to be a regular aspect of competition, the defense for the club would be inherent risk.

Assumption of Risk

Because risks are associated with sport, participants make an **assumption of risk** when they decide to participate. If they know the risk and voluntarily consent to expose themselves to those risks, they have assumed the risk (Cotton, 2007a). It is important to note that participants consent to expose themselves only to the known risks, not other variables that could cause harm. For example, a participant in soccer exposes himself to the risk of being tackled during a game, but he does not expose himself to a dangerous playing surface. If he is injured and a dangerous playing surface was the proximate cause of the injury, the club can be found liable.

assumption of risk—When participants are aware of the risks associated with an activity and voluntarily consent to expose themselves to those risks.

Ultra Vires Acts

Earlier in the chapter ultra vires acts were discussed as a legal principle. The concept is also a defense for a club against a plaintiff's claim. If the club believes that the actions of an employee were beyond the scope of that person's responsibilities, the club can use ultra vires as a defense (Cotton, 2007a). Basically, the club is putting the onus on the individual employee rather than the club. If the court agrees, the club is no longer a party in the suit, and the plaintiff would seek damages from the individual employee. If a club coach takes minors out to drink and a minor is harmed in some way as a result, the club can use the ultra vires defense because that type of activity is not within the scope of the coach's responsibilities.

Procedural Noncompliance

Certain rules, standards, and procedures must be followed within the legal system to avoid having a claim thrown out. One of the most important is the **statute of limitations.** In the case of a civil suit, a plaintiff has a time frame known as a statute of limitations, within which a suit must be filed. If that time expires, the plaintiff cannot file the suit (Cotton, 2007a). The length of the statute of limitations varies by jurisdiction, but in most cases it is between five and seven years.

statute of limitations—The time frame within which a plaintiff must file a suit.

Immunity

Immunity implies a freedom from penalty based on a person's or an organization's status or situation (Cotton, 2007a). In the sport environment several forms of immunity may be applicable: governmental immunity, voluntary immunity, and recreational use immunity

Federal, state, and local governments are free from suits based on governmental immunity. Only in the case of gross negligence can a person seek damages from governments. Sport clubs that are aligned with government entities may receive this immunity.

A club volunteer can be granted immunity for an action if she was unpaid, acted in good faith and within the scope of her duties within a specified position for which she was trained, and was appropriately supervised. Coaches who are paid lose this form of immunity because they are considered professionals.

In terms of recreational use immunity, a person injured at a facility that is open for recreation use cannot sue the organization unless gross negligence is present. A person who is running on a field for personal exercise and is injured when he steps on an uneven part of the field cannot sue the owner of the facility, but a person who was invited to that same facility for a lacrosse game and is injured on the same spot could. The recreational use immunity was lost when the scheduled game was set.

Agreements to Participate and Waivers

agreements to participate—Forms participants sign prior to taking part in an activity that notify them of the inherent risks associated with participation in the activity.

Agreements to participate are forms that participants sign prior to taking part in an activity that notify them of the inherent risks associated with participation in the activity. The person's signature creates a primary assumption of risk defense for the club, because the participant is made aware of the risks associated with the activity and agrees to participate anyway. Cotton and Cotton (2005) cited the following elements common to all agreements to participate: the nature of the activity, possible consequences of injury, behavioral expectations of participants, the condition of the participant, and a concluding statement. This document provides a strong defense if a suit is filed.

waivers—Forms that participants sign to waive their rights to sue the sport club.

Waivers differ from agreements to participate in that, when participants sign them, they are waiving their rights to sue the club. This does not mean that they can never sue the club, however. The plaintiff may sue for something that was beyond the activity described in the waiver, in which case the waiver is not valid. It is very important that the club make the waiver conspicuous, so that the participants know they are signing a waiver. The language on the waiver form must be clear so the participants know what they are waiving. Clubs should hire attorneys to draft both their agreements to participate and their waivers, because if a suit is filed, the plaintiff will have an attorney looking for flaws in the documents to make the case. A sample waiver is shown on page 103.

Most participants in sport clubs are minors, who cannot sign binding contracts (agreements to participate and waivers). Neither can one person sign away the rights of another. Yet, it is still important that the parents or guardians of minors complete and sign these forms. They are acting in the best interests of their children when they assume the risks and waive the right to file a claim.

Contracts

contract—A legal document that turns a promise into a legal obligation.

Contracts are an essential aspect of operating a sport club. All clubs enter into contractual agreements on a regular basis. A contract is based on the promises of two parties, whether it be the club promising to pay a coach a specified amount of money for a specified time frame and that coach promising to coach to the best of his abilities, or a trash removal company promising to come twice a week to

Sample Waiver

I, _____ (parent/guardian), am the parent or legal guardian of _____ (minor child).

In order for my child to participate in the leagues, camps and clinics or any other activity organized by the Blue Star Sport Club, I agree that neither my minor child nor I will make a claim against, sue, or seek prosecution against Blue Star Sport Club LLC, and their agents, sponsors, building contractors, suppliers, and employees for damages, death, personal injury or property damage which my minor child may sustain as a result of his or her participation in these sporting activities.

This release is intended to discharge in advance Blue Star Sport Club and their agents, sponsors, building contractors, suppliers, and employees from and against any and all liability except for liability that may be caused by the willful or wanton actions of Blue Star Sport Club and their agents, sponsors and employees.

I further understand that sport involves physical contact and exertion and there is the potential for injury, bodily harm, and death and property damage. Having been made aware of the above stated risks, I assume those risks and agree to allow my minor to participate in the activities organized and sponsored by the Blue Star Sport Club. I confirm that my child is physically fit and has no known medical conditions which would prohibit his or her participation in activities sponsored by Blue Star Sport Club LLC. I understand that this waiver is effective for the duration of my child's participation for the current program for which he or she is enrolled. I fully understand its contents and that I am agreeing to release Blue Star Sport Club from liability for my child.

Parent/Guardian Signature: _____

Date: _____

Print Name: _____

Based on waivers from Blue Star Sports Club LLC.

empty the club's dumpster in return for the club's promise to pay a monthly fee. (A sample contract is provided on page 104.)

A club manager must understand that contacts are binding. A contract turns a promise into a legal obligation for both the club and the other party. To create this obligation, four elements must be present (Sharpe, 2007), as listed here and shown in the sidebar on page 105:

1. An *offer* has to be made from one party to another.
2. There has to be an *acceptance* on the part of both parties to the terms of the contract.
3. There also has to be a *consideration*, or an inducement, for each of the parties to enter into the contract.
4. There needs to be *intent* on the part of both parties to fulfill their obligations.

SOUTH CHARLOTTE SOCCER ASSOCIATION (SCSA)
Financial Contract

Player's Name: _____

Parent's Name(s): _____

Address: _____
           (Street)   (City)   (State)   (Zip code)

2008-2009 Team Assignment

U-_____ Men / Women   Team Name/Color_____   SCSA Fees_____

Club Fees are paid directly to SCSA and cover expenses such as, but not limited to, field rental, training fees, uniforms, player registration, additional SCSA training (i.e., speed & agility, technical, goalie, etc). These fees are set by the association based on the various levels of play offered at SCSA. The fee structure and fee schedule will be posted on the SCSA website prior to May tryouts.

Team Fees are separate expenses paid directly to your assigned team. The Team fees cover expenses such as tournaments, referee fees, coach's travel, team parties/player awards, etc. These fees will vary from team to team and are based on the amount of tournaments and travel your team participates in.

All expenses to travel with the team to and from practices, scrimmages, games and tournaments are your responsibility. This includes gas, food, room & board, etc.

By signing this contract, you acknowledge you have read and understand this form and the 2008 SCSA fee structure in its entirety and agree to the following terms and conditions:

1. You are financially responsible for all Club fees as stated for the _entire_ playing year.
2. Refunds will only be offered as follows:
    a. Player signs with SCSA, but withdraws before June 15, 2008. SCSA keeps $100.
    b. Player signs with SCSA, but withdraws after June 15 but before August 11, 2008. SCSA keeps $300.
    c. Players with a season ending injury are eligible for a refund to be determined.
    d. Players moving more than 50 miles during the season are eligible for a refund to be determined.
3. Players will not be released from SCSA unless all Club fees and team fees are up to date at the time of the request in accordance with the SCSA fee schedule.
4. All fees will be paid when payment is due. Any payments that are delinquent may be cause to remove player card from the team. If this should occur, a service charge of $50 to reinstate a player card may be charged.
5. Statements will not be mailed. Requests for withdrawls must be presented to the SCSA office in writing.

_____   _____
(Parent Signature)   (Date)

_____
(Print Parent's Name)

Reprinted, by permission, from South Charlotte Soccer Association.

To demonstrate the elements of a contract, a swim club offers a contract to a person to become the club's technical director. The club wants the new technical director to produce national-level swimmers; the person is induced to enter into the contract because she will be paid a handsome fee for the length of the contract. Finally, the club intends to pay the person the set fee for the length of the contract, and the person intends to offer the best coaching possible to the swimmers of the club. The person accepts the terms of the contract presented by the club.

> **Elements of a Contract**
>
> Offer
> Acceptance
> Consideration
> Intent

Clubs may enter into a variety of contracts including employee contracts, game contracts, service contracts, rental contracts, and loans. The four elements will be present in each type of contract.

Employee Contracts

Sport clubs negotiate contracts with their employees. Caughron (2007) identified several areas that can be addressed in a sport club employee contract: compensation, length, benefits and fringe benefits, bonuses, provisions for outside income, and termination clause.

▶ *Compensation.* Compensation is what most people associate with an employee contract. Compensation can come in the form of a salary or hourly wage. In the case of a for-profit venture, it also may come in the form of stake in the value of the company.

▶ *Length.* Length is the duration of the contract. A contract can be for one year or multiple years. Rollover provisions may also be available—for example, an employee can sign a three-year contract that consistently rolls over, making it an annual three-year contract. Terms that would end the rollover can be addressed in the contract—either one party can end it, or both parties must agree to end it. This means that the contract would become terminal at the end of three years. Club managers generally have multiyear contracts, whereas coaches and other employees often have annual contracts. Coaches and independent contractors may have contracts for the length of a season and thus may have multiple contracts over the course of the year.

▶ *Benefits and fringe benefits.* An employee contract should also stipulate other benefits beyond compensation, such as health insurance, a pension or retirement, vacation time, and whether vacation time is paid or unpaid. Fringe benefits are those items that are beyond the scope of normal benefits, such as a car, a loan on a home, membership to a local fitness center or golf club, or discounts with local businesses.

▶ *Bonuses.* Sport clubs can also provide incentives in the form of bonuses. Employees who reach certain performance measures may receive added compensation. For example, if membership increases to a certain number, a team wins a championship, or athletes set records, the people responsible are compensated at an agreed-upon level. Bonuses are tied to club goals. If the club wants championships or top performances, bonuses should be tied to those goals. If the club wants market share, bonuses should be tied to increases in the number of participants.

▶ *Provisions for outside employment.* Sport clubs must communicate in their contracts what, if any, outside employment employees may hold. Does a club want one of its trainers or coaches working for another club or running personal training sessions with athletes off or on site? Employees who do so may be benefiting from their associations with the club to get additional work, and the club is not being compensated. Employee contracts should clarify what is appropriate outside employment to be able to determine whether a breach has occurred.

▶ *Termination clause.* The stipulation of what an employee can be dismissed for and under what terms is covered in a termination clause, as is the compensation due an employee if the contract is terminated early by the club. If the contract stipulates that having a sexual relationship with a member or the parent of a club participant is a dismissible offense and an employee does so, the club can terminate the employee without compensation. If the club wants to hire someone else for a position and the current employee has not committed a dismissible act, the club would have to pay the remaining amount on the contract.

Event Contracts

Clubs often enter into contracts related to games and tournaments. The most important part of these contracts is the date, time, and location. This ensures that both parties will be at the right place on the right day at the right time. Along with these important details, event contracts also stipulate officials for the contest as well as any special accommodations or amenities that will be provided, and by whom (McMillen, 2007). A host club may provide locker room accommodations, water on the sidelines, athletic training services, and lodging for the visiting team. These promises enable visiting teams to plan accordingly. The event contract may also present scenarios for canceling the contest or event (most commonly for weather), as well as the terms for canceling and rescheduling.

Service Contracts

independent contractors—People who are not employees of a club and are paid only for the services they provide to the club.

Club may enter into promises with entities or individuals for the purpose of managing or executing certain aspects of the club, including trash removal, lawn care, laundry, and accounting. The club may also hire people to provide services such as coaching, personal training, and strength and conditioning. These are known as **independent contractors;** they are not employees of the club, but are paid only for the services they provide. Service contracts can be negotiated annually.

Rental or Leasing Contracts

A club may enter into a rental contract as either the renter (the person renting the facility or equipment) or the rentee (the entity paying for the use of the facility or equipment). A club may be a tenant at a facility and make monthly rent payments to use the facility. An important element of the rental agreement is who is responsible for the upkeep of the facility and for improvements. A contract may stipulate that the landlord has to pay for general maintenance of the facility and anything that breaks from normal wear and tear, whereas the renter has to pay for improvements to the facility and damage beyond normal wear and tear. It is important to communicate clearly what falls into each of these categories, because when the time comes, one of the two parties will have to pay, and disagreements can occur.

A club may be the entity doing the renting—for example, if an outside group is interested in using the club's facilities for an event. Important elements of this type of contract include the date, time, and duration of use; the intended use of the facility; and the provisions the club will provide to the renter. The rental contract should stipulate that the entity renting the facility must carry insurance that names the club as well. If someone is injured while participating in the activity at the club, the renter's insurance covers the club. Such insurance policies should be for $1 million or more, depending on the event.

A lawsuit can be either premise related or activity related. If the person's injury is the result of a fault in the facility (e.g., a hole in the ground, unsafe equipment), the club is liable; if it is related to the supervision or instruction of the activity, the renter is liable.

Loans

A loan is a contract between a club and an individual or a financial institution. The club is obligated to repay the loan according to the terms of the loan agreement. The club may have a mortgage on its facility and may also take out loans to pay for capital expenditures such as equipment and start-up costs.

Breach of Contract

A **breach of contract** occurs when one side breaks the promise that was made in the contract. For example, a soccer club hires a lawn care company to maintain the fields. The company does not do it weekly as promised in the contract, but the club has made all of its payments. The lawn care firm is in breach, and the club has the right to file suit to seek damages. The club can either seek **restitution,** meaning to have its money returned, or damages resulting from the lawn care company's failure to meet its obligations (e.g., the lawn dies and must be completely replaced).

A club may make a contract for a well-known athlete to come to the club. After the club spends money promoting the event and pays for travel, the athlete does not show. The club is entitled to seek damages in the amount of the money spent promoting the event.

Clubs may also seek the potential revenue lost because the other party did not meet its obligation. A club may hire a marketing firm to sell naming rights and sponsorship opportunities for the club. The firm does not make any effort to sell these items as promised. The club can sue for the amount of what it could have made if the firm had met its promise.

breach of contract—When one party does not meet the obligations of a contract.

restitution—In the case of a breach of contract, one party seeks reimbursement from the other party of the money it has paid.

Summary

Knowing the legal aspects of running a club is important to the operation of any club. Many club managers overlook this aspect and in so doing put their clubs as well as the participants at risk. Club managers who know their legal responsibilities and act with common sense ensure that their clubs meet their responsibilities and offer safe and positive experiences to all involved.

Club leaders must have a working knowledge of tort law and liability, contract law, risk management, and the actions necessary for reducing the club's liability. The club owes participants the highest level of care. If the club goes below that level and a participant is injured, the club is liable. Club leaders must also understand that, based on the doctrine of respondeat superior, the club itself may be found liable for the actions, nonaction, or harmful actions of its employees. Therefore, hiring employees is one of the most important decisions a club manager will make. Clubs that use the services of volunteers must take the appropriate steps to ensure that those volunteers are protected under voluntary immunity.

Clubs enter into contractual agreements with a variety of parties and must understand that they are bound by the terms of those contracts. If they breach a contract, they may be forced to pay damages. Club managers should also know the legal actions at their disposal if other parties do not meet their obligations. Certain risks are unforeseen, but measures should be taken to develop a risk management plan to reduce the uncertainty of situations that may arise.

The sport club has a legal and moral responsibility to do everything in its power to make the club experience as safe as possible for participants.

Rick recognizes that the actions of his coach are against the law and that the minor's civil rights are being violated. After researching the legal issues, Rick understands that knowing about the illegal behavior and doing nothing can make him a guilty party in a criminal case, and the club and he could be found liable of deliberate indifference in a civil suit. Realizing this and the fact that he has not been living up to his responsibility, he fires his friend of 10 years and reports his actions to law enforcement officials.

By the end of the chapter, the sport club manager will be able to do the following:

- Explain the importance of budgeting and accounting.
- Identify potential revenue streams and operating expenses for the club.
- Describe the basic financial statements associated with running a club.
- Appreciate the importance of developing a deferred maintenance plan.
- List the five elements of the marketing mix and explain how each functions independently as well as how they rely on one another.
- Recognize the importance of developing a database and conducting market research.

6

Business Aspects of Club Management

Ronny Jones is a former college basketball player who has coached basketball for more than 15 years. He has trained under some of the best college coaches in the United States and is a sought-after speaker on developing basketball players. He is a great coach. Ronny started the Sharpshooters Basketball Club 10 years ago. During that time the club has won regional championships and placed in national championship tournaments in several age groups. Also during that time the club has produced several athletes who have earned college scholarships and a few who have gone on to the professional ranks. The Sharpshooters is a quality club.

Despite the club's on-court success and Ronny's ability to develop players and offer a quality experience, the club is in significant financial trouble. Three years ago, the Sharpshooters decided to buy and renovate the facility it had been renting. The Sharpshooters now has to cover its debt services as well as the expenses of operating the club. Also, despite the quality of the Sharpshooters program, other clubs in the area attract and retain more players, so revenues are not sufficient for operating the club and keeping up the facility. If the financial situation of the Sharpshooters does not improve dramatically within the next year, Ronny will have to declare bankruptcy, and the Sharpshooters will no longer exist.

Successful sport clubs recognize that they are business enterprises that must meet the needs of their clients—in this case, the parents who are paying the fees and the children who are participating. This goes back to the need for the club to understand why it exists. Is it in the business of training world-class track athletes, preparing young people to earn college athletic scholarships, or offering participation opportunities for kids of every age and skill level to promote healthy lifestyles and character development?

revenue—The income the club generates from the services it provides.

A club also must be conscious of how it plans to make money (**revenue**) and spend money (**operating expenses**). Revenue and operating expenses are closely tied. When revenues are greater than expenses, the club turns a profit and remains a viable business enterprise. When expenses are greater than revenues, the club operates at a deficit, jeopardizing its longevity, sustainability, and ability to offer a quality experience.

operating expenses—The cost of providing services to members.

In the case of the Sharpshooters, Ronny offers clients a quality basketball experience, but the expenses of operating the club are greater than the revenue being generated. Other clubs in the area may not have as good a product as the Sharpshooters, but they market themselves more effectively. So, despite Ronny's success as a coach, his weakness as a businessman is preventing the Sharpshooters from remaining a viable club. Successful clubs identify and maximize potential revenue streams and determine and control the expenses associated with the operation of the club.

If the leadership of a club does not recognize that it must both meet the needs of its clients and manage its business affairs, the club will not remain viable. Chapter 1 describes the various business structures for a club (e.g., nonprofit 501[c], limited liability corporation [LLC]). Regardless of the business structure, a club must follow sound business practices to survive, grow, and succeed.

Budgeting and Accounting

budgeting—A precedent financial process that enables club leaders to plan, coordinate, and control the club's activities based on projected revenues and expenses.

Ham (2005) indicated that budgeting and accounting are both financial processes. Because the two are directly related, sport clubs need to coordinate them. Generally, **budgeting** is a precedent activity that enables club leaders to plan, coordinate, and control the club's activities. However, this planning is based on the previous year's accounting of revenues and expenses, assets and liabilities, and the net worth of the club. Whereas budgeting involves planning, **accounting** focuses on record keeping, classifying, and understanding and interpreting financial statements. If a club manager is not versed in finance or accounting, the club should hire an accounting firm to handle this aspect of club management. Even if an outside firm handles the club's accounting, the club manager should still have an understanding of the overall financial picture of the club.

accounting—The financial process that focuses on record keeping, classifying, and understanding and interpreting financial statements.

Budgeting

Ham (2005) defined a budget as a management plan for revenues and expenses. This plan should present a detailed forecast of how the club will spend funds on items such as labor, materials, and services. Further, Ham (2005) stated that a budget should also indicate how and how much the club plans to generate in revenue. A budget also makes a statement about the priorities of the club by indicating where it will spend its money as well as how it plans to make its money. Such a statement of priority enables the club to plan its activities. Consider one club that allocates significant funds to pay qualified coaches, and another that relies solely on parent volunteers to coach. It can be argued that quality instruction is a priority of the first club and not of the second club. The first club will have to charge higher registration fees to cover the expense of paying the trained and qualified coaches.

Sport clubs receive revenues from registration fees, concession sales, sponsorships, fund-raising, camps, tournaments, special programs, and facility rentals. Each of these will be discussed in more detail later in the chapter. After identifying its revenue sources, the club needs to determine the amount the club expects to make from each source. This process is known as **forecasting**. According to Fried, Shapiro, and DeSchriver (2003), forecasting is based on assumptions, but forecasting that is close to being correct is better than not forecasting at all.

Fried and colleagues (2003) stated that forecasting involves (1) gathering information from previous financial statements; (2) projecting revenues as increasing, decreasing, or staying the same; (3) projecting profits and losses; (4) comparing

forecasting—Determining the amount the club expects to make from each of its revenues sources. Forecasts are based on the previous year's revenues, which are then adjusted up or down or kept the same for the coming year.

SUCCESSFUL STRATEGY

Sound Business Plans

Club leaders must understand that their clubs are businesses and must act as such, understanding the ramifications of the decisions they make. In July of 2009, the Premier Soccer Academies (PSA) in Lorain, Ohio, was sued by a bank for over $7 million in unpaid loans. The $10 million PSA facility and program were started by former USA national team goalkeeper Brad Friedel in 2007. Friedel is viewed as one of the greatest goalkeepers in U.S. soccer history and has had a successful career playing in the English Premier League.

PSA's plan was to host annually up to 30 gifted players between the ages of 12 and 17 from around the world. The athletes would receive scholarships to attend PSA and were to be recruited based on ability and skill level and not their parents' ability to pay. This was a unique approach to player development for the United States. The PSA facilities include three and a half soccer fields, an indoor field house, a 5,000-square-foot elite training center, student housing, and an academic learning center.

Unfortunately, the launch of PSA coincided with a global economic downturn. The academy lost a significant source of income with the loss of corporate sponsors and entities that had previously been willing to pay for participants' scholarships. As a result, PSA was unable to generate the revenue to cover its expenses and pay down its debt service. In light of the suit, the club shut down operations in the summer of 2009 with the hope of launching again in the fall of 2009. PSA's leadership is working to restructure its business plan and will offer new services to generate revenue, such as a fitness club on site, while still offering a scaled-back version of its soccer programming.

Although Mr. Friedel is well compensated as a professional soccer player in the English Premier League, the business he established has not fared as well. PSA was established as a nonprofit corporation, so the suit has been filed against PSA and not Friedel as an individual. The concept of PSA was unique to the United States and promising, but unfortunately, the economic climate kept it from succeeding. Although this example doesn't highlight a *successful* strategy, it does illustrate the need for a plan in place to guarantee revenue streams.

industry norms; and (5) determining capital needs. For example, after gathering information from previous financial statements, the club can project a 10 percent increase in participant registration and a 30 percent drop in sponsorship revenues as a result of the global financial crisis. The club also knows that a 20-year loan will be retired at the end of the current fiscal year and that a trade-out sponsorship will eliminate 10 percent of operating expenses. Finally, the club must replace the HVAC system in the indoor facility in the upcoming year. Club leaders will account for all of these factors as they forecast for the coming year.

Budgets also helps club leaders coordinate among themselves when making spending decisions. A director of coaching who wants to order new uniforms for a travel team will need to discuss the matter with the club manager, who will refer to the budget. The budget shows how much the entire club plans to spend on uniforms, and the manager can then determine how much of that can be spent on travel uniforms and how much on in-house T-shirts. The amount available for travel uniforms will determine the style or quantity of uniforms and from which company to buy.

Lastly, a budget controls the activities of a club by restricting spending to certain areas and amounts. In fact, a budget makes many decisions for the club manager. When a coach asks for money for a particular activity or item, the budget provides the answer by stipulating clearly whether the activity or item is a budgeted item, and if it is, how much can be spent on it.

Elements of the Budget

Budget categories are broadly defined, such as personnel, contracted services, utilities, equipment, and facility management. Within those broad categories are specific items. For example, under personnel, budget items would include the salaries of the club manager, director of coaching, administrative assistant, and part-time coaches. A given amount is associated with each item. (See the sidebar on pages 115-116 for a sample budget.)

fixed cost—A cost that will not fluctuate over the course of a budgetary cycle.

Within the budget are fixed and variable costs. Moyer, McGuigan, and Kretlow (2003) defined a **fixed cost** as one that will not fluctuate as the level of the club output changes. **Variable costs** vary in close relationship with changes in the club's output level (such as an electric bill). The sidebar on page 117 shows various fixed and variable costs.

variable cost—A cost that will fluctuate based on usage over the course of a budgetary cycle.

capital expenditures—Major one-time purchases that are outside the normal operating expenses.

A club also has to plan for the purchase of long-term assets such as equipment. Moyer and colleagues (2003) called these purchases **capital expenditures.** Capital expenditures pay for such items as major equipment and facility renovations. A club may purchase a scoreboard one year with the hope that it will last 10 to 20 years. The club can develop a capital project budget that addresses capital projects each year—for example, directing 20 percent of forecasted revenues to capital projects. If the club needs an item that will cost $60,000 and its capital project budget yields only $30,000 per year, club leaders may forgo capital projects for two years to save for the needed item. Chapter 7 addresses another approach to paying for capital projects such as new buildings or field expansions: holding capital fund-raising campaigns.

Revenue			
Item	**Amount**	**Part**	**Cost**
Youth recreation league registrations	75,000	750	100
Adult recreation league registrations	15,000	150	100
Summer camp registrations	50,000	250	200
Holiday tournaments registrations	10,000	50	200
Elite training registrations	40,000	100	400
Select team registrations	100,000	200	500
Select team tryout fees	7,000	350	20
Sponsorship	40,000		
Fund-raising	20,000		
Concession stand	10,000		
Facility rental to outside groups	10,000		
Other	500		
Total revenue	**377,500**		
Expenditures			
Salaries	**Amount**	**Part**	**Cost**
Executive director	70,000		
Director of coaching	30,000		
Business and office manager	22,250		
Benefits	12,225		
Facility			
Facility maintenance	10,000		
Field development and repair	7,000		
Equipment replacement	3,000		
Competition costs			
Uniforms	22,000	1,100	20
Equipment	7,000		
Officials' fees: recreation leagues	3,000		
League registration fees for select teams	3,000		
Officials' fees: select teams	2,000		
Tournament fees	4,000		
Office expenses			
Postage	525		
Office supplies	1,000		

(continued)

Sample Budget *(continued)*

Expenditures			
Utilities	**Amount**	**Part**	**Cost**
Electric	75,000		
Phone	3,000		
Water	8,000		
Internet	1,000		
Cable	1,000		
Contracted services			
Accounting and tax prep	3,000		
Legal	3,000		
Sports medicine professionals	10,000		
Web design and management	3,000		
Strength and conditioning coach	12,000		
Trash removal	2,500		
Lawn care service	5,000		
Awards			
Individual trophies	5,000		
Team trophies	1,000		
Coaching awards	200		
Club patches	300		
Staff development			
Subscriptions	300		
Memberships	1,000		
Conferences	2,000		
Travel	1,000		
Mileage	2,000		
Concessions			
Cost of concessions	5,000		
Tournaments			
Cost of tournaments	3,000		
Fund-raising			
Cost of fund-raising	3,000		
Sponsorship			
Cost of sponsorship	500		
Insurance	4,000		
Debt service on facility	24,000		
Club advertising	1,000		
Savings	700		
Total expenditures	**377,500**		

Fixed Costs Versus Variable Costs

Fixed Costs	Variable Costs
Salaries	Utilities
Rent or mortgage on a property	Equipment and uniforms
Contracted services such as trash removal and lawn care	Officials
	Professional development
Debt service	Office supplies
League or association fees	Travel
Insurance premiums	Awards

The Budget Process

As mentioned earlier, budgeting is a precedent activity. Ham (2005) suggested that the process be completed months in advance of the actual implementation. Further, Ham (2005) identified the following important steps in the budget process:

1. Referring to the mission
2. Reviewing the previous years' budgets
3. Getting input from club leaders on the needs for the coming year
4. Using the predetermined budget type established by the club
5. Assessing the budget in terms of accuracy, feasibility, and reality
6. Preparing a final budget
7. Presenting the final budget to the club's board for approval
8. Implementing the approved budget
9. Auditing and evaluating the budget implementation

Accounting

Another aspect of the business of a sport club is the gathering, recording, classifying, summarizing, and interpreting of financial data. Ham (2005) termed these activities *accounting*. Accounting is done on a daily, weekly, monthly, quarterly, and annual basis. At its most basic level it deals with the debits and credits of the club. **Debits** are the revenues generated. Accounting involves reconciling these on a given day (e.g., online registration for an upcoming season resulted in 50 registrations at $250 per registration, all paid by credit card). **Credits** are the expenses that have been budgeted for and must be paid. From a larger perspective, accounting also involves determining the club's assets and liabilities.

debits—In accounting, the revenues generated by a club on a daily, weekly, monthly, and annual basis.

credits—In accounting, the expenses that have been budgeted for and must be paid.

Financial Statements

Club managers must be aware of four main financial statements: balance sheets, income statements, cash flow statements, and statements of net worth. These provide an overview of a business's financial condition in both the short and long term.

balance sheet—A statement of the financial position of the club that presents the club's assets and liabilities and how much equity the club has at a fixed point in time.

assets—Items of value that the club owns.

current assets—Items the club can convert into cash within one calendar year.

fixed assets—Assets used to operate the club that, if sold, would affect how the club operates.

liabilities—The financial obligations the club has to other entities.

Fried and colleagues (2003) defined a **balance sheet** as a statement of the financial position of the club that presents the club's assets and liabilities and how much equity the club has at a fixed point in time, usually the end of a fiscal year. (See the sidebar at the bottom of this page for a sample balance sheet.) **Assets** are items of value that the club owns. Assets come in three forms: current, fixed, and long term (Ham, 2005). A club's assets may include its facility and the land it is on, sport equipment in the facility, uniforms, computers, and office furniture. Assets also include the cash on hand and any investments the club has made.

Assets can be classified as current, noncurrent, or fixed. **Current assets** are those items the club can convert into cash within one calendar year (Ham, 2005). This would include cash on hand, the inventory in the concession stand, licensed products the club sells to its members, and positions on a team. Long-term assets are any investments such as bonds or certificates of deposit that have fixed dates of maturity. Finally, **fixed assets** are those assets used to operate the club that, if sold, would affect how the clubs operates. Fixed assets include such things as the facility and training or fitness equipment. The club would not be able to offer its services if these assets were sold.

Liabilities are the financial obligations the club has to other entities. These obligations can include loans from banks to upgrade the facility, rent on the facility, and promises to provide services in the future. Current liabilities are those financial obligations the club plans to pay off within a year (Ham, 2005), such as taxes, interest, and accounts payable items to service providers. Long-term liabilities, on the other hand, are those that will take more than a year to retire. These would include most of the club's fixed assets (e.g., real estate, equipment). A club manager can determine the club's net worth by determining how much money would be left if the club sold all of its assets and paid off all of its liabilities.

Sample Balance Sheet

Assets		Liabilities	
Current assets		Accounts payable	10,000.00
Cash	20,000.00	Short-term loans	25,000.00
Accounts receivable	10,000.00	Interest payable	44,000.00
Concessions inventory	3,000.00	Accrued payroll taxes	5,000.00
Short-term investments	8,000.00	Long-term liabilities	50,000.00
Prepaid expenses	3,000.00	Loans payable	1,000,000.00
Total current assets	44,000.00	Investor equity	100,000.00
Fixed assets		Investor equity	50,000.00
Facility and building	1,200,000.00	**Total liabilities and equity**	**1,284,000.00**
Facility equipment	30,000.00		
Maintenance equipment	10,000.00		
Total fixed assets	1,240,000.00		
Total assets	**1,284,000.00**		

Net worth is calculated by subtracting total liabilities from total assets. The net worth makes an important statement about the overall value of a club by indicating how much has been invested in the club and what is still owed. A positive net worth indicates a club that it is in a strong position to take on new projects, whereas a negative net worth indicates a problem with the overall viability of the club.

Income statements are financial statements that indicate how a club has performed over a given period of time (Moyer, McGuigan, & Kretlow, 2003). The financial performance of the club is determined by how the business generates revenues and incurs expenses through both operating and non-operating activities. It also shows the net profit or loss incurred over a quarter, a fiscal quarter, or a year. A sample income statement is in the sidebar below.

Cash flow statements show the exchange of money between a company and the outside world also over a period of time. Cash flow statements for a sport club would show the revenue made at the concession stand and from player registration fees and tournament entry fees. They would also show the money paid to creditors and vendors.

income statement—A statement showing the money a club made and spent over a period of time.

cash flow statement—A statement that shows the exchange of money between a company and the outside world over a period of time.

Sample Income Statement

Revenue

Registrations	262,000.00
Tournaments and camps	60,000.00
Sponsorship	50,000.00
Fund-raising	25,000.00
Concession sales	10,000.00
Facility rental to outside groups	10,000.00
Gross profit	**417,000.00**

Expenses

Salary and wages	121,000.00
Facility costs	20,000.00
Competition costs	41,000.00
Office expenses	1,500.00
Utilities	88,000.00
Contracted services	38,500.00
Concessions	3,000.00
Debt service	30,000.00
Awards	6,500.00
Professional development	6,000.00
Insurance	4,000.00
Fund-raising/marketing	750.00
Advertising	1,000.00
Total operating expenses	**361,250.00**
Net income (profit)	**55,750.00**

Revenue Streams or Cash Flow

A sound business plan identifies the potential sources of income for a club as well as the percentage of the total revenue that will be generated by each of those sources. The club needs to set realistic goals for revenues over the course of a fiscal year and also determine which are essential. Revenues deemed essential are those that must be generated to cover expenses vital to sustaining the club on a daily basis. **Ancillary revenues** are extra sources of income that can be directed to special projects or used to offer special benefits to members. Each club must determine for itself which revenues are essential and which are ancillary.

ancillary revenues—Extra sources of income that can be directed to special projects or used to offer special benefits to members.

The most common revenue sources for clubs are registration fees, sponsorships, fund-raising strategies and donations, public support, concessions, the sale of licensed products, camps, tournaments, special programs, and facility rentals. (Sponsorship is covered in chapter 7.)

Registration Fees Sport clubs are in the business of providing participation opportunities. The cost of that participation is in most cases the primary source of revenue for a club. A club needs to set a fee and then attract enough players at that fee to sustain the basic offerings. For example, a registration fee of $200 may cover the costs of a 10-game season for a player in an in-house league. Determining the cost of participation will be discussed in more detail later in the chapter.

Fund-Raising Strategies and Donations Every club needs to determine whether it will rely on fund-raising as an essential revenue source. Clubs that decide to do so must establish the means to raise the funds, set goals, and make achieving those goals a priority. Many organizations hold one major special event such as an auction or golf outing to raise funds. Fund-raising strategies are discussed in detail in chapter 7.

Concession Stands A concession stand can be a great money maker or a great money loser depending on how it is managed. Taking a professional view of the stand will enable a club to generate revenue. Professionalism involves appropriate staffing and selection of merchandise, as well as a knowledge of purchasing, controlling, and storing inventory.

If possible, a club should consider hiring a full-time concession manager, even if the stand is staffed by volunteers or students. The full-time person establishes a professional relationship with vendors, makes purchases, and arranges to have them delivered to the club. He can also keep track of the inventory and reconcile the number of items sold to the profits generated.

Sale of Licensed Products Participants and parents are often interested in apparel and items with the club logo. These items allow them to demonstrate their affinity with the club while also helping the club promote itself. Many clubs turn over the sale of licensed products to local sporting goods stores, but another option is to develop an inventory of items and advertise them on the club's Web site. The club can generate a profit by marking up the price of licensed items.

Camps Camps can be a significant revenue source for clubs. Some clubs allow employees to run camps and either charge them a rental fee for the use of the

Courtesy of the Brandywine Youth Club

A snack bar or concession stand staffed by volunteers is one way for a club to earn additional revenue.

facility or let them use it free of charge. A more lucrative approach is to make the camp a revenue stream for the club and assign the responsibility of organizing the camp to a paid coach or club director. The club may give a percentage of the gross profit to that person in exchange for running the camp, thus giving the person an incentive to attract participants. Given the number of families in which both parents work, summer camps for youth are in high demand.

Tournaments   Tournaments can also be effective revenue generators for sport clubs. The revenue from the tournament is driven by registration fees. Ancillary revenues are generated from concession sales and sponsorships. Tournament revenues do not come without hard work; tournaments require the commitment of full-time personnel supported by committees of club volunteers.

Special Programs   Special programs are activities beyond the primary purpose of the club for which the club charges extra. They may support the primary purpose of the club or offer extra assistance to club members. Special programs that support the primary purpose of the club would include speed, agility, and strength training programs; out-of-season conditioning programs; individual skill development sessions; sport psychology sessions; and nutrition lessons. Such programs are targeted to members who take the sport more seriously than regular members and whose parents are willing to pay extra to pursue their interests.

Special programs that offer assistance to club members may come in the form of after- or before-school care programs. After-school care programs can be helpful if there is a block of time between the end of the school day and the beginning of a training session. Some clubs provide homework guidance sessions, free play sessions, or conditioning or individual training sessions depending on the wants and needs of participants.

Facility Rentals Clubs that own or lease their facilities can consider renting them to outside groups. It is important for the club to determine how often and for what type of events it is willing to rent its facilities. Renting during nonpeak times is ideal. In most cases club activities are concentrated on weekends and weeknights; other times would be considered nonpeak times.

The club needs to determine how important facility rentals are to the operations of the club. Is the club willing to bump a club activity to accommodate an outside group that is willing to pay a significant rental fee? Also, is the club willing to have its facilities used for activities not consistent with the purpose of the club? For example, is a soccer club willing to rent its field for an American football or lacrosse tournament, or to rent its facilities for a nonsport purpose? Clubs with indoor facilities have the most to offer. Nonsport organizations are often looking for open space in which to hold meetings, trade shows, tournaments, and social events.

Deferred Maintenance Planning

deferred maintenance planning—Projecting future major projects and setting aside the necessary funds to pay for them.

At some point a club may acquire a fixed asset in the form of a facility and should invest in maintaining and sustaining it. The club can establish a proactive approach to protecting its assets by developing a deferred maintenance plan. **Deferred maintenance planning** entails projecting future major projects and setting aside the necessary funds to pay for them.

Deferred maintenance planning begins by determining the replacement cost for the facility. The club sets aside a percentage of that cost in a deferred maintenance fund. Say, for example, a club's facility replacement cost is $5 million. One percent of that replacement cost would be $50,000. If the club wanted to be more aggressive, it could set aside 5 percent, or $250,000. Those funds can be set aside for capital improvements or saved for major projects.

A deferred maintenance fund allows the club to replace or fix the infrastructure of the facility such as mechanical, electrical, and HVAC systems as the need arises. The club can also begin to address the expansion of and enhancements to the facility such as adding new fields, improving locker rooms, or expanding the concession or social area.

Clubs are businesses and need to be run as such. Club managers who accept this reality can thrive, and those who don't may ultimately fail. Understanding the financial aspects of the club is vital. Leaders of the club should be well informed of the financial status of the club and consistently look to identify future revenue streams. The club should also demonstrate the discipline to adhere to the budget. If taken seriously, the budget can be a great help to a club manager, indicating what she can spend the money on and how much she can spend on it. This is as important as knowing the sport the club offers.

Marketing

Marketing can be defined as activities that meet the wants and needs of consumers (Mullin, Hardy, & Sutton, 2007). Because the wants and needs of sport club consumers vary, there is no magic bullet or a cookie-cutter model for developing a sport club's marketing efforts. The club must understand its customers' wants and needs and then offer the right product at the right price and in the right place, and promote that product and use public relations in the right way. To achieve this goal, the sport club must develop a **strategic marketing management plan.** This plan helps the club determine how to position itself in the marketplace.

Positioning is how consumers view the product—in this case, the club (Mullin, Hardy, & Sutton, 2007). Is the club viewed as an expensive, highly competitive club that produces high-level players, or as an inexpensive club that focuses on participation and fun over competition and player development? Perhaps consumers view it as a multisport club that achieves both of those objectives. With its vision of a position in mind, the club can then develop goals and objectives to achieve that position in the marketplace. These goals can be related to the number of customers in the club; the number of college scholarships awarded to players; or the number of regional, state, or national championships won. Once the club has created these goals, it can develop a plan that incorporates the five Ps of sport marketing (see figure 6.1) to achieve them (Mullin, Hardy, & Sutton, 2007).

marketing—Activities that the club offers that meet the wants and needs of consumers.

strategic marketing management plan—A club's strategy to offer the right product at the right price in the right place and to promote that product and use public relations in the right way.

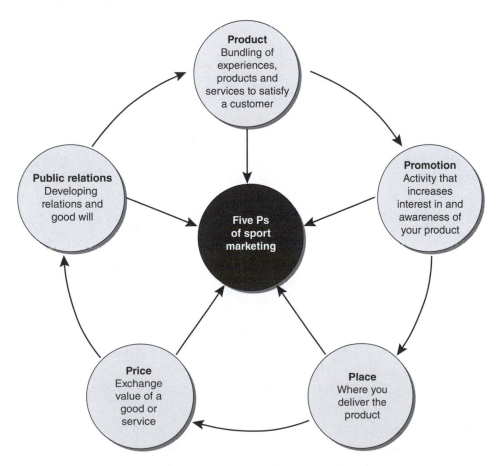

Figure 6.1 The five Ps of sport marketing are most effective when they are coordinated.

Next, the marketing plan needs to be incorporated into the larger strategic vision of the club. In fact, the marketing piece is central to the achievement of the larger strategic plan. The marketing plan drives the revenue streams, which ultimately funds all of the club's initiatives, services, and long-term plans.

The club may spend a great deal of time developing a strategic marketing plan, but it must also manage it and evaluate it. Managing the plan means being sure club leaders do what they said they were going to do. Evaluation involves an ongoing review of the plan as it is being implemented and at the end of the year to determine what worked and what didn't work.

Product

product—A bundle of experiences, products, and services that will satisfy club members.

The sport club as a **product** can be defined as a bundle of experiences, products, and services that will satisfy club members (Mullin, Hardy, & Sutton, 2007). What makes marketing a sport club different from marketing a traditional product such as toothpaste is that the wants and needs of customers vary. Toothpaste consumers want clean teeth and fresh breath. Sport club customers, on the other hand, have a variety of wants and needs, and the experience itself is intangible and subjective. One player may be very satisfied that her team won the majority of games in a season, whereas another may be disappointed because she did not improve as much as she would have liked. They were both on the same team, but their experiences were quite different.

Price

price—The exchange value of a good or service.

Price can be defined as the exchange value of a good or service (Mullin, Hardy, & Sutton, 2007). A soccer club charges a $250 registration fee for an in-house recreation league. In exchange, an eight-year old gets a T-shirt, a water bottle, 10 games, training from a volunteer coach, and a trophy at the end of the season. The pricing of a product is important because consumer satisfaction is usually tied to value. Value is the measure of the worth of the product in the mind of the consumer. If the customer believes he got what he deserved for the price he paid, he is satisfied. If he believes he did not get what he paid for, he is dissatisfied. Club managers must be able to explain to consumers the connection between the price and the services offered.

Price can be easily manipulated depending on the circumstances. A club may originally announce that it will charge teams $500 to enter a tournament it is hosting, but that fee can be increased to $600 for teams that do not pay by a set deadline or reduced to $450 per team for a club that enters more than three teams.

Price is also highly visible and plays an integral part in the positioning of a product (Mullin, Hardy, & Sutton, 2007). One of the first questions a customer will ask about a product is, How much? If she believes the price is too high, she may not even inquire further. If she believes the price is too low, she may question the quality of the product.

Because a club is a business, it needs to charge a price that will at the very least cover the costs associated with providing the experience to participants. When determining the price to charge participants, the club needs to consider expenses associated with the coaches, facility fees, uniforms, registration fees, and the overall operations of the club. To earn a profit, the club must add a markup to the cost of providing the experience. Nonprofit clubs can use a markup to fund future capital projects.

The club must also consider what its customers can afford to avoid pricing itself out of the market. An awareness of what competitors are charging will help club leaders position the club. If a club views itself equal to another club in terms of quality and services offered, its pricing should be in the same range as that of the other club. If a club is looking to position itself as affordable and less competitive than other clubs, it should be charging less than those that are considered high end and competitive. On the other hand, if the club wants to be viewed as the Cadillac of clubs, it should price accordingly to position itself as better than or of a higher quality than other clubs.

Pricing should also consider the goals and objectives of the club. The club may be interested in having the most players of any club in the state. In this case it desires a large market share. The club may decide not to charge as much to achieve the desired market share. On the other hand, the club may want to be selective and offer a high-quality experience to a few. If this is the case, it should price accordingly.

Consider a club that can charge $100 per player for a season and get 1,000 players in the club. In doing so, the club will gross $100,000. Another club may select only 100 players and charge each player $1,000. That club, too, will gross $100,000. Both clubs have met their goals.

Lastly, the strength of the brand dictates the willingness of people to pay. A club known to have great coaches, a tradition of success, and a first-class facility can charge accordingly. A club that does not possess those traits may not be able to charge as high a fee until its brand is stronger and more people make positive associations with the club.

Promotion

Promotion is any activity that increases interest in and awareness of the club and that ultimately leads to someone deciding to become a member. Promotional media include print and electronic advertising, printed and electronic materials, mailings, telemarketing, and personal selling (Mullin, Hardy, & Sutton, 2007). All of these media can communicate the benefits of the club to potential customers and play an important role in the positioning of the club in the mind of the customer. A printed brochure or a 30-second advertisement on a local cable station that has images of kids having fun playing a sport and that explains that the cost of participation in a 10-week league would equal the cost of babysitting positions the club in the mind of the potential customer as an affordable, enjoyable experience. A brochure or television ad with images of past players who are now intercollegiate athletes or of teams holding up trophies positions a club as one that is competitive.

Because promotion does have a cost, it should be accounted for in the budget. The success of a club's promotional efforts is based on the ability to reach the

promotion—Any activity that increases interest in and awareness of the club and that ultimately leads to someone deciding to become a member.

target audience, generate a return on the club's investment, position the product in the mind of the consumer, increase consumer awareness, and most important, affect sales or registration fees. To reach a target audience, club leaders need to know who they are targeting and then determine the best way to reach them. What newspapers and magazines do they read? What Web sites do they visit? What radio stations do they listen to, and at what times? The club can also acquire the names, addresses, e-mail addresses, and phone numbers of potential clients and reach them either through phone calls, mailings, or e-mail blasts.

market research— Communicating with customers to assess the effectiveness of marketing efforts, understanding the wants and needs of current members, and providing valuable information in preparing corporate partnership proposals.

The most effective way to gather information to communicate with current customers and to assess current marketing efforts is through **market research.** (The sidebar on pages 127-128 provides a sample marketing survey.) Clubs can initiate a market research study of current club members by distributing a survey via e-mail or at the facility.

Mullin and colleagues (2007) identified the following promotional efforts that a club could incorporate into its marketing efforts:

▶ *Advertising* entails paying for publicity in newspapers and magazines and on television, radio, billboards, the sides of buses, and the Web. The larger the circulation of a medium, the more expensive it will be because the club is paying for exposure. An ad that 1 million people will see will be more expensive than one that only 1,000 people will see. That means that an ad in a major metropolitan daily newspaper will be more expensive than an ad in a local weekly newspaper. A radio ad that is played during people's morning commute, from 8 a.m. to 10 a.m., will be more expensive than an ad that is played at 2 a.m. The club should see a return on its investment in an ad.

▶ *Mailings and e-mail blasts* forward information on the club via the postal system or through e-mail. The key is having "good" addresses, those of people who are likely to purchase your product. The club should develop a database of information on anyone who has ever interacted with the club. Another way to secure good addresses is to partner with businesses related to the business of the club. For example, a soccer shop may have contact information on customers that the club could purchase. The store's list may be smaller than, say, a list of everyone in a given area, but the potential of securing one as a customer is greater because the people on the store's list most likely have a specific interest in soccer. The beauty of e-mailing is that it is free. The downside is that an e-mail could be identified as spam and never be seen by the potential customer. (See page 128 for a sample e-mail blast.)

▶ *Personal selling* involves any person-to-person interaction in which a club representative has the chance to persuade a person to join the club. A coach may see a quality player and approach that player's parents, or a club representative may respond to an inquiry from someone looking for the right athletic environment for her daughter.

▶ *Sales promotion* includes a variety of techniques that make the product attractive to a potential consumer. These may include price discounts, coupons, and added benefits. A common sales promotion practiced by clubs is decreasing

Sample Marketing Survey: Tornado Soccer Club

Gender:____ Male ____ Female

Age:____ Under 18 _____ 19-34 _____35-50 _____ 50-65 _____ Over 65

Program of which you are a part ____ Recreational Program ____ Elite Team

How many years have you been with the TSC?

What is the annual household income? (Combined incomes of spouse or partner)

____ Student _____Less than $30,000 _____ $30,000 to $49,999 ____$50,000 to $74,999

____$75,000–$99,999 _____$100,000–$149,999 ____ $150,000-$199,999 ____ Over $200,000

How far do you live from the TSC complex?

____ Less than 5 miles ____ 6–15 miles ____ 16–30 miles ____31–45 miles ____ More than 45 miles

Mark all of those promotional methods that have made you aware of TSC.

_____ Word of Mouth	_____ Web site
_____ Success of past players	_____ Direct mailing
_____ Newspaper ads	_____ Telemarketing
_____ Newspaper articles	_____ Public appearances by players
_____ TV ads	_____ Community relations efforts of TSC
_____ TV reports	_____ Recommendation from a friend
_____ Radio ads	_____ Other _____

List three publications that you read or subscribe to.

_____ _____ _____

In which section of the newspaper do you look for recreation or entertainment options?

____ Front section ____ Local section ____ Entertainment section ____ Sports section

Which radio station do you listen to most frequently? List call letters, number, or both.

_____

Please rate the following factors based on how important they were in your decision to join TSC.

5 = Very Important   4 = Important   3 = Neutral   2 = Unimportant   1 = Very Unimportant

Price	5	4	3	2	1
Quality of coaching	5	4	3	2	1
International reputation of the program	5	4	3	2	1
National reputation of the program	5	4	3	2	1
Local reputation of the program	5	4	3	2	1
Success of TSC teams	5	4	3	2	1
Sale promotions	5	4	3	2	1
Time with family or friends	5	4	3	2	1
Love of soccer	5	4	3	2	1
Proximity to home	5	4	3	2	1
Quality of facilities	5	4	3	2	1

(continued)

Sample Marketing Survey: Tornado Soccer Club *(continued)*

Please rate the following aspects of your experience with TSC.

5 = Very satisfied   4 = Satisfied   3 = Neutral   2 = Unsatisfied   1 = Very unsatisfied

Quality of coaching	5 4 3 2 1
Willingness of staff to assist	5 4 3 2 1
Courtesy of staff	5 4 3 2 1
Off-field programs	5 4 3 2 1
Price	5 4 3 2 1
Facilities	5 4 3 2 1
Availability of fields	5 4 3 2 1
Availability of coaches	5 4 3 2 1
Development of skills	5 4 3 2 1
Other	5 4 3 2 1

What three words would you use to describe the TSC experience?

_____   _____   _____

What three words would you use to describe the TSC soccer complex?

_____   _____   _____

What three words would you use to describe the TSC staff and coaches?

_____   _____   _____

From M.J. Robinson, 2010, *Sport Club Management* (Champaign, IL: Human Kinetics).

Sample E-Mail Blast

Newark Stars Volleyball Club

FOR IMMEDIATE RELEASE

February 8, 2010
Contact: Troy Smith
tsmith@newarkstarsvb.com
555-555-1212

STARS VOLLEYBALL TO HOLD TRYOUTS

The Newark Stars Volleyball Club will hold open tryouts for its elite-level club teams on February 13, 2010, starting at 6 p.m. at the Newark Volleyball Center.

Tryouts will be held for open, 16-and-under, 14-and-under, and 12-and-under teams. There will be a $20 tryout registration fee, and minors must be accompanied by a parent.

The Newark Stars have been in existence since 1986 and participate in the Middle States Elite Volleyball League.

Questions can be directed to Club Director Troy Smith at 555-555-1212 or visit www.newarkstarsvb.com.

-30-

the cost for more than one child from a family. Coupons for a reduced cost for admission can be mailed in a brochure or printed in a newspaper ad. Increasing the value of membership is a good strategy that can enable the club to increase its customer base while not lowering its prices. Included in the membership fee for a league may be a ball, a trip to a professional game, or several individual training sessions.

▶ *Sampling* gives the customer an opportunity to experiment with the product. One way to do this is to invite a potential player to come for a tryout and work with a coach to get a sense of what the training would be like and get a feel for the facility. Another approach is to hold a free clinic to give potential customers a chance to experiment with the product. If they enjoy the experience, they may make the commitment to join the club.

▶ *Tabling* incorporates personal selling, advertising, sales promotions, and sampling. In this case the club pays for the right to have a presence at an event. A club representative attends the event and interacts with potential customers and distributes brochures. Again, the key to successful tabling is targeting. What types of events do families attend? Parades, community events, and minor league games are potential places. The idea is to be where potential customers are to make it easier for them to learn about the club.

Public Relations

The image of the club in the mind of the consumer is important to the marketing efforts of the club. Effective **public relations** involves developing relations and goodwill. The club must be proactive about creating these relations and monitoring the thoughts of those who can help the club achieve its goals and objectives (Mullin, Hardy, & Sutton, 2007). Proactive steps through public, community, and media relations can foster goodwill with both internal and external publics and stakeholders.

> **public relations—** Developing relations and goodwill with those publics and stakeholders who can help the club achieve its goals and objectives.

Publics

A **public** is an individual or entity that has an interest in the club. Publics can be external to the club, such as the members of the community in which the club resides, civic leaders, businesses, and others in the sport community. Publics can also be internal, such as members of the club, past members of the club, board members, coaches, and staff members.

> **public—**An individual or entity that has an interest in the club.

Public relation efforts should be directed at these publics. To influence external publics, the club may participate in a project that benefits a local charitable organization or a particular cause. It may encourage club members to raise funds for a charitable cause by soliciting donations and running in a 10K race that supports the cause. It could also adopt a highway and make a commitment to keeping it clean. The club executive director also may be willing to appear at or speak at functions in the community or donate his time for a worthy cause. All of these efforts are directed at making the club a part of the local community by reaching out to people and organizations in the community.

Positive relations with internal publics, those within the club, are also paramount. The club can recognize the efforts of volunteers or boards members by developing recognition awards for exemplary volunteers or those who have contributed the most to the club. Players too can be recognized for excellence on the field or for demonstrating behavior the club wants to promote such as fair play or teamwork. Awards and recognitions can be posted on the club's Web site.

Media Relations

The club can create awareness of club activities by using media outlets. Club leaders can send press releases to newspapers either to announce upcoming events or to share the successes of the club. (The sidebar below shows a sample press release.) The goal is to make it easy for the media to print stories about the club by providing as much information as possible and making members of the club accessible for interviews. Ultimately, the media outlet will determine whether an event is newsworthy, but it can't make that decision unless it is aware of the event. Media relations should be the responsibility of a full-time staff member or the priority of a volunteer.

Place

place—Where a club delivers its product.

The **place** a club delivers its product is an important part of the marketing mix. The concept of place includes the accessibility, quality, and safety of the facility. A field or gym that is easy for families to get to in terms of traffic and distance has an

---

Sample Press Release

Newark Stars Volleyball Club

FOR IMMEDIATE RELEASE

April 7, 2010
Contact: Troy Smith
tsmith@newarkstarsvb.com
555-555-1212

Newark Stars to Host Volleyball Marathon for Cancer Research

The Newark Stars Volleyball Club will host the 5th Annual Volleyball Marathon for Cancer on May 15, 2010, starting at 11 a.m. at the Newark Volleyball Center.

Money raised from the event will be donated to the National Cancer Foundation. Members of the club will play matches for 24 consecutive hours, and donations are based on the number of games played by a sponsored participant or team.

In the previous four years, the club has raised over $80,000 for the cause. The goal for this year's event is to raise $25,000.

Donations can be made to the club directly or by supporting an individual player. There are also event sponsorship opportunities. Questions can be directed to Club Director Troy Smith at 555-555-1212, or visit www.newarkstarsvb.com.

The Newark Stars Volleyball Club has been in existence since 1986 and is a USVBA-certified club. It participates in the Middle States Elite Volleyball League.

-30-

increased chance of gaining customers, as does a modern, well-designed, spacious facility. On the other hand, a poor location and low-quality facilities negate such positives as a great product (in terms of instruction) that is priced and promoted well. If the club views tournaments and camps as an essential revenue stream, place takes on an even more important role in the marketing mix, because teams may decide not to sign up for a tournament because of the condition of the field, the difficulty associated with getting to the facility, or a poor parking situation.

Arguably, place is the hardest P to change. New facilities may cost millions of dollars, and renovations are costly as well. A club that has to rent a facility (e.g., a for-profit facility) or use a public facility (e.g., a recreation park or school) is at the mercy of someone else's schedule and has little control over the quality and location of the facility. A facility that is off the beaten track or a great distance from the club's target audience presents a marketing challenge.

Another concern related to location is the safety of the area. Will parents feel comfortable leaving their cars when dropping their kids off at the facility? Will they be concerned about the safety of their children while they are at the facility? Again, these concerns can negatively affect the marketing efforts of the club.

The condition, size, and number of playing fields and their surfaces are important. Eight teams sharing a soccer field or three teams trying to practice on one basketball court takes away from the experience and the quality of instruction. Also, practices scheduled at odd hours to get gym, field, or ice time can be a deterrent to potential customers.

The ideal situation is for a club to have its own facility that is designed to meet the expanding needs of the club. See chapter 7 for more on generating revenue to pay for the facility, chapter 8 for more on operating and managing the facility, and the earlier discussion in this chapter on developing a deferred maintenance plan to ensure that the facility stays in good condition.

Club leaders must also consider the viewing accommodations. Does the facility need bleachers or a seating area? Parents of young athletes often bring their own chairs to outdoor games. This is not the case at indoor events. If the club plans to use its facility for competitions, customer seating should be addressed. The risk management aspect needs to be considered as well. Spectators should not be sitting so close to the fields that they might be injured.

Many new outdoor facilities designate one field as a stadium field. It may have permanent bleachers or be positioned so that portable bleachers can be brought in if needed. The installation of bleachers can be viewed as an investment given that other sporting events may be looking to rent venues that have seating. If the club is interested in generating revenue from renting its facilities and hosting events, it can see a return on an investment in bleachers.

Along with the playing and viewing aspects of a facility, parking is another important consideration. The amount of and ease of parking can affect marketing efforts. The ideal situation is to have enough parking spaces that members are not parking on side streets. Also, the quality of the parking lot is an issue. Is it blacktopped with clearly marked spaces and arrows directing traffic flow, or is it a dirt field with holes and no clear plan for parking or exiting?

Ancillary facilities such as an indoor playing area at a primarily outdoor complex or a playground area to entertain kids before, during, or after contests or practices can add to the club experience. Having an indoor space to offer shelter in case of rain or to hold practices or games is also an important option.

Concession stands can generate significant revenue for a club, but the size and quality of the space can determine the level of success. A modern stand with a place to cook or warm food, refrigeration, and a clean and accommodating space in which customers can sit and eat will be attractive to customers. The design of a stand should be a consideration in the planning of a new facility or the renovation of an existing one.

Social space for members has become of increased importance as sport clubs increasingly become social outlets for participants and their parents. Clubs can offer spaces where parents can meet after events or come to even when there is not an event. In the design of a club facility, a space can be created that overlooks the playing areas. It can serve as a spot from which to view the action, a space for club events, or a rental space.

Manipulating the Five Ps

The goal of the club is to develop the right product at the right price in the right place, and to promote and publicize it in the right way. Each of the five Ps of sport marketing must be examined to determine the best way to manipulate it to meet the wants and needs of potential consumers. This involves an ongoing analysis of the club's marketing efforts. Is the club offering the services that members want? Is it charging too little and as a result being viewed as low quality? Is the Web site easy to navigate, and does it provide the information club members need and want? Should the club add lights and an artificial surface to increase programming? All of these questions are related to the manipulation of each of the five Ps.

Mixing the Five Ps

Even if each of the five Ps is strong as an independent entity, issues may arise when they are mixed together. Club leadership must understand the relationship among the Ps and work to ensure that mixing them promotes the efforts of the club. For example, a club may have the best coaches and training program in the region (product), but if it does not advertise, if the Web site is of poor quality, and if the club leadership is not willing to tout its great abilities and great experience (promotion), the club may never get the membership it needs to sustain itself. This is an example of a bad mix between product and promotion. On the other hand, a club with inferior coaches and programs whose leaders are knowledgeable and savvy about marketing may be more successful in attracting members than the club that offers better programs although customers might be disappointed once they join because the product is inferior. Figure 6.2 shows an example of an ideal marketing mix. If a particular marketing mix wasn't positive, the club should determine what modifications are needed.

	Product	Price	Place	Promotion	Public relations
Product		Great soccer club, great coaches, good facility, and the price is reasonable.	Great coaching and training methods with a modern facility	Great club that is well promoted.	Successful club with a positive reputation of contributing to the community.
Price			The club is in a convenient, safe location and is priced to meet consumer needs.	The first 200 to sign up will get a reduced rate.	The club is able to reduce its costs without compromising services.
Place				The facility is highlighted in promotional materials.	Facility is viewed as first class, and that is the image being sent out to potential customers.
Promotion					Club promotes its image, and public relations initiatives create awareness of the club.
PR					

Figure 6.2 Marketing mix of the five Ps in a sport club setting. This matrix shows how the five Ps of marketing can work together.

Importance of Market Research

Market research is vital to club success. It enables the club to assess the effectiveness of its marketing efforts, enables it to understand the wants and needs of its current members, and provides valuable information for preparing corporate partnership proposals (Mullin, Hardy, & Sutton, 2007).

A variety of methods are available for conducting market research. The method used should be based on the type of information the club desires. Surveys can serve multiple purposes and can be administered on site, sent by electronic and regular mailing, or sent home with kids. Surveys are an effective way to gather information to assist in the development of corporate partnership proposals. A survey enables the club to gain the demographic information that potential partners desire. The partner needs to know whether the people associated with the club are the same people who are likely to purchase its product. The survey can also ask about the brands club members buy, the stores at which they shop, and the likelihood that they would patronize a business that sponsors the organization.

Surveys are also an effective way to gather information to develop an advertising strategy. A survey can ask how a customer became aware of the club, the team, the tournament, or the summer camp. The survey can ask what media customers use, what radio stations they listen to and at what time, and what Web sites they visit. This information can help the club determine which marketing strategies have been effective and where they should be putting their advertising money.

Surveys can also be used to assess the quality of the customer's experience. Questions related to how well the club keeps to the schedule, the effectiveness of the coaches, and the quality of the food at the concession stands can be included. Also, surveys can provide information on customer desires. What times should league games start? Should the club add an in-house recreation league? Because marketing is based on meeting customers' wants and needs, the club should know what those wants and needs are.

focus group—A group of customers brought together to answer questions and provide detailed feedback to an organization.

Another marketing research method is a **focus group.** A focus group brings together a group of customers to answer questions and provide detailed feedback (Mullin, Hardy, & Sutton, 2007). The focus group provides more information than a survey, because the participants can go into more detail. Often, a survey can provide the insight into the questions that can be asked in a focus group. For example, the quality of coaching may receive a low score on a survey. In a focus group the club manager can ask about the quality of coaching. The participants may communicate that volunteer parents coaches are not sufficient and that a rival club is hiring licensed coaches or high school or college assistant coaches. The focus group participants may even communicate that they are willing to pay more to have quality coaching.

It is wise to have a person not affiliated with the club lead a focus group to keep the process objective and ensure that participants are not inhibited in their responses. With both surveys and focus groups, it is a good investment to use trained professionals who know how to design and administer surveys and ask good questions in focus groups.

Observation is another method of market research. **Observation** entails having the club manager walk around the club facility during the hours of operation to determine whether practices and competitions are being run well, the parking lot is organized, the concession stand is meeting the needs of the customers, and seating is adequate. These observations offer valuable information.

Finally, one of the most important sources of market research is customer complaints. Club leaders' first reaction to a customer complaint is often to explain away the complaint or blame the source, but most complaints offer an opportunity to improve. Leaders must look past the emotion in the complaint to determine whether an unmet want or need is at the heart of the complaint. Is the complaint from a parent about the starting time of training sessions an issue related to the delivery of the product? It may be a scheduling oversight that results in this child's team having an undesirable training time or location while another team has a favorable one all of the time. Perhaps the training time is not conducive to working parents who have to transport their children to the training sessions. Complaints are worth listening to because they may give the club an opportunity to better serve its members. Also, listening to complaints is good public relations. Even if the club leadership cannot make changes to address the complaint, at least the customer has had the chance to present the concern.

> **observation**—A market research technique in which the club manager walks around the club facility during the hours of operation to evaluate the services being provided.

Database Marketing

An important aspect in marketing is the development of a database of current, past, and potential customers. The database has long-term benefits for the club in other aspects of club management also, such as fund-raising, sponsorship sales, and attracting volunteers. A basic database includes contacts' names, mailing addresses, e-mail addresses, and phone numbers. The club can reach these people through a direct mail campaign or an e-mail blast to announce an upcoming event.

The database can move beyond the basics and include demographic information such as age, education, occupation, place of employment (for parents), and income. This information allows the club to know who its members are. Why is this important? The club can use the experience of a member to help advance the club's efforts. Consider a database that indicates that a parent of a club member is a senior executive with a national corporation based in the city. That corporation has a foundation that financially supports initiatives that promote youth activities, such as a sport. This person may know more about the foundation, the leadership of the foundation, and how best to prepare a grant proposal that will be favorably reviewed. This person may also have a personal relationship with the marketing area of that corporation and could facilitate a meeting that could lead to a sponsorship deal for the club.

Summary

Sport clubs are businesses and need to be run as such. Those that accept this reality will thrive, whereas those who do not may face financial challenges and put themselves in jeopardy of not existing. Understanding revenue streams and expenses as well as the basics of marketing is important for sport club managers.

Clubs must have plans for generating revenue and for controlling their operating expenses. A club manager must either become versed in finance or accounting or hire an accounting firm to handle the financial aspect of the club, while still being aware of all of the club's finances.

The budget process for any club starts with reviewing the previous year's budget to determine whether the projections were accurate in terms of the actual club expenses. Within any budget there are fixed, variable, and capital expenses, and all must be taken into account when planning for the following year. Adjustments should be made based on the budget issues from the previous year.

Club managers should figure out ways to increase revenue through income-generating activities such as operating concession stands, licensing and selling team products, and organizing camps, to name a few. Club managers that implement ancillary revenue–generating activities will likely reap greater financial benefits for their clubs.

In determining the best strategy for generating income for the club, managers should use the five Ps of sport marketing: product, promotion, place, price, and public relations. The goal of the club is to develop the right product at the right price, offer it in the right place, and promote and publicize it in the right way. Each of the Ps must be examined to determine the best way to manipulate it to meet the wants and needs of the potential consumer.

Finally, the club should conduct market research to assess whether it is meeting the wants and needs of its consumers and develop an effective database to communicate with customers and track their levels of involvement with the club.

Although Ronny was a successful basketball player and now a coach, a businessman he is not. After coming to terms with this, Ronny hires an accounting firm to manage all of the accounting and finances of the organization. The firm works with Ronny to develop the annual budget, set up a payment plan to retire the debt, and prepares his taxes. In addition, Ronny hires a marketing director for the club who is responsible for developing and implementing a marketing plan that will enable the Sharpshooters to meet the wants and needs of its existing customers while attracting new ones. In the end, the Sharpshooters is being run like a business, and in turn, its long-term viability has been ensured.

By the end of the chapter, the sport club manager will be able to do the following:

▶ Explain the difference between sponsorship and fund-raising

▶ Explain what a sport property desires in a corporate partnership.

▶ Evaluate the effectiveness of a corporate partnership.

▶ Organize a successful fund-raising campaign.

▶ Explain the rule of thirds in fund-raising for a capital project.

▶ List the elements of a grant proposal.

▶ Describe the types of funding agencies.

▶ Write a grant proposal.

7

Sponsorship and Fund-Raising

The Santa Rosa Swim Club needed to renovate its indoor pool complex: the pool operating systems were out-of-date; a zero-level entry was needed to service the club's special needs participants; the locker room shower area and lockers were in need of replacements as was the flooring; and the building needed a new roof. Along with those infrastructure issues, the facade and lobby of the facility were aesthetically unappealing. To do the job right, the club would have to spend $900,000. Club leaders realized they would not be able to pay for the renovations from the existing revenue streams, and they were not sure the current members would be willing to contribute to the renovations through donations or increased fees.

M any sport club leaders have great ideas about how to make their clubs better by enhancing program offerings, increasing staff, or expanding facilities. However, many great ideas are left on the drawing board because the funds are never secured to make those ideas a reality. Essential revenue streams (discussed in chapter 6) in most cases cover the day-to-day costs of operating the club. To fund new initiatives or to enhance the current offerings, the club has to move beyond those revenue streams and generate external funding through corporate partnerships, fund-raising, and grant writing.

Clubs that have been able to build complexes, add fields or buildings to their complexes, or add staff members in many cases have been able tap into funds from external sources. Such funds come from selling naming rights to a facility, hosting annual events such as auctions or golf outings, or writing grants to request funds from corporate foundations.

Sponsorships Versus Fund-Raising

As stated earlier, many club leaders are interested in expanding their clubs but are either not willing to put out the effort to generate the revenue to do so, or do not know how. Two primary sources of revenue are sponsorships (or the more commonly used term these days, *partnerships*) and fund-raising. The club manager needs to understand the difference between the two.

corporate partnership—A cash or in-kind fee paid to a property in return for access to the exploitable commercial potential associated with the property.

A **corporate partnership** is a cash or in-kind fee paid to a property in return for access to the exploitable commercial potential associated with the property (Mullin, Hardy, & Sutton, 2007). In the case of a sport club, the club approaches an entity, in most cases a business or corporation, about entering into a business proposition that will benefit both the sport club and the business. Leaders of the business are interested in exploiting an aspect of the club for the purpose of generating revenue for the business. It is not a charitable deed on their part; they are looking to gain.

fund-raising—A request to an entity or individual for a charitable contribution for a worthy cause.

Fund-raising, on the other hand, is a request by a club to an entity or person for a charitable contribution for a worthy cause. In theory, such a donation is a philanthropic gesture from which the entity or person does not seek commercial gain. In reality, though, the person or entity may want something in return for the donation, such as a field named in her honor or a position on the board of directors.

Knowing the difference between a corporate partnership and fund-raising is important when it comes time to approach a partner or potential donor. Club leaders need to be clear about whether they are negotiating a business deal that will benefit both the club and the business or asking for a contribution to a worthwhile program (i.e., the club or an aspect of the club).

Creating the Corporate Partnership

In corporate partnerships, both parties are looking to benefit. Entering into a partnership, the club needs to know what it expects to gain from the relationship as well as what it can offer the business or corporation.

SUCCESSFUL STRATEGY

Emergence of Corporate Sponsorship

Sponsorship has been a part of youth sport on a small scale for a long time in the form of local businesses sponsoring teams in youth leagues. In recent years, corporations are seeing the benefits of partnering with sport clubs and their facilities and have made more significant investments in the environment in an attempt to communicate with potential customers while supporting local communities.

In 2007, Citizens Bank entered into a five-year naming rights deal for a 16-field Massachusetts Youth Soccer Association (MYSA) complex in Lancaster, Massachusetts, with a goal of targeting parents, coaches, and youngsters. The $9.5 million complex was named Citizens Bank Fields at Progin Park. Although the financial terms of the deal were not disclosed, a significant commitment was made by Citizens Bank. In a *Boston Globe* article on the deal, Citizens Bank of Massachusetts chair and CEO, Bob Smyth, stated, "We really look at 'Where do our employees and customers live and work? And how do we enhance those communities?'"

Banks and soccer are not the only benefactors of corporate partnerships. In February of 2008, the Hardee's restaurant chain purchased the naming rights to an ice rink in the St. Louis area and renamed it the Hardee's Iceplex. On the Hardee's corporate Web site, Hardee's president and CEO, Andy Puzder, stated, "This is a natural fit as Hardee's has always been an avid supporter of local sports."

"Our facility is very excited about the extraordinary impact this new partnership can have on youth sports and tourism in St. Louis," said Lloyd Ney, general manager of the Hardee's Iceplex. "With the immediate credibility that the Hardee's Iceplex name will bring our business, we will now have a unique advantage in bringing national events to our facility."

Lastly, in 2008 Coke became a founding partner with Fieldhouse USA, a $14 million multisport facility located in Frisco, Texas. With the deal Coke gets exclusive pouring rights for carbonated beverages and bottled water and year-round brand exposure inside the facility. Coke will have signage incorporated into the building, including electronic signs on flat screens above competition areas, and it will have a presence on the facility's Web site.

Identifying Potential Partners

Partners for a club fall into product categories. For example, what are the brands of soft drinks? The question really is, Who are the potential partners in the soft drink category? Sponsor categories go beyond soft drinks, however; they include office supplies, automobiles, insurance, computers, banks, financial services, upscale restaurants, fast-food restaurants, and insurance companies, to name a few.

Benefits for the Sport Club

The sport club receives several benefits from entering into a partnership agreement. The first is a guaranteed source of revenue. Partnership deals can range from 1 year to 30 years (in the case of naming rights deals on major stadiums and arenas). The club will know that on an annual basis the agreed-on amount will be paid based on the contractual agreement.

Another benefit of securing a corporate partnership is the credibility a partnership brings to the club. A partnership with a global or national brand such as Adidas, McDonald's, or All-State, or a well-established local grocery store or insurance agent, makes a statement about the club's legitimacy. A reputable brand will not partner with a disreputable entity because of the potential damage to its brand. In fact, securing a reputable partner gives a club leverage to secure partnerships with other businesses.

trade-out—The exchange of a product or service for a partnership with a sport club, eliminating an expense for the club or creating a revenue stream.

Finally, a corporate partner does not always provide money. It can provide a product to eliminate an expense for the club or allow the club to turn the product into a revenue stream. This is known as a **trade-out.** No money is exchanged. Products, services, or benefits are traded to the benefit of both partners. If a sport club can enter into an agreement with an office supply company to be an official partner in the club, the office supply company can eliminate the annual budget expense of office supplies for the year in return for the relationship with the club. Club leaders can look at the annual budget to identify product or service categories and then approach the providers of those products or services about creating in-kind partnership deals.

The money the club would have spent on products and services traded out can be spent on other aspects of the club or directed to one-time major expenses. If $20,000 worth of expenses could be traded out through corporate partners, that money could be spent on two part-time coaches' salaries or put away annually for a capital project (in five years the club would have $100,000). Trade-outs should either eliminate expenses for the club, as discussed, or generate revenue for the club. A donation of 100 cases of soda provided as in-kind sponsorship to a club that sells them at $1.00 a can is worth $2,400. What can the club provide to the soft drink company in return for the $2,400 in product if provided? That question will be answered with the information provided in the rest of the chapter.

Recognizing a Partner's Objectives: Solving Problems

As stated, a corporate partnership is based on both parties having their needs met. Many clubs make the mistake of focusing only on their own needs and not the needs of their partners. Partners whose needs are not met are highly unlikely to continue the relationship beyond the original contract. Each potential partner has unique needs, and a sport club can play the role of a problem solver by listening to the partner and developing a proposal that addresses their needs. Addressing needs must be at the core of the proposal.

Mullin, Hardy, and Sutton (2007) identified the following corporate partner needs:

▶ *Brand awareness.* The business wants more people to know more about its product. Customers must know a product exists before they can seek it out and purchase it.

▶ *Image enhancement.* A business may be known, but not in the positive manner it would hope to be. Consumers may know about the brand but do not purchase it because they do not relate to it or feel negatively about it.

- *Product trials or sales.* The business wants to have potential customers either sample or purchase its product or service. Customers may be aware of the product and have positive views of it, but they haven't had a chance to experience it.

- *Increases sales.* A business will be interested in a partnership if the partnership directly affects its bottom line through increased sales. This is one of the truest measures of the success of a partnership agreement.

- *Access to potential customers.* The opportunity to communicate with potential customers directly is extremely appealing to corporate partners. Granting access to the mailing addresses, phone numbers, and e-mail addresses of club members enables the partner to communicate directly with potential customers.

- *Entertainment.* Businesses seek unique ways to communicate with, entertain, and reward important customers. A sport club's activities and facilities offer these unique opportunities.

- *Employee morale.* Businesses seek ways to reward loyal or outstanding employees with incentives or to boost the morale of the entire workforce. As with the entertainment objective, a sport club offers partners unique reward and incentive opportunities.

- *Return on investment (ROI).* Ultimately, a business wants to see a return on its investment in the partnership. What did it get in return for the money or product it provided? Was it worth the investment? Was the objective it desired achieved? If the answers are yes, the partner will be back to renew the deal; if the answer is no, the partner will seek out a deal with a better ROI elsewhere.

Assessing the Potential Inventory

Meeting the needs of the partner is based on using the club's inventory. A sport club needs to determine what elements are in its inventory and which ones it is willing to offer a potential partner to meet that partner's needs. Each inventory item has the ability to be a part of a partnership deal depending on the individual partner's needs. The old partnership model was "One deal fits all," and often the partner's specific needs were not met. Being a problem solver involves assessing each situation independently and using the inventory to meet each partner's needs.

Facility

Securing the naming rights of a facility is a great opportunity to build brand awareness. The business that purchases those rights will have its name used every time the facility is referenced by a person or a media outlet. The partner can also use the facility to entertain and build employee morale. A swim club could trade memberships to a local computer dealer in return for laptops, printers, and service on those computers. The memberships could be used for employee morale, and the pool could be used for a swim party to entertain clients. A soccer club could allow a local business to use its facility for pickup employee soccer games two nights a week or during lunch breaks.

Events

Clubs can sell naming rights to club events as well. This builds brand awareness because the brand's name is used with every mention of the event. What is the name of the all-star basketball game in which the top players in the country compete? Did McDonald's come to mind pretty quickly?

Signage

A business can gain brand awareness by having its brand or logo strategically placed in the facility—on the boards of an indoor soccer complex, the scoreboard of a baseball field, the T-shirts of the coaches and participants, or the bumpers and sides of the equipment that prepares the playing surfaces. The value of a sign is based on the number of people that will see it and is figured as a cost per thousand. If the cost per thousand is $10, and if the club's facility has 50,000 visitors a year and each of those visitors will see the sign three times a visit on average, the sign is valued at $1,500 annually.

Publications, Public Relations Materials, and the Web Site

A business can also gain awareness by having its logo placed on all printed and electronic items produced by the sport club. This could include registration forms, programs, and advertisements for the club or its events; yearbooks; and the club's Web site. A link to the business can also be placed on the club's Web site so members or visitors can access the partner's Web site easily.

Coupons, Special Benefits, and Affinity Programs

As part of a partnership with a sport club, a business can distribute coupons in club mailings, provide links on the club's Web site, and give out goody bags at club tournaments or events. The club, for its part, may be able to offer special benefits to its members. In each case, the value of the partnership is determined by the number of coupons redeemed and the number of club members who take advantage of the special benefits.

Consider a local restaurant that pays $5,000 for a partnership deal. A benefit of the partnership is the right to distribute 1,000 $5-off coupons over the course of the year. Suppose 75 percent off those coupons are redeemed. The average meal for a family of four costs $30; minus the $5 coupon, the gross profit for the restaurant on the meal is $25. The restaurant has generated $18,750 in business from the $5,000 partnership with the club. The key to the partner's success is the club encouraging members and visitors to patronize its sponsors.

Another partnership deal could involve giving club members a 10 percent discount on purchases from the corporate partner. That discount may encourage the club members to purchase from the corporate partner rather than another business.

Finally, a partnership designed to promote loyalty to the club and enable the business to contribute also involves a member discount. In this case, however, 10 percent of every member's purchase from the corporate partner is donated to the club. To support the club, members patronize the business, and in turn, the business may develop customers for life.

Unique corporate partnerships such as those discussed in this section may take time to develop. The club may need to patronize the business before approaching it about a partnership. A club may hold its monthly board of directors meeting at a restaurant to form a relationship with the business. The next step would be for club leaders to present how a partnership could expand the business the club generates for the restaurant.

Stands or Tables at Events

Setting up a table or a display at a club venue during events so that attendees can sample, take home samples of, or purchase a product is called **tabling**. This form of corporate partnership provides brand awareness and also offers product trials and sales opportunities. To identify potential tabling partners, club leaders should think in terms of the products club visitors might be interested in buying. They could range from home improvement products to food to automobiles.

tabling—Setting up a table or a display at a club venue during events so that attendees can sample, take home samples of, or purchase a product.

If a club is comfortable, as part of a corporate partnership a car dealership could strategically place cars around an outdoor facility or in the parking lot of an indoor facility. A salesperson would be on site to talk about the cars and offer test drives. This arrangement benefits both the car dealer and members. With all of the kid activities on the weekend, members may have no time to visit a car dealer, so the club has brought the car dealer to them. The car dealer, for its part, gets 30 good leads and sells five cars.

Contests and Sweepstakes

A corporate partner can increase sales and product awareness by hosting a contest for the members of the club. The sweepstakes may involve inviting club members to go to the business's Web site to fill out an entry form, or offering club members eligibility for a major award if they use a product 10 times. The business gains information on potential customers for future contacts, promotes its product, and increases awareness of its product among members of the club.

Use of the Facility

If a club has its own facility, it can offer a corporate partner the use of the facility as part of the deal. The club is giving up revenue from renting it out, but it is not spending any money. The corporate partner can use that time in the facility to improve employee morale (e.g., with pickup games) or to entertain clients.

Community Relations Programs

If a club has an interest in supporting a worthy cause or offering opportunities to those who may not be able to afford to participate in club activities, it can approach a corporate partner to sponsor the initiative. In the case of a league for special needs kids, the corporate partner can cover league expenses in exchange for having its name embedded in the league title. The partner is making a valuable contribution to the local community and enhancing its image by supporting a worthy endeavor.

Synergistic Packages

The partnership proposal may include one or several of the inventory items that were presented (e.g., tabling, signage, coupons) if the partner has multiple needs. As stated earlier, the key for a club is to be a problem solver. By listening to the potential partner's needs and using the inventory to meet those needs, the club becomes a true partner for the business.

Fund-Raising

Fund-raising for a sport club can take on many forms. It can be an essential revenue stream if the club determines that a percentage of its operating revenue will be generated through annual campaigns, sales, or a special event. Fund-raising can also be viewed as an ancillary revenue stream if the club determines that money raised from fund-raising efforts is extra to the operating budget and will be used to pay for an added benefit such as a special trip or a minor capital improvement. Finally, fund-raising plays an integral role in the funding of capital projects such as buildings and new fields. In this case, the club organizes a one-time campaign to reach a goal. When that goal is reached, the campaign disbands and the funds are used to pay for the project. It is important to note that in almost all cases a club must be classified as a 501(c) nonprofit entity to initiate fund-raising efforts. This is especially true when it comes to grant writing, which is discussed later in this chapter.

Courtesy of the South Orange County Wildcats

Extra money raised through fund-raising efforts can be used to pay for trips for a club's athletes.

Fund-raising should be centralized, and all efforts should be approved by the club leadership or board and managed by the leadership. Capital campaigns, annual donations, sales, and special events that are managed centrally make better use of time and resources than those that are managed separately. In fact, fund-raising should be the responsibility of a full-time club employee. This ensures a common theme running through the organization and that the money coming into the club is used as the club leadership determines. A full-time club employee focused on fund-raising can also ensure that potential donors are asked to make a donation that best fits their financial situation; a person who may be willing to donate $1,000 may donate only $10 if that is what a club asks for. Donations also should be for the good of the entire club and not individual entities within the club. Multiple teams approaching similar potential donors for funds can become counterproductive and annoying, turning potential donors into nondonors. For example, a potential donor should not be approached by an individual athlete and asked to make a donation to the athlete's team and also be approached by the club to make another donation to the club; a potential donor should only be asked once to make a donation.

The keys to successful fund-raising are researching, planning, organizing, implementing, and evaluating. The researching phase involves learning more about potential donors and fund-raising methods and developing a strategy to best reach donors through the appropriate methods. From this the club can develop effective quid pro quo, what the donor wants and receives in return for the donation. A donor must have the motivation and the means to donate. To understand this, the fund-raiser must consider the geographic area, demographics, and psychographics of the potential donor. This will help the fund-raiser determine what the person or entity can donate and why they might be willing to.

The following sections describe some ways to raise funds for a sport club.

Annual Donations

Annual donations are usually secured through an annual solicitation campaign. Traditionally, an aspect of the club is targeted for the funds, such as scholarships for participants or an annual event. The key to the success of the annual campaign is keeping a database of current and past members of the club. The campaign uses that database to communicate with potential donors by mail, e-mail, phone, or personal interaction. Mail has the lowest success rate, and personal interaction has the highest. A common method is having current members call past members to ask for donations so that the new generation at the club will have the same positive experience that former members had. Annual donation campaigns have a start date and a completion date. Some clubs set up call centers and have groups of volunteers come in to make calls in the evenings for a week.

The club should keep track of who donates and how much and, at the very least, send thank-you notes. The club can also establish giving levels and offer gifts based on the amount of the donation—for example, for a $10 donation, the donor gets a club bumper sticker; for $100, the donor gets a club shirt; and for $500, the donor gets all of the items offered at the lower levels as well as a club warm-up suit. These gifts are incentives for people to donate. The key is having a donor base beyond the current membership list. Current members can solicit past members or those who have an interest in the sport or the club.

Sales

Product sales is a common means of fund-raising. Companies specializing in providing products for sales allow fund-raising groups to keep a percentage of the proceeds. These companies provide not only the product, but also the promotional and sign-up materials. The downside of sales fund-raisers is that the marketplace is saturated with sales from other organizations and schools, and club members themselves or their family members end up purchasing the products.

The sales product should be something of value to potential donors. Coupon books and wrapping paper at the holiday season are often valuable products.

Club leaders need to decide how club members will be involved in a sales fund-raiser because its success depends on their participation. Some clubs require that each participant be responsible for the sale of a predetermined amount; if they do not sell that amount, they must pay the difference. The money members make beyond the sales amount can be put toward their registration fees.

An effective strategy in sales is to create a contest among either individuals or teams within the club. The individual or team that sells the most products is rewarded.

Special Events

If done well, a special event can be a successful fund-raiser as well as a positive social event for the members of the club. Special events include golf outings, picnics, auctions, and trips. Keys to the success of special events are the use of volunteers, getting as much donated as possible (e.g. the venue, the items to be auctioned, food and drink), building a tradition for the event, making the experience worthwhile for participants, and most important, making sure the club generates a profit that is worth the time and effort of organizing the event.

The event should be run and staffed by the members of the club, and members should reach outside the club to get attendees beyond the club membership. Clubs can set a goal of each club member inviting two guests. Also, through sponsorships, the club should get as much donated as possible to eliminate the overhead. If a club can get a golf course to donate the course for the day, a major expense has been eliminated. In terms of auctions, all items should be donated so that the profit is 100 percent.

Solicitation

solicitation—The act of identifying an individual or entity, cultivating a relationship with that individual or entity, and then making a request for a donation.

Solicitation entails identifying an individual or entity, cultivating a relationship with that individual or entity, and then making a request for a donation. Club leaders can spend hundreds of hours of their own time and other employees' and club members' time selling products and organizing annual campaigns and special events, when they could have developed a relationship with a person who has the means and the motivation to write a check for the amount that all of the other functions would have generated combined.

Learning about a person's means and whether that person even has an interest in donating to the club requires research. Cultivating a relationship involves taking the time to play golf, inviting the person free of charge to attend club functions, and inviting the person to join the club's board of directors. In the end, if the person makes a major donation to enhance the club, the club has worked smarter rather than harder.

Centralization is important when soliciting from a potential donor. A club member may identify the person, and the club itself may arrange and pay for the cultivation, but club leaders must determine the best person to make the request. Should it be the member who has a personal relationship with the person, or the director of coaching who is well respected in the local community? Each situation is unique, and much thought should be given to the approach because the club may get only one chance to make the request.

When asking for a major donation, the person should communicate how the donation will be used. Solicitation is a common approach for capital projects such as buildings and new fields. The person requesting the donation should also explain how the solicitation factors into the strategy. In the case of an **endowment,** the donated money is invested and the club uses the interest off the principal to fund aspects of the club. The interest may pay for facility enhancements on an annual basis, scholarships for players who cannot afford the registration fees, or college scholarships for deserving members. Again, each situation is unique. The donor may have an idea about how the endowment should be used, or may accept the suggestions of the club.

> **endowment**—A sum of money invested for a club; the club uses the interest off the principal to fund aspects of the club.

Capital Campaigns

Fund-raising plays an integral part in enhancing or enlarging sport clubs' current facilities. The revenue needed for adding fields, constructing buildings, or refurbishing aspects of the facility is not generated through the club's operating revenue. A club must initiate a **capital campaign** to raise the funds to complete such projects. (See the sidebar on page 150 for a sample capital campaign letter.) A capital campaign is a one-time campaign to reach a goal. When that goal is reached, the campaign disbands and the funds are used to pay for the intended project.

> **capital campaign**—A one-time fund-raising campaign undertaken to fund a major project such as a field or building.

An effective capital campaign is a well-researched, well-planned, and well-executed initiative with a clear goal in mind. The first step in the process is to determine the amount needed for completing the project, and the next is to determine whether raising that amount is achievable. This step involves a **feasibility study** to identify potential donors and determine whether they have an interest in the project and the means to contribute.

> **feasibility study**—A study conducted to identify potential donors to a capital campaign and determine whether they have an interest in the project and the means to contribute.

The **rule of thirds** in a capital campaign relates to breaking down the desired amount into three segments of donors and developing cultivation, solicitation, and fund-raising methods for each segment (see figure 7.1 on page 151). Consider a club that is interested in raising $900,000 for the addition of synthetic fields and upgrades to the current indoor facility. The rule of thirds states that $300,000

> **rule of thirds**—Breaking down the desired amount into three segments and developing cultivation, solicitation, and fund-raising methods to achieve the goal of each third.

Sample Capital Campaign Letter

Dear members of our community:

The Kerry Lacrosse Club (KLC) is a nonprofit organization that has organized and supervised youth lacrosse teams and leagues for boys and girls for more than 25 years. KLC has influenced the lives of more than 15,000 youths since its inception. Many have gone on to play high school and college lacrosse, but most have grown to be outstanding citizens of the city of Kerry.

In the early years of KLC, games and practices were held on a variety of school and community recreation fields and the club did not have a home base. In 1990, KLC was able to secure property and build a clubhouse and five fields.

Because of the incredible growth of lacrosse in the area, there has been a 200 percent increase in female participation in the past two years and a 120 percent increase in male participation. The existing facility is not sufficient to meet these needs.

KLC plans to expand its facility in 2012 resulting in 16 outdoor fields (four with artificial surfaces and lights) and an expanded clubhouse to include locker rooms and more meeting spaces. The approximate cost of the project is $8 million.

Your financial assistance and support will be crucial to ensure a successful capital drive. Either you or your children have benefited from the KLC experience, and we want to ensure that future generations will have the opportunity for the same positive experiences.

Also, please contact your employer. Many companies support nonprofit organizations if their employees have benefited, can benefit, or will benefit from the organization. Your support in these two areas will be key to our success.

Please fill out the enclosed donation card or visit www.kerrylax.com to make a donation online.

Thank you for contributing to this important cause.

Saul Measley
Kerry Lacrosse Club
Capital Campaign Chairman
555-555-1213
emailmeasley@kerrylax.com

will come from large donors such as wealthy people and foundations. The next $300,000 will come from donors that have an interest and the means to donate, but not to the degree of the donors in the first group. These donors may be individuals and foundations, but special events can also be used to achieve this third's goals. The final $300,000 will come from those that have the interest but moderate means to donate. Again, solicitation, special events, and sales will play a role in reaching this segment. The rule of thirds also contends that fund-raisers will be successful only a third of the time with requests for funding; they will get six no responses for every three yes responses.

Club managers using the rule of thirds should work from the top down, approaching the donors with the greatest ability to donate first. Donations from these sources add legitimacy to the campaign, not to mention the fact that if the

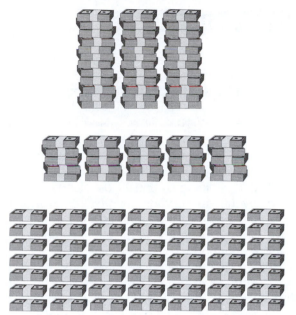

1. Can you get 10 sources to donate $30,000 or 30 sources to donate $10,000? This equals $300,000. Understand that you will need to approach 30 potential donors to eventually get 10 donors, or 90 donors to eventually get 30 donors.

2. Can you get 100 sources to donate $3,000 or 300 sources to donate $1,000? This equals $300,000. Again, understand that you will need to approach 300 potential donors to eventually get 100 donors, or 900 donors to eventually get 300 donors.

3. Can you get 1,000 sources to donate $300 or 3,000 sources to donate $100? This equals $300,000. Understand the club will need to approach 3,000 potential donors to eventually get 1000 donors, or 9,000 donors to eventually get 3,000 donors.

Figure 7.1 Using the rule of thirds can help an organization reach a $900,000 fund-raising goal.

goal for this third is met, the campaign is a third of the way there. Sometimes, too, wealthy donors are willing to fund the entire project.

The rule of thirds gives everyone with an interest in contributing a chance to donate. A person who can contribute only $100 plays a part in reaching the goal as much as the person who gives $1,000 or $10,000.

A capital campaign does not happen overnight, and it costs money. The club should plan to spend at least 10 percent of its desired goal on the campaign. Expenses include creating promotional materials, cultivating potential donors, and hiring professionals to conduct the feasibility study and assist in executing the campaign.

Grant Writing

Funds are available to a club through **grant writing**, a formal process of requesting funds from a grant-funding agency looking to support a cause or causes. Club managers must understand that grant writing is a competitive process. Other organizations are submitting grants against which the club's grant is competing. Entities that offer grants include corporate foundations, government agencies, and charitable foundations. A club also can respond to requests for grant proposals from organizations. Grant proposals can often be very long; a sample of a part of a grant proposal is shown in the sidebar on page 152.

grant writing—The formal process of requesting funds from a grant-funding agency looking to support a cause or causes.

Corporate Foundations

Corporate foundations are the charitable arms of corporations. In addition to seeking benefits from partnerships with sport clubs, as discussed earlier, corporations also establish foundations or endowments from the revenue generated by

> ## Sample Grant Proposal: Statement of Need
>
> Youth sport programs in recreational environments play an integral role in U.S. society. Sport reinforces lessons taught in classrooms and at home. In most cases children are introduced to sports through recreation sport leagues sponsored in local communities.
>
> Those who participate in sports in the United States benefit away from the field of competition. Research indicates that student-athletes have higher grade-point averages than nonathletes, are less likely to be absent from school or class, are less likely to drop out of school, and are less likely to behave inappropriately in class. Along with the physical benefits of sport participation and the development of sport skills, children who participate in youth sport programs develop skills needed for communicating and interacting with their peers and adults, self-confidence, self-discipline, a positive self-image, a sense of achievement, leadership skills and qualities, the ability to cooperate and compete within a group, and the ability to make decisions and accept responsibilities.
>
> The Blue Star Basketball Club calls for the development of youth recreation leagues through the introduction of the After-School Basketball Initiative (ASBI). The ASBI will emphasize that sport can bring out the best in both boys and girls and can inspire many to achieve their fullest potential as students, as athletes, but most important, as human beings. The ASBI also wants to make a meaningful and sustainable contribution to the growth of basketball in the region. In responding to the call for proposals from the Office of Community Development in the state's Bureau of Educational and Cultural Affairs, the Blue Star Basketball Club welcomes the opportunity to champion the importance of youth sport in proposing the After-School Basketball Initiative.
>
> The Blue Star Basketball Club has a long tradition of promoting social development through sport. The ASBI emphasizes fundamental skill development, teamwork, fair play, and positive interactions with adults with the goal of providing a fun and rewarding youth basketball experience in which young players can create a bond with the game while also learning what it takes to be successful away from the court.

their business. This money is invested and the interest from those investments is used to fund worthwhile activities. Corporate foundations have boards that review grant proposals and vote on which projects to fund. They specify the types of projects they will fund as well as the regulations for submitting proposals and the deadlines for submissions. A sport club can benefit from knowing who sits on these corporate boards and whether they have any ties to the sport or club.

Charitable Foundations

Charitable foundations serve the same purpose as corporate foundations, but their funding sources differ. Some are created by wealthy people who leave money in their wills to establish such foundations; others are established by 501(c) nonprofit organizations and are similar to corporate foundations. The US Soccer Foundation was created from revenue generated by the 1994 FIFA World Cup hosted in the

United States. Annually, the foundation funds projects that help grow the game of soccer in the United States.

Government Grants

Grants are offered by government agencies at the local, state, and federal levels. In most cases the requirements in writing are very detailed, and those receiving grants must keep detailed records of the execution of the grant. For a list of government agencies that offer funding, visit www.grants.gov/ and www.governmentgrants. com. Grant guidelines can often be found on the organization's Web site as well as through a grant search. Depending on the entity, grants are awarded quarterly, semiannually, or annually. It is up to the club to research funding sources and submit grants when required.

Requests for Proposals

Another way to secure a grant is to respond to a **request for proposals (RFP)**. In this case an entity announces a grant competition and welcomes organizations to submit proposals. The RFP clearly states the types of projects it will fund and what the intended outcomes should be. The RFP is a competitive process, and as with foundations, a review committee evaluates the proposals and determines which best meet the desired outcomes of the agency. Clear guidelines stipulate how to structure proposals as well as the deadlines for submission. Government funds are often granted through the RFP process.

request for proposals (RFP)—The announcement of a grant competition that welcomes organizations to submit proposals for funding.

The Grant Writing Process

Because the grant writing process is time consuming, the club would do well to give the responsibility to a full-time staff member or qualified volunteer or to subcontract the task out to someone experienced in writing grants. The sidebar on page 154 provides some suggestions for writing grants.

Most granting agencies are seeking information from applicants for funding. At the heart of a request for proposals are these questions that the granting agency wants answered:

- ▶ Who are you?
- ▶ Do you qualify for funding?
- ▶ Why do you want the funds?
- ▶ How much do you want, and how will you spend it?
- ▶ What do you want to accomplish?
- ▶ How will you determine whether you achieved your stated objectives?
- ▶ To what degree are your goals compatible with the funding agency's goals?
- ▶ Is your program sustainable?

Adhering to the following steps can help club leaders answer these questions.

Suggestions for Writing Grants

- *Research and plan.* Before writing a grant, the club needs to know what grants are available, what needs to be done to submit the grant, and when the grant needs to be submitted.
- *Write for the granting agency.* Most important in writing a grant is communicating that the club meets the requirements of the funding agency. It is not what the club wants but what the funding agency wants that is important. Also, grant writers must address all of the areas requested in the grant, make sure that all required documents are submitted, and pay attention to how the proposal is formatted. A great idea may never be reviewed if the guidelines are not followed.
- *Research the agency.* Clubs should take the time to learn what types of projects the granting agency has funded in the past and why so they know before writing and submitting a grant whether their ideas fit with those of the granting agency.

Conduct a Grant Search

The club needs to develop a database of all potential grants from government agencies, corporate and charitable foundations, and entities that have offered RFPs in the past.

Determine Which Grants the Club Is Eligible For

There are many granting agencies, and each clearly states the types of projects it funds. Sport clubs should identify granting agencies that list sport as a potential project. But a club can be creative by using sport to promote other initiatives, such as activities for disadvantaged or special needs population, AIDS awareness, childhood obesity, or the promotion of cultural understanding.

Contact the Agency

If contact information is provided or someone from the club knows someone from the granting agency, having a conversation about the types of projects the agency is interested in funding or what it has funded in the past can be helpful. If the idea the club has for a proposal is not of interest to the granting agency, writing and submitting a grant would be a waste of time. A conversation may also clarify for the club how to develop a proposal that piques the agency's interest.

Prepare and Submit the Grant

The key to preparing a grant is proving that the club has a significant need and can achieve the goals of the funding agency. The club must also communicate its ability to execute what it is proposing by demonstrating that it has the human resources and facilities to do what it says it is going to do in the proposal.

Some grant proposals are only one page long, whereas others are very detailed, describing the project in detail, outlining the budget, and explaining how the outcomes of the program will be evaluated. Included in the grant is usually a description of the idea and an explanation of how it fits with the goals of the granting agency. The grant proposal also includes a time line of the grant and, finally, a realistic budget.

Grant proposals sometimes include **overhead.** These are costs incurred in executing the grant such as electricity, computer use, and use of office space. Overhead is a percentage of the overall cost requested. A granting agency will usually communicate the amount of overhead allowed in a grant. For example, if a club figures it will cost $50,000 to execute an after-school soccer program for disadvantaged children and the granting agency allows 15 percent overhead, the club can add $7,500 to its request, for overhead. Sometimes the club can factor human resources into the grant. If an assistant club director earns $30,000 annually and she will devote 10 percent of her time to executing the grant, the grant proposal can request $3,000 to pay for that time.

Some granting agencies request matches from the entities applying for grants. Matches can come in the form of the human resources allocated to executing the grant, facility use, or product. For example, the club can communicate in the grant that if it is granted $50,000, it will match with the assistant director devoting 10 percent of her time to executing the grant (which is worth $3,000). In addition, the club will match with 30 hours of rental fees of $100 per hour for field use, for another $3,000, and provide 100 club T-shirts and balls valued at $3,000. The granting agency is awarding $50,000, but the club is willing to match that amount with $9,000, which is 18 percent of the request. The higher the match, the more attractive a grant becomes, because it shows a level of commitment on the part of the club; it is giving as well as receiving.

> **overhead**—Costs incurred by the club in executing the grant such as electricity, computer use, and use of office space. It is a percentage of the overall cost requested.

Execute the Grant

If a grant is awarded, the club must do what it said it would do with the funds. A detailed record of the use of funds must be kept during the execution process, and any changes in what was presented in the proposal must be communicated and approved by the granting agency. Misuse of granted funds is a criminal offense.

Once a grant is awarded, the club should designate a person as a project manager, who may or may not be the person who wrote the grant. This person may even be interested in forming a committee to help execute the grant. Responsibilities should be assigned, time tables set, times reserved, and documentation kept.

A key to successful grant execution is buy-in by the club on the project. The staff as well as members should be aware of the grant award as well as their roles in executing the grant. Also, during the execution phase, it is smart to update the granting agency on the progress of the project and even invite a key person to the facility to see how it is developing.

Report on the Benefits of the Grant

The granting agency will require a report on how the funds were spent. Again, the depth of this report will vary by funding organization. Most agencies ask for the summary of the activities, an account for how funds were spent, a measurement of the outcome or benefits of the program or project, and any media coverage that the project garnered. The key is to assure the funding agency that its money was well spent. If that is the case, the likelihood of a grant being awarded again is good not only with the current funding agency but with other funding agencies as well. The club is developing a track record of delivering on what it promises.

A club should not be discouraged if a proposal is not accepted by a funding agency the first time. Reviewers' comments are always available to help strengthen a proposal for resubmission. A club that makes the revisions and resubmits the proposal may be successful the next time around.

Summary

As stated at the beginning of the chapter, sport clubs may have great ideas and plans, but if they cannot fund them, they will remain on the drawing board. Club leaders must know about funds available through sponsorships and fund-raising and how to secure them.

First, club leaders most know the difference between fund-raising and sponsorships and understand that the strategies for generating revenues from these sources differ. When looking to secure sponsorships, the club must view its efforts as business transactions. It must understand its need to increase revenue or eliminate or reduce expenses, but it must also appreciate the needs of the potential corporate partner. Each potential partner has unique needs. One partner may be interested in building awareness of its product; another may want product trials. To meet the partner's needs, the club must know what it can include in a corporate partnership package.

The club needs to determine which method of fund-raising it is prepared to execute. These methods range from soliciting donations to holding special events. To raise a significant amount of money for a major project such as the renovation of the pool operating system, the club will have to apply the rule of thirds in developing a capital fund-raising campaign. The club also needs to be aware of the funds that are available via grant writing and understand the grant writing process, know the potential funding agencies, and execute the grant appropriately once it is received.

The club must make a commitment in the form of human resources to tap into these resources. It may need to hire a staff member whose sole responsibility, or one of her responsibilities, is partnership sales or fund-raising. In the end, it is worth the investment if the club is able to grow and prosper by maximizing these revenue streams.

To make the project a reality, the Santa Rosa Swim Club initiated a capital fund-raising campaign that tapped into local charitable and corporate foundations as well as past participants and their families. The club also secured a corporate sponsorship by selling the naming rights to the indoor pool to a national corporation looking to create a presence in that market, and eliminated a number of club expenses by establishing business-to-business relationships. Any revenues not being spent on operating expenses were directed to the renovations. In the end, the club had the funds to pay for the renovations before the project even started.

By the end of the chapter, the sport club manager will be able to do the following:

- ▶ Determine whether renting or owning a facility is best for the club.
- ▶ Describe the steps in planning, designing, and constructing a club facility.
- ▶ Explain the various financing models and sources of funding for a club facility.
- ▶ Recognize potential partners for financing a facility.
- ▶ Describe scheduling strategies for the facility.
- ▶ Appreciate the importance of risk management in the management of a facility.
- ▶ Develop a deferred maintenance plan for the facility.

8

Club Facilities

Matt Robinson and Christopher A. Sgarzi

The FC Adamsville is the fastest growing soccer club in the state. The municipality in which the club is located has seen a dramatic population increase over the past 10 years, and projections are that the growth will continue. There are plans for several more large housing developments to be constructed on the open land in the municipality.

Currently, FC Adamsville rents outdoor fields from the local school district and has been granted access to open space in a municipal park. For indoor soccer in the winter, the club again rents gym time from the local school district, but the schedule is irregular because of the high demand for the gym by the school's basketball program. The club rents office space in a local business park, where a staff of five shares two offices and a conference room. The club has to rent space at a local fire hall to hold board of directors meetings and for general club member meetings. Prior to renting that location, the club's business was conducted out of the executive director's home.

As the club has seen an increase in participants, club members have expressed dissatisfaction with the quality of the fields on which they train, as well as the lack of access to the fields. Members complain that there are no restrooms at the outdoor sites, and that they cannot buy concessions while watching games or practices. The club is interested in hosting tournaments but does not have the facilities to do so. In its travels to other tournaments, the leaders of FC Adamsville have seen other clubs' facilities and would like to have their own facility but don't know how to go about planning and paying for such a project.

The leaders of a sport club may have visions of their dream facility. They may envision several lighted fields; multiuse indoor facilities; ample office, meeting, and storage space; a modern concession area; and ample room for spectator viewing. Such dreams often do not become reality because the leaders of the club do not know how to start the process of making a dream a reality. Those who do get started on realizing their dreams sometimes end up in a nightmare because they do not manage, operate, or maintain the facility in a professional manner.

This chapter describes the processes associated with planning for, designing, financing, managing, maintaining, and operating a sport club facility. In terms of the marketing mix addressed in chapter 6, the facility is the *place*. The quality and location of a facility are extremely important in determining whether a club can meet the needs of its members. A club may provide a good product in terms of coaching and training, promote that product well on its Web site, advertise in the local media and through public relations efforts, and charge prices its customer are willing to pay, but if the club does not have a facility to accommodate practices or games, or if its facility is in an undesirable or inaccessible location, customers may go elsewhere.

A facility also plays an integral role in helping the club achieve its mission and goals, concepts addressed in chapter 1. If a club's mission is to train elite athletes as well as offer sport opportunities to participants of all skill levels, it will need a facility large enough to accommodate these purposes. In a nutshell, a facility contributes to the overall success of a sport club.

Rent or Own

The decision to rent or own a facility is often based on the financial status of the club. (Table 8.1 shows some pros and cons of both renting and owning a facility.) The ideal situation is to own a facility because of the many benefits that come with ownership. By owning the facility and the land it is built on, the club has an asset (see chapter 6) that will in most cases increase in value. In addition, ownership gives the club the autonomy to make decisions about expanding or improving the facility. These enhancements will further increase the value of the facility. Also, the club and its activities have priority in its own facility. Although the club may rent its facility out to generate revenue, the club's activities and its members should remain the priority.

Table 8.1 Pros and Cons of Renting and Owning

	Pros	Cons
Renting	• Has no debt service • Is not responsible for maintenance costs	• Is not the primary tenant • Pays rent to another party instead of investing in an asset
Owning	• Has an asset that will increase in value • Is the primary tenant and has control over scheduling • Can rent out as an additional revenue stream	• Takes on the debt services of the facility • Is responsible for maintenance and upkeep • Takes on the liability for accidents that may occur at the facility

Renting is an option for a club that is not interested in or does not have the revenue to take on the responsibility of owning a facility. Common sites clubs rent are local school facilities, municipal fields, and the facilities of other sport clubs. The renting model can be either pay as you go or a set fee. In the pay-as-you-go model, the club pays a rental fee for the use of fields or a facility. The owner or operator of the facility determines a rental fee, and the club pays that fee every time it uses the facility. A common pricing method is either by the game or by the hour. In the set-fee model, a one-time fee is paid based on the projected use over the course of a given time, such as a sport season. In either model the operator should have the fields or facility ready for use and is responsible for their upkeep and maintenance.

In terms of liability, the owner or operator of the facility is liable for any facility-related negligence, but the operator in most cases requires the club to have an insurance policy in excess of several million dollars and to name the facility owner on that policy. As a renter, a club has limited responsibility, but little control over the upkeep and scheduling of the facility. Another issue to consider is the fact that the rent the club is paying could be used toward paying for its own facility. Also, by renting the facility, the club may be second or an even lower priority to the facility operator and as such may get the least desirable times or the poorer quality fields or playing spaces. This could affect its ability to meet the needs of customers. Who wants to play or practice at odd hours, on a poor field, or in a rundown gym?

© Human Kinetics

Owning a facility can provide many assets, including opportunities to earn additional revenue through renting the facility. However, owning has its cons, too, so a club manager must carefully consider renting versus buying.

Finance Partners

The most daunting part of owning a facility is figuring out how to pay for constructing a new one or renovating an old one. Regan (1997) indicated that building a sport facility requires public, private, and joint public and private financing because of the high cost. Thus, the club needs to be proactive and creative in identifying new revenue streams and potential partners. Revenue sources include capital campaigns and naming rights (discussed in chapter 6) and loans, which are paid off with revenue generated by the club, as well as public partnerships.

Every situation is unique, so there is no cookie-cutter model of securing financing to build, buy, or renovate a sport club facility. A municipality may have land to offer but may not be willing to offer bonds, or a club may have access to capital through a large charitable donation but no land to build on. Every option should be considered, and a realistic financial plan should be developed that does not place too great of a burden on the club to repay, thus jeopardizing its viability.

Private Funding Sources

One of the main reasons for building a facility is to enhance the quality of the club members' experiences. Therefore, it makes sense for the club to pass some of the expense of the new facility on to its members. This can be done by directing an existing revenue stream or a part of one toward the cost of purchasing or building a facility. For example, a percentage of registration fees and annual events (such as tournaments and camps) are two ways a club can generate extra money to save in a capital project account for a future building project:

An additional $20 added to 1000 athletes' registration fee = $20,000

Annual events = $15,000

Total generated = $35,000

Interest earned will not build a facility, but it begins to build capital.

The club can also look to generate revenue from the sale of naming rights for the facility and aspects of the fields. It can sell naming rights to businesses for a given period of time stipulated in a contract. When that contract expires, the businesses can enter into a new deal, or the club can look to sign another sponsor. Another option is to name the facility or aspects of the facility for a business in exchange for a donation made during a capital campaign. Both of these strategies are discussed in greater detail in chapter 7.

Next, the club can borrow money from a financial institution. Just like with any loan, there will be a fixed rate and term. The club will make monthly payments on principal and interest. The payment of the loan becomes a major operating expense for the club and should be factored into how it prices the services it offers to members as well as external groups. Budgeting and accounting are discussed in more detail in chapter 6. Ideally, the club should secure as much funding as possible from private and public sources so that its debt service is not too burdensome or does not makes the club too expensive for members.

SUCCESSFUL STRATEGY

Maryland SoccerPlex

In October 2000, the Maryland SoccerPlex opened with 19 full-sized irrigated soccer fields. The dream of a high-quality multifield soccer facility in suburban Maryland began in 1988 when a group of local soccer clubs successfully advocated for the facility to be added to a park master plan. At that time there was no public or private funding for the project. However, with a local youth soccer community of 25,000 and more than 100,000 in the Washington metropolitan area, a soccer complex was destined to be built.

In 1998 a group of soccer parents led by Maureen and John Hendricks, the founders of Discovery Communications, established the Maryland Soccer Foundation (MSF), a nonprofit corporation whose mission was to build, manage, and maintain the 24-field soccer complex. A public–private partnership was formed with the Maryland-National Capital Park and Planning Commission (M-NCPPC), and a location for the complex was identified in a suburb of Washington, DC. Nine local soccer clubs provided time and resources to ensure the building of the complex. Along with the soccer complex, the Discovery Sports Center was also built. The facility is able to host indoor soccer, basketball, and volleyball leagues; camps; and tournaments.

Today, the Maryland SoccerPlex welcomes more than 600,000 visitors a year. The majority of visitors come from the local soccer clubs and leagues that play more than 4,500 matches at the complex annually. However, teams from all over the country come to participate in some of the most competitive youth soccer tournaments in the country. The complex is not used only for soccer; it also hosts leagues in flag football and lacrosse. The fields are organized in clusters of four or five fields with parking and a comfort station for each cluster. The parking was built at 75 spaces per field to ensure that teams coming for the next game would have ample parking.

A major attraction of the complex is the Championship Stadium. The stadium sits in a natural bowl with a paved, lighted plaza surrounding it. The field was constructed using a sand-based under-drainage system that drains an average of eight inches of water an hour. There is seating for 3,200 spectators. The Championship Stadium has hosted a U.S. Olympic qualifier, MLS Open Cup matches, a CONCACAF Champions League match, the ACC Men's Soccer Championships, USL and W League matches, training sessions for Argentina's Boca Juniors, and the New Zealand National team. In addition, the U.S. Youth Soccer National Championships were held at the Maryland SoccerPlex. In 2009 the Championship Stadium became home to Women's Professional Soccer and the Washington Freedom. In anticipation, the stadium will undergo a series of exciting improvements. The seating capacity will increase to 5,200 with corresponding restroom facilities, and a formal press box and box office will be added.

The Maryland SoccerPlex is a premier sport facility in the United States and a model for future facilities.

Public Funding Sources

The sport club can rely on the municipality in which it is located to assist in the financing of the facility. The municipality can benefit from the building of a modern facility. First, it improves the quality of life of residents, increasing the recreation opportunities for children and adults. Second, the facility can have a positive economic impact on the area. When businesses look to relocate or open branch offices or factories, they consider the quality of life of an area. If a sport club facility attracts a business to the area, the municipality benefits from the business itself and the taxes it and its employees pay.

Municipalities can issue bonds and use designated tax revenues to help clubs finance facilities. They may also have land the club can use. It is in the public interest to support sport clubs in this way because the public may reap benefits such as use of the facility, economic stimulation of the community, increased tax revenues, and a better quality of life for the residents.

Another way a sport club benefits a municipality is by offering events that attract outside visitors to the area. If the club hosts a three-day tournament for 50 teams, local businesses such as hotels, restaurants, grocery stores, gas stations, and malls all reap the benefits. Along with the initial injection of money into businesses, there is a ripple effect through the economy. The businesses buy the products they offer to customers, and their employees spend and save the money they make. Whether the club is a nonprofit entity or a for-profit LLC, the local municipality may benefit from the construction or renovation of a facility and thus can be called on to contribute.

A local municipality can contribute in a number of ways depending on the club's needs and the ways and means of the municipality, including land acquisition and access to capital. A municipality may own land that it can lease to the club at a very low rate for a long period of time. It is not uncommon for a county to lease a tract of land for $1.00 a year for 30 years. This type of arrangement eliminates a significant expense related to the construction of the facility; the club only has to focus on the cost of building a facility or making fields playable. Ideally, the land should be accessible to club members.

Municipalities have access to capital in three forms: grants, bonds, and taxes. Grants are discussed in chapter 7. In the case the club can apply for grant funds from a municipality, it may be at the local or state level that will assist the municipality in achieving its goals such as economic development, job creation, or land regeneration. The club and its facility can attract visitors to the area for weekend or weeklong tournaments, attract new businesses to the areas and thus create jobs, or take an undeveloped or dilapidated tract of land and make it usable for the benefit of the residents of the municipality. All three cases are win–win situations for the club and the municipality.

bond—A debt instrument used by an entity to generate funds, usually for the purpose of financing a long-term investment.

A **bond** is a long-term debt instrument that promises to pay the lender a series of interest payments in addition to returning the principal upon maturity (Moyer, McGuigan, & Kretlow, 2003). It is used to generate funds, usually for the purpose of financing a long-term investment, and is the most common way for a municipality to generate money for a sport facility (Miller, 1997). Unlike stockholders, who are the owners of the company, bondholders are lenders to the issuer. In compensation for this, issuers usually pay interest to bondholders on a periodic basis. A variety of bonds are available to a municipality, all of which are attractive to investors because their investment are guaranteed by the municipality and are tax exempt.

general obligation bond—A bond that is paid back by increasing tax revenues in the municipality.

General obligation bonds are backed by the full faith and credit of the issuing body and normally are paid back by increasing taxes in the municipality (Regan, 1997). These bonds must have voter approval, and the way to acquire that is to demonstrate that the municipality as a whole will benefit from the facility.

A **revenue bond** is paid for from a predetermined revenue stream usually tied to the new facility, such as a hotel-motel tax, property tax, or user tax (Regan, 1997). That revenue pays off the bond. **Tax increment bonds** are paid back by increasing property values and ultimately taxes in the area around the facility. If the facility is likely to attract new construction or housing developments to an area or increase the property values of existing properties, this is a viable option.

As stated earlier, the club must explore all public and private funding options and put together a plan that will not only lead to the building of the facility, but also ensure the longtime financial viability of the facility.

Planning the Facility

With any construction project the most important decisions are often made early in the process (figure 8.1). Careful planning by the club will reduce the surprises and allow for accurate budgeting and scheduling for the construction of the facility. The club should create a committee of board members and staff and designate one person, usually a full-time employee, as the project manager. (See the sidebar on page 166 for a list of who should be part of the design team and their roles.) This committee can begin to conceptualize the ideas for the facility, hire a design team, and develop a conceptual design for the facility. Considering all of the options early and making sound, well-informed decisions will result in fewer surprises as the project progresses. Experimenting with ideas and exploring alternatives is relatively inexpensive when conceptualizing a project, especially when compared to the high cost of construction errors or, worse, building the wrong facility that does not adequately meet the club's needs.

White and Karabetsos (2002) presented the following eight guidelines for the planning of a facility that could help the club in these early discussions and also drive the overall planning process:

- ▶ Comply with the requirements of the Americans With Disabilities Act (ADA).
- ▶ Operate off a master plan.
- ▶ Use a participatory planning approach.
- ▶ Research funding options.
- ▶ Organize a project planning committee.
- ▶ Understand when it is best to renovate, retrofit, or replace.
- ▶ Develop a problem statement for the architect.
- ▶ Use planning professionals in the design of the facility.

The Plan

To prepare for fund-raising and establish a budget, the committee may consider hiring a professional **design team** to create a better understanding of the vision and establish a realistic cost for completing the project. The first step for this team is to develop a formal, comprehensive building scheme that identifies all the club's facility needs and establishes priorities for the construction or renovation. This

revenue bond—A bond that is paid for from a revenue stream generated from the new facility.

tax increment bonds—A bond paid back by increasing property values and ultimately taxes in the area around the facility.

```
Need
  ↓
Concept
  ↓
Cost
  ↓
Funding
  ↓
Site
  ↓
Design
  ↓
Construction
  ↓
Manage and maintain
```

Figure 8.1 The process of building and maintaining a facility has many steps, and it's important to make sure all of them are covered.

design team—A group created to initiate the facility planning process.

Members of a Design Team

Member	Role
Architect	Leads design team and develops conceptual designs based on input from the team.
Mechanical engineer	Assists with plans for heating, ventilating, air-conditioning, plumbing, and fire protection.
Structural engineer	Prepares a report on the basic systems and written descriptions of alternatives for study and cost-estimating purposes.
Electrical engineer	Prepares a report on the basic systems and provides written descriptions of alternatives for study and cost-estimating purposes.
Geotechnical engineer	Contracts for borings or test pits to examine the soil's characteristics and determine whether traditional building systems will be sufficient or if there will be a higher fee because of the soil composition.
Environmental engineer	Determines whether there are any preexisting environmental conditions.
Civil engineer	Assists with evaluating the site for the building and, often with a landscape architect, determining where on the site a facility will be located along with fields, parking, roadway layouts, and other infrastructure components.
	Files local permits with planning boards, zoning boards, and environmental departments.
Real estate attorney	Assists with preparing contracts and legal agreements.
Builder	Based on input from the design team, prepares a cost estimate for the project.

master plan—The plan the club has for multiple buildings and fields and site improvements that may be developed over several phases.

facility plan—A plan for the building or renovation of a facility.

conceptual design—An artistic rendering of the vision of what a facility can be.

is known as the **master plan** (White & Karabetsos, 2002). Not all of the projects outlined in the master plan may be completed, but it provides foresight for future projects.

From the master plan the design team can develop a **facility plan** for the building or renovation of one facility. This step is most effective when it involves the development of a **conceptual design,** an artistic rendering that depicts the design vision including floor plans, building elevations, building sections, field locations, and parking areas. The conceptual design can be done either by hand with watercolors or markers, or by computer as a static or dynamic three-dimensional model with walk-through. It should also include a written description of the anticipated building systems (e.g., HVAC) and materials. The more information included in the conceptual design, the better understanding there will be for the project issues, including the budget.

It is important that the design team have experience with sport facilities from both a use and construction standpoint. A common misperception is that all facilities are the same. Because sport facilities are unique, a design team with experience is essential in designing a first-class facility.

The design team should challenge the committee with ideas and work creatively to develop a graphic representation of a vision that supports the committee's vision as well as the overall vision of the club. Sharing attractive renderings, models, or computer animations depicting future facilities with club members, potential investors, and funding sources can excite these important constituents and encourage them to participate in the dream of making the proposed facility a reality. Club leaders may have an idea for a building or field layout on a site, but no matter how much they explain it, nothing is as effective as a picture or model to ensure that others understand the vision. With the software available today, designers can show realistic views of the outside and inside of the facility and complex complete with moving people, advertising graphics, and landscaping.

Design Team Members

Usually an architect has the prime role on the design team and hires the other team members, or the club may hire them directly. Another option is to include on the team a club member with a particular area of expertise who is willing to donate her time. The team should include mechanical (encompassing heating, ventilating, air-conditioning, plumbing, and fire protection), electrical, and structural engineers, whose roles are to understand the basic systems and prepare written descriptions of alternatives for study and cost-estimating purposes. These consultants do not typically have large jobs or produce any drawings for the conceptual design, unless there is a particular concern or goal for these trades, such as a special structural expression or a particular mechanical system that is primary to the design idea.

A civil engineer familiar with the local utilities and municipality can also be a valuable member of the design team during the study phase. This person assists with evaluating the site for the building and, often with a landscape architect, determining where on the site to locate the facility as well as fields, parking areas, roadways, and other infrastructure components. Locating the building advantageously on the site can result in significant cost savings. The civil engineer often takes the lead in filing for local permits with planning boards, zoning boards, and environmental departments. Understanding this process can save a great deal of time and improve the chances for local approvals and community acceptance. If there are significant political issues or controversial zoning interpretations, a real estate attorney with local experience can help during the permitting process as well.

The soil conditions on the site, which dictate the necessary structural and drainage systems, can have a substantial effect on the cost of any construction project, but especially one with a large footprint, outdoor playing fields, large parking needs, and intense public use. Understanding soil characteristics and their impact on foundations and storm water systems requires the collection of data on the soil profile in various locations around the site. Geotechnical engineers on the design team contract for borings or test pits to examine the soil's characteristics and determine whether traditional building systems will be sufficient or if the construction will require costly alternatives because of the soil composition. If the soil will not support the building loads with traditional spread footings, deeper foundation systems such as piles or caissons may be required. Other issues that geotechnical engineers unveil include the height of the groundwater and the soil's ability to drain.

A site's history may suggest that the soils have previously been contaminated and might threaten the health of users or be structurally unstable. Environmental issues can take many paths depending on the pervasiveness and the makeup of the problem, and regulatory agencies and additional consultants may need to be involved. These processes can take a great deal of time and red tape and be very costly to mitigate. If a club is buying or leasing a piece of land, it should know the history of the site. It is critical during the purchasing and negotiation phase to know of any preexisting conditions because in most cases the previous owner is responsible for making the land environmentally safe.

In addition to the designers and engineers, the club's design team needs a professional to estimate construction costs. If the club has a builder in mind for the project, the builder, or a construction manager, takes the work of the design team and uses subcontractors and his own expertise to determine the projected costs of the project. At the appropriate time in the process and after the design has progressed, the builder may be asked to develop a guaranteed maximum price (GMP) to complete the project. The GMP consists of basic costs of labor, materials, overhead, and profit (Sawyer, 2002). This project delivery method is commonly known as construction manager at risk.

design-bid-build or design/build—A method in which the club bids the entire scope of work once it is designed to a preselected group of general contractors. The design and construction entities work together under a single contract with the club to provide one price and then work together to complete the project.

Another method that the club may elect to pursue involves bidding the entire scope of work once it is designed to a preselected group of general contractors (**design-bid-build** or **design/build**). The design and construction entities work together under a single contract with the club to provide one price and then work together to complete the project. Each method discussed previously has its benefits, and the club should choose based on existing relationships, design issues, construction issues, and of course schedule and cost. Some contractors provide the cost-estimating services at no cost during the conceptual design phase, but it is generally a better idea to pay for these services to avoid implied obligations to the builder prior to fully establishing the project scope and delivery methods.

soft costs—Costs in addition to land acquisition and construction that include costs for design, cost estimating, permitting, furniture, equipment, printing, financing, and project management.

Cost estimations should always have a contingency allowance to cover unpredictable or unforeseen items or changes required by the owner (Sawyer, 2002). In addition to the cost of the land and construction, the club should have a budget that includes all of the **soft costs.** These are costs not directly related to the actual construction but necessary for completing the project. They include costs for design, cost estimating, permitting, furniture, equipment, printing, financing, and project management. Soft costs vary depending on the needs of the project or site, but generally they amount to an additional 20 to 30 percent of the construction costs for a new facility.

Conceptual Design

Once the design team is in place, it can initiate the creation of the conceptual design. The first step in developing a conceptual design is to establish the goals for the project. What are the priorities for the building program components (spaces in the building) and the design characteristics? This information can come from club documents such as the mission statement and strategic plan and also from the staff and members or even surveys or focus groups. Is the club a single-sport club that just wants to offer training and competition opportunities, or is it a multisport club that has both indoor and outdoor needs as well as plans to offer strength and conditioning and social activities for its members? Club leaders need to ask, "Do we have a project budget, or do we need to determine a budget that will fulfill our vision?" (For example, "Do we have $10 million to complete this project? Or, do we design a project and determine it will cost $10 million?") Usually it is a combination of both questions that requires a process of testing and cost estimating during the planning phase.

Activity Space Considerations

The starting point for the design process is determining the primary activities that will take place in the space. In an indoor facility, each activity will have particular requirements in terms of room size and shape, ceiling height, surfaces, mechanical systems, and lighting. The club needs to consider which activities can be accommodated in similar spaces. For example, an indoor space could accommodate basketball and volleyball, whereas an outdoor space could accommodate both soccer and lacrosse. Multipurpose spaces can maximize use; however, there may be sacrifices in performance as a result of accommodating more activities. For example, basketball players and coaches prefer a high-performance wood flooring system specifically designed for athletic activity. This may also work well for volleyball, but it does not work well for indoor tennis. If indoor tennis must occur in that same space, the club may select a synthetic surface that can work for all of those activities, but the surface will be less attractive to the basketball market.

If basketball is the club's main focus, it might choose a high-quality wood floor system to draw in customers and additional revenue. Although outdoor sport purists may prefer natural grass, a synthetic outdoor surface can meet the needs of all outdoor sports and can be used without the concern of burning out a field. Although the installation cost is greater, a synthetic surface offers a greater saving over the long term than a natural grass field. Over the lifetime of the field, there is a payback from reduced maintenance costs (e.g., mowing, seeding, aerating, chemical treatment, lining).

Spectator Space Considerations

In addition to the activity spaces, the club needs to consider what to offer spectators or participants' families. Parents making the decision to register for a club's programs will likely respond positively to a comfortable spectator space. In addition to comfortable seating and good sightlines to the play areas, parents and spectators appreciate game rooms, wireless Internet access, and a food concession area. Some even view these amenities as necessities. Offering these amenities can also generate revenue for a club. A well-considered menu, for example, can provide the club with supplemental income. The food operation can be outsourced, but if an experienced manager can run it well, the club can realize a higher profit.

Another question the club has to ask in the design phase is whether it plans to host large events with many participants and spectators either outdoors or indoors. Will the building be used for special events such as concerts, speakers, or trade shows? If the answer is yes to any of these questions, building access, exiting, and restrooms must be addressed during the conceptual design. Restrooms are expensive to construct, and exiting may involve stairs. Both must meet the building code requirements for the number of people the site will support, and they must be appropriately located.

Spectator Management Considerations

Spectator management includes considerations for where spectators will sit or stand and how they will be kept away from the playing surface and players' bench areas. Locating spectators too close to a playing area can lead to liability concerns if play goes out of bounds and a spectator is injured. Also, although parents are usually well intended, most coaches prefer to have a degree of separation from parents, who like to yell instructions, as well as from younger siblings, to prevent them from running around the team's space. Some playing surfaces, such as new wood floors, will last longer and perform better if access onto them is controlled and shoes are cleaned before walking on them. For indoor facilities, mezzanines and overlook balconies can be a nice asset for providing good views and separating spectators from the activity area.

Structural Considerations

One of the primary considerations when planning indoor facilities is how large to make them and what to include. Outdoor fields have the benefit of open space; games to be played indoors, however, are limited by the clearances inside the building. In colder climates, indoor soccer has grown in popularity. Many indoor fields are enclosed by dasher board systems, similar to ice hockey, and many use multipurpose flooring surface. These systems offer the benefit of containing the balls on the playing field and can be used by a variety of sports and recreational activities. Today, many soccer clubs are designing and building indoor soccer facilities that are more similar to outdoor facilities. Clubs are finding that traditionalists prefer fields that are not surrounded by dasher boards, so players develop the appropriate ball control skills, including sideline control, throw-ins, and corner kicks.

Some clubs are building full-size facilities to accommodate 11v11 games. In this type of facility at least 40 feet of ceiling clearance is required. The large fields have the benefit of performing like outdoor fields and can be subdivided into cross fields for 6v6 or 8v8 competitions. Suspended netting systems are a common solution for controlling flying balls and protecting the building and spectators.

Some clubs are using the latest infill turf systems on their indoor fields, which consist of a green nylon fiber carpet that is infilled with small rubber (and sometimes sand) pellets to give it added cushion and playability. These are the same systems that are used outside on many professional football and baseball fields. This limits the use of the facility to sports that compete on grass. If a club wants the space to be multipurpose, these surfaces can be rolled up and stored revealing a rubberized surface underneath. In this way, a space used for indoor soccer could also be used for street hockey, basketball, or volleyball. Depending on the size of the space, the labor and storage space required for the rolled-up surface can be significant. The club would have to consider the cost benefit. Multipurpose playing surfaces increase offerings for club members as well as options for generating revenue from rentals from outside groups.

Clubs must also consider safety margins around the playing areas. Because athletes fall and balls fly, safety must always be considered when determining the field size in relation to the indoor space. Space is the best remedy for safety concerns, because it gives players time to react and reduces their momentum. Padding may also be needed if there are projections such as large steel columns near the playing areas.

Indoor Facility Design Considerations

A large indoor field or even a smaller one obviously requires a structural system that allows long spans without columns in the playing areas. The most cost-effective building type for long spans is a pre-engineered system of bent-frame steel beams or light-gauge truss systems that include flat ceilings.

The bent-frame system is the most popular and is a common structural system for large warehouses and hangar-type buildings. This system includes a metal panel exterior skin and insulation that is either included in a sandwich of metal panels or enclosed more loosely in vinyl cloth. In addition to being cost effective, the bent-frame system has the benefit of creating a large space that is open to its peak.

Truss systems also are integral with their metal panel skin and barrel-type roof. Although they do not have the interior volume that the bent-frame systems do, their flat ceiling can help keep in heat and can be more energy efficient, especially for skating rink construction.

Both systems can accommodate many openings for daylight, although the truss system does not allow skylights. Daylight, if properly controlled with durable translucent panels in the roof and walls, can add a nice quality of light to the space, even enough to decrease the need for artificial lights. This can lead to significant energy savings during the day.

Preengineered structures are most cost-effective when the design uses their standards. This means that the preengineered portion of the building should be located on a flat site, and wherever possible, its metal siding should be incorporated. Masonry may be desired around the lower parts of the building to help protect inside and outside faces from damage. Preengineered structures can save on building costs, which means more money is available for custom designs around the entry and spectator areas, giving the building a less plain appeearance. These custom portions can help mask the massiveness of the simple box structures and add character to the building design.

Other Design Considerations

In addition to the specific requirements of the programs offered, facility designers must give some thought to qualitative considerations as well. What level of quality is desired for the building? How important is durability, longevity, appearance? Is the club willing to spend more up front for amenities that will offer long-term benefits? And if so, what is long term—does the payback need to be within 5 years, 10 years? These questions may relate to how long the club intends to own the facility, but they also address the issue of the resale value of the facility. Payback analysis is often done for mechanical systems such as heating, ventilating, and air-conditioning units as well as light fixtures, but they are also relevant for building materials. The design team needs to consider how often a surface requires cleaning and how long a surface can be used before it must be replaced. These considerations will help the design team determine the initial capital costs for construction.

In addition to the potential long-term cost benefits of using better systems and materials, there is often an environmental benefit. Better equipment may use less energy, and if does not need to be replaced as soon, the energy that goes into manufacturing the equipment and transporting it is reduced, not to mention the savings in landfill waste. Builders and owners are becoming more aware of the impact of these decisions as they consider construction alternatives. The club's position on environmental issues will assist the design team in establishing a budget for construction.

The mechanical consultant needs to understand how the facility will be used operationally and the level of quality and sophistication that the club desires in the heating, ventilating, and air-conditioning systems. Whether to install an air-conditioning system is an important decision that is best planned early because it will have an impact on the cost and the space needed for equipment. The design team may decide to air-condition smaller spaces (e.g., offices, fitness centers, conference rooms) and not larger spaces, or to use a lower level of cooling for larger spaces to provide dehumidification to decrease the impact of the heat during high-humidity days. Another option is to design the system so air-conditioning can be added later—by using a system that can easily be adapted and allowing proper duct sizing and space for the future units.

The decision about air-conditioning will have an impact on operating costs as well as construction costs. The mechanical and electrical engineers will determine the building's demands for fuel and electricity so the club can discuss these with the local utilities and negotiate how these services can be delivered to the site. This cost can be significant if these services are not currently nearby. Sometimes a utility will waive or reduce these charges if there will be enough use from the new facility or if there are other potential customers in the same area.

Life Safety and Emergency Considerations

Once the design team has established a concept for the life safety systems (e.g., sprinklers, fire exits, width of stairwells, and so on) and a design approach to the various code requirements, it is usually helpful to bring the building and site layout to the local fire and building officials to discuss the proposed approach with them and develop an agreement on these strategies. Buildings that are large or that accommodate large numbers of people require fire protection systems (sprinklers). During the study phase the projected height of the building and a study of the nearby water pressure will determine whether a fire pump will be required in the building to support the system. Fire department personnel will review how they will approach the building, where they will enter it, and how they would fight a fire if such a catastrophe occurred. Working with these officials is critical to a successful project and construction process, because ultimately, local authorities have jurisdiction and the last say on the requirements for life safety measures.

Ideal Design

The success of the facility will depend on creative programming and high usage. That means that the design must meet the club's needs. Spaces that can be used for multiple purposes will allow the club to adapt to changing needs and new ideas. In addition to the occasional special events mentioned earlier, there may be clients who are looking for regular use during times that are not popular for sports leagues. Corporate clients may be interested in team building, stay-at-home parents may be looking for activities during the day, local high schools or colleges may need sport practice space, and families may need a place for birthday parties. If the facility offers a variety of possibilities and enough storage space and access to support unforeseen demands, the club will have a better chance of not just surviving, but prospering.

Site Selection

The site on which the facility will be built is as important as the design. Businesses that involve on-site customer participation benefit from a convenient and visible location (Mullin, Hardy, & Sutton, 2007). Sites that offer both visibility and easy access from primary traffic routes and for pedestrians will be the most expensive sites to purchase in a region, but the club should weigh the benefits against the extra cost.

Depending on the club's offerings, its location can be an advantage from a marketing standpoint. If the marketing plan includes nonorganized activities such as parties, preschool or infant programs, professional team building, or special spectator events, a visible location may be an important part of selecting a site. Passersby become familiar with the facility by seeing it, and if signage includes event and function postings, they may consider them when planning.

Club facilities that are primarily used by leagues and organizations typically do not rely on an overly obvious location because they are scheduled destinations that are familiar to participants; others are directed to the facility for specific events. The ability to find a building by travel teams or tournaments based on easy directions or high visibility is only a benefit to those traveling to the event and doesn't become a point of frustration for those who are organizing the leagues or events. The easier you can make it for the visitor, the more likely they will make their event a regular occurrence at the facility.

Site Selection Considerations

Aside from the importance of locating a club based on marketing and exposure to passersby, and the typical due diligence and existing conditions documentation needed when purchasing any significant real estate such as title reviews, surveys, property use history, soils conditions, and wetlands, a series of considerations can be particularly relevant to locating a sport club. With an increasing awareness of energy consumption, a location near public transportation can be a benefit for easy access and for participants who are too young to drive or do not have access to a vehicle. Also, planners should consider bicycle access paths and parking, because many participants may be inclined to use them to travel to and from the facility as part of their sporting activity.

Access to public transportation and accommodations for bicycles will help reduce the amount of traffic and the number of cars parked on the site, but parking should still be given a great deal of consideration. Chances are good that the local zoning requirements may not have a specific model for determining the appropriate number of parking spaces for this building type. Therefore, the club may need to develop realistic estimates for parking demand that will be acceptable to those approving the local permits and, more important, that will work well for customers. Although it may feel like a hardship during planning and construction to provide a generous amount of parking, not having adequate parking will result in inconvenienced, hurried, and frustrated customers.

The parking quantity and configuration should take into account the fact that teams often arrive before the previous games are completed. As a result, the demand for parking may exceed the amount predicted based on the level of activity the building supports. The configuration, including the exiting, should also address the fact that many events or games may end at the same time, resulting in a queue of patrons leaving the parking lot at one time. If the facility hosts large spectator events, this issue is even more critical. The design team should consider a traffic light at the exit or double exit lanes so cars that are turning right don't get stuck behind those that are waiting longer to turn left across the traffic.

The town or city approval process often requires a traffic report (produced by a traffic consultant hired by the club) to study the impact of the project on the local roadways and nearby intersections. The municipality may even require the landowner to contribute design funds or construction contributions to improve the conditions created by the additional traffic. Such requirements can seem like an unfair burden when trying to pay for the building and site, but in the end it would be a detriment to the success of the building to have a negative impact on the community. Additional information about a site, such as stormwater runoff, wetlands encroachment, historical value, earthwork (e.g., leveling a surface), and zoning that is typically required during the permitting process should be evaluated by the design team with calculations provided by the civil engineer.

The construction costs of the facility will also be influenced by the availability and capacity of nearby utilities. Gas, electricity, and sewer are the primary utilities that will either be available in a nearby street or require special provisions to bring them to the site. The club may want to consider alternative energy sources such as solar, wind, and geothermal. These may have an initial premium cost, but the payback and the environmental benefits may be appealing. The club can enhance its reputation in the local community by using renewable energy sources.

Site Conditions and Layout Considerations

Ideally, the site will have a significant flat area for cost-effectively locating the long span portions of a building (indoor field or gymnasium or synthetic turf field). Access to the front door from the parking area should be convenient—especially in colder climates—because players often arrive wearing shorts and prepared to play indoor sports. If future expansion is a possibility—even remotely—the building should be located and the utilities routed with that in mind. Buying a slightly longer route for a sewer line is much more cost effective when the initial earthwork and piping is done than digging it up later and relocating the line when enlarging the existing facility.

Another consideration in the positioning of a facility is solar orientation. Where will shading be helpful, and where is it problematic? A north-facing entranceway to an indoor facility is often darkened by shade and is not only less welcoming but also has less chance for snow and ice melt in the winter. Also, the solar orientation of indoor facilities will influence window locations. The design should provide open views and desirable day lighting without causing unwanted glare, heat gain, or unsafe direct light in players' or spectators' eyes.

For outdoor facilities, shading can provide a cool seating area that is welcoming to spectators in the heat of the summer. Outdoor fields should be oriented north-south so participants never have to look directly into sunlight. The club should also separate spectator sides and player sides. If fields are side by side, the interior areas (between the fields) could be designated as team space and the exterior edges as spectator space. Outdoor fields may need toilets to accommodate players and spectators, depending on local requirements. Outdoor fields also need handicap accessibility, including pathways to spectator and player areas. Clubs may want to plan for large netting systems to contain balls, especially behind nets, and low fencing around the perimeter to keep people off the playing area.

Site selection involves not only good visibility and access, but also an advantageous layout for the building, parking areas, and other associated outdoor areas such as fields. Designers should take advantage of the natural surroundings such as scenic views, but most important, they should make sure that the layout works well for the building operations and the convenience of club members and visitors.

Facility Management

When a club takes on the ownership of a facility, it takes on a whole new set of responsibilities beyond the sport itself. The management of the facility includes scheduling, maintenance, risk management, operating expenses, and deferred maintenance. In most cases the management of the facility will require either a full-time staff position or a position in which the management of the facility is the majority of that person's responsibility. (See chapter 3 for a discussion of job designs.)

Scheduling the Facility

Once a facility is built, it will be used. How it will be used, by whom, and when are some of the decisions facing club leaders. As discussed in the design part of the chapter, the needs and priorities of a club should determine how the facility is designed. These needs and priorities may change over the course of the year especially in the case of a multipurpose facility or all-weather fields. In the case of a multisport club, the sport that is in season should have first priority in the use of the facility for practice and competition. If other sport teams want to use the facility, they should be scheduled when it is not being used by the in-season sport teams. (See the sidebar below for a sample scheduling matrix.)

A common mistake clubs make is overusing outdoor natural grass fields until they become worn, unplayable, and even unsafe. At this point they are undesirable to members, visitors to club-hosted tournaments, and potential renters. Ideally,

Scheduling Matrix for a Soccer and Lacrosse Club

Program	July	Aug	Sept	Oct	Nov	Dec	Jan	Feb	March	April	May	June
Fall soccer recreation league		X	X	X	X							
Fall soccer competitive teams		X	X	X	X							
Fall soccer adult league		X	X	X	X							
Out of season soccer conditioning program					X	X	X	X				
Outside rentals	X	X	X	X	X	X	X	X	X	X	X	X
Lacrosse pickup games	X	X	X	X						X	X	X
Summer soccer camps	X	X										X
Summer lacrosse camps	X	X										
Spring soccer recreation league									X	X	X	
Spring lacrosse recreation league									X	X	X	X
Spring lacrosse competitive league							X	X	X	X	X	X
Spring soccer competitive league								X	X	X	X	X
Soccer tournaments			X		X						X	
Lacrosse tournaments			X							X		X
State championship					X							X

X represents programs that need access to fields during that time.

a club should develop a field rotation schedule so that a few to several fields are dormant at any given time so they can be seeded, aerated, and watered. Members may wonder why a field is not in use, but the long-term benefits to the life and quality of a field make the sacrifice worth it.

A club looking to generate revenue to grow or pay off debt may want to rent its facility to outside groups. A local high school that needs field space for girls' and boys' varsity, junior varsity, and freshmen soccer teams; a girls' field hockey team; an American football team; and an out-of-season lacrosse team may be willing to pay $250 hourly for the use of the fields. In this case the club has the potential to generate over $2,000 per week in rental fees. The club may also bid on events such as regional or national championships for particular sports to generate income through sales of concessions and rental fees while also bringing greater recognition to the club. Club leaders would have to keep in mind, of course, that these uses come at the expense of club members, who would not be able to use the facility during those events.

A facility schedule is based on time and use. The standard approach to scheduling is to develop one-hour blocks for the overall facility as well as subunits of the facility. (See the sample facility schedule in the sidebar on pages 178-179.) For example, a 12-field soccer complex will have a schedule for the overall facility as well as for each of the fields. A three-day weekend tournament may reserve all of the fields for 10 hours each day. For the club's own teams, fields can be assigned in two 1-hour blocks for three days of the week.

Risk Management

Ensuring the well-being of those who will use the facility should be a club's major priority. This is accomplished by developing a comprehensive risk management plan that addresses the facility itself as well the activities held in the facility. Risk management entails identifying and eliminating the activities, aspects of the facility, or actions of others that may cause harm. Risk management means being proactive as opposed to reactive to these potential problems and addresses issues related to the access to, maintenance and upkeep of, and use of the facility.

Access to the Facility

As stated in chapter 5, the sport club is liable for the actions of anyone who enters the facility. If harm is done to a club member because of the actions of a trespasser (e.g., assault and battery), the club can be found liable. For this reason, the club must ensure that only people associated with the club or an activity sponsored by the club are on the premises. Indoor facilities should have a single access point and a membership card swipe system to ensure that only club members enter. Visitors for events can be required to sign in before entering. Outdoor facilities are harder to monitor, but a single point of entry can be established for all fields. A common outdoor facility design is providing access through a clubhouse area from the main parking area. Limiting the access to the facility will ensure that members are safe from trespassers, criminals, and general troublemakers.

Sample Facility Schedule

Date _____

Time	Field 1	Field 2	Field 3	Field 4	Field 5	Field 6	Field 7	Indoor field 1	Indoor field 2	Club room	Fitness facility
10 a.m.											
11 a.m.											
12 p.m.											
1 p.m.											
2 p.m											
3 p.m.											
4 p.m.											
5 p.m.											
6 p.m.											
7 p.m.											
8 p.m.											
9 p.m.											

Schedule Key

Fall soccer recreation league	1
Fall soccer competitive teams	2
Fall soccer adult league	3
Out-of-season conditioning	4
Outside rental	5
Lacrosse pickup	6
Summer soccer camps	7
Summer lacrosse camps	8
Spring recreation soccer league	9
Spring recreation lacrosse league	10
Spring competitive lacrosse league	11
Soccer tournaments	12
Lacrosse tournaments	13
Other	14

From M.J. Robinson, 2010, *Sport Club Management* (Champaign, IL: Human Kinetics).

Facility Inspection

A club facility should be inspected on a daily basis to ensure that nothing is in disrepair, has been modified, or is unsafe. The inspection should include all areas of the facility as well as the equipment that may be used by participants and should focus on function, cleanliness, and safety. The inspection can lead to the detection of a leaky roof, a broken piece of training equipment, or broken glass or a sinkhole on an outdoor field. A facility inspection sheet can ensure that all areas of the facility are checked. If staff members find problems, they should notify the club manager that repairs are needed or a risk needs to be reduced—for example, by closing off the area or putting a sign on equipment stating that it is out of service.

Emergency Procedures

The sport club also needs to develop procedures to follow in the event of an emergency. The law requires that the club have an emergency evacuation plan in place and on file that has been approved by local authorities. Staff members should be familiar with the plan so that if an emergency does occur, they can lead the evacuation of participants or direct them to appropriate shelter. The most common emergency is fire, but other types of emergencies may arise. The emergency plan should consider weather-related emergencies such as tornados, as well as environmental concern such as chemical spills and gunfire.

The emergency plan is unique to the facility. For example, a club's facility may be located next to a major interstate highway. If a chemical truck overturns and toxic fumes are released, the club should have a plan for evacuating participants from the area. A club in a secluded area may not have this concern but may have others related to its seclusion. Also, if severe weather comes during club activities, the club should have a plan to direct participants to appropriate shelter. The International Association of Assembly Managers (IAAM) has established protocols that can serve as the basis for a sport club emergency management plan. Visit www.IAAM.org to acquire the standards and to learn about the organization's resources.

Maintenance and Upkeep

maintenance plan—A detailed plan that ensures that the facility remains clean and safe for the participants as well as viable over the long term.

Every sport club should have a detailed **maintenance plan** to ensure that the facility remains functional, clean, and safe for participants, as well as viable over the long term. (See the sidebar on page 181 for a sample maintenance checklist.) Without a maintenance plan, a facility becomes rundown and aspects of it may no longer be functional or safe, at which point fixing the facility could cost more than building or buying a new one.

The maintenance plan addresses the maintenance of the facility on a short-term basis (daily, weekly, and monthly) as well as over the longer term (annually, every 3 years, every 5 years, every 10 years). The plan should also designate who is responsible for the actual maintenance. It may be a staff member's responsibility, or it may be contracted out to a professional service. For example, a staff member may be responsible for mopping the concession area and restrooms at closing each night. A staff member at a swim club may be responsible for checking the pool chemicals daily. The club may hire a landscaping company to mow its field weekly in season and to chemically treat the fields quarterly.

Because most staffs lack such expertise, many sport clubs enter into contractual agreements with HVAC companies to provide annual service to equipment and to be on call if the equipment breaks down. Every five years, the club may close for a week during an off-peak time and paint all of the offices, locker rooms, restrooms, and hallways. Finally, the club may seek bids from local roofing companies to replace the roof of the facility 10 years after it was last replaced.

A facility's appearance and ability to function make a statement about the club. A facility with holes in the roof, chipped paint, uncut fields, and filthy restrooms is viewed negatively, and so is the club. Club members and visitors deserve better.

Equipment Management

equipment management—The effective inventorying, storing, repairing, replacing, and maintaining of the club's equipment.

To operate effectively and offer its services, a club must have equipment. **Equipment management** can fall under the responsibility of the person who oversees the facility. Olson (1997) classified equipment as either capital or expendable. Capital equipment includes items such as scoreboards, goals, bleachers, and backboards. Expendable equipment includes uniforms, balls, and bats. Keeping an inventory of the capital and expendable equipment as well as storing and maintaining it properly can save the club significant revenue.

Equipment can also be related to the operations of the facility. Lawn mowers and floor cleaning machines should also be stored properly and maintained so that the club gets the full life out of them. In fact, it is wise to enter into a maintenance contract on such items to ensure their longevity.

An important area that is often neglected in the design of a facility is an equipment storage space. Many clubs use a closet here or there or the hallways of the

Sample Precontest Maintenance Checklist for Soccer and Lacrosse Artificial Surface Stadium Field

Item	Functionality	Safety	Cleanliness	Maintenance needed	Comments
ADA access	Y	Y	NA		
Field conditions	Y	Y	NA		
Bleachers	Y	N	Y		Loose railing in Section D, Rows 10-14
Goals and nets	Y	Y	Y		
Scoreboard	Y	Y	NA		
Concession stand	N	Y	N		Clogged drain, eating area needs mopping
Lights	Y	Y	NA		
Team benches	Y	Y	Y		
Field markings	N	Y	NA		Lines have faded, need touchup
Electrical systems	Y	Y	NA		
Restrooms	N	Y	N		Sink in men's room not working, both not cleaned after last contest
Parking lot	N	N	Y		Pothole on left side of lot needs to be filled in and covered.
Team locker rooms	Y	Y	N		Locker room not mopped after last contest.
Ticket booth	Y	Y	Y		

Y = Yes

N = No

NA = Not applicable

club for storage, which can lead to the neglect of equipment and equipment disappearing. In colder climates, a soccer club should disassemble its portable goals and store them inside for the winter. This will ensure a longer life for the goals. Most clubs don't, however, because they don't have the space. In the design process, the club should include ample space for equipment storage and distribution. It should even designate a room as an equipment room. A space like this will help the club distribute, store, and inventory the equipment and reduce wear and tear and theft. For outdoor equipment, the club can build a large, secure shed. If the building is strictly for storage, it may require only limited electric and no HVAC.

Deferred Maintenance

If the club owns its facility, it is a fixed asset. As such, the club should protect it by developing a deferred maintenance plan. **Deferred maintenance planning** entails projecting future major projects and setting aside the necessary funds to pay for them. To do so, the club leaders must determine a replacement cost for the facility if imploded into the ground. Based on that cost, the club sets aside a percentage of that replacement cost in a deferred maintenance fund.

Let's say, for example, that a club's facility replacement cost is $5 million. One percent of that replacement cost would be $50,000. The club sets this amount aside annually to be directed to capital improvements to the facility or saved for major projects. By adhering to this strategy, the club can fix and replace the infrastructure of the facility such as mechanical, electrical, and HVAC systems. It can also begin to address an expansion or enhancements to the facility such as adding new fields, improving locker rooms, or expanding the concession or social area.

Summary

A facility is essential to the overall operations of a club. Planning, funding, designing, building, and managing a facility may seem like daunting tasks, but taking the appropriate steps in the earliest stages will enable the club to meet the needs of its members as well as visitors for many years to come.

One of the most important decisions for a club is whether to rent or own its facility. The club needs to be sure it can cover the expenses associated with owning and operating a facility before it takes that step. A wrong decision could threaten the financial viability of the club.

If club leaders decide to build a facility, the club needs to conduct a **feasibility study** to determine the cost of construction. With this done, the club needs to consider all financial sources and consider entering into public and private partnerships. The club has the ability to generate revenues and has the professional experience to run the facility, and the public can provide the land or favorable financial resources such as tax-free bonds, or both. At the end of this study phase, the club should develop a design plan that includes an artistic rendering of the facility, the costs, and how it will pay for it.

A design team should be created consisting of stakeholders in the club (e.g., board members, the executive director), each of whom brings a unique perspective to the building of the facility, as well as professionals who have experience in the design and operations of such a facility (e.g., architects, civil engineers). This team develops a conceptual design that meets the goals and needs of the club and also addresses structural considerations associated with the building of a sport facility.

Whether a club owns or rents a facility, it must develop sound facility management policies and procedures related to scheduling, inspections, risk management, equipment management, and maintenance. The club should also appreciate the importance of developing a deferred maintenance plan to ensure that it has funds to modernize and address facility wear and tear.

In the end a club's facility has a great deal to do with the overall success of the sport club. Decisions made in relation to the facility—in terms of ownership, design, and management—will be some of the most important that club leaders will make.

---

deferred maintenance planning—Projecting future major projects and setting aside the necessary funds to pay for them.

feasibility study—A study to determine if building or renovating of a facility is a viable option.

After a vote by the board, FC Adamsville decided to embark on a plan to build, own, and operate its own facility. Through good relationships with the local government, the club was able to secure 80 acres of land that the city was looking to develop. The club secured a 30-year lease for $10 a year. The club organized a committee to plan the facility and then hired a firm to develop a schematic plan for the layouts of the fields and the indoor facility and offices. Ultimately, the complex would include 14 outdoor fields and an indoor playing complex. The club raised funds and also took on debt to pay for the facility. FC Adamsville now has a facility that other clubs in the region, and even the country, envy.

Brand X Pictures

By the end of the chapter, the sport club manager will be able to do the following:

▶ Describe the benefits of implementing a long-term athlete development (LTAD) program.

▶ Provide an optimal competition structure for the various stages of an athlete's development.

▶ Provide optimal training, competition, and recovery programs throughout an athlete's career.

▶ Recognize the gaps and shortcomings of current player development systems.

▶ Appreciate the importance of developing physical literacy in youth athletes.

▶ Recognize maturation differences among athletes.

▶ Describe the LTAD stages of development, and determine what coaches should be doing with players in each stage.

▶ Incorporate LTAD into the player development strategy of the club.

▶ Integrate elite sport, community sport and recreation, scholastic sport, and physical education in schools which impacts the entire sport continuum.

9

Long-Term Athlete Development

Richard Way and Istvan Balyi

• • •

Midtown Soccer is one of the largest sport clubs in its regions. The club has always prided itself on the success of its youth teams in tournaments. The coaches at this level focus on winning, which has always led to success. The club requires youth players to make a year-round commitment to soccer and the team, and they are expected to play in leagues and tournaments in the fall, attend indoor tournaments in the winter, and take part in league play in the spring.

Despite the great success of Midtown's youth teams, many players leave the game as teenagers. Midtown's older teams do not fare as well as the younger players, and those who still want to play are not skilled enough to play at the intercollegiate level. Should the leadership of Midtown reevaluate its player development strategies?

• • •

Chapter 1 addresses the importance of understanding and communicating the reason for a sport club's existence and its continuing purpose. One of the most important purposes of a club is the development of those who participate in and compete for the club. This chapter presents the long-term athlete development (LTAD) model for athletes across multiple sports. This model ensures that athletes achieve their true potential while developing skills that will enable them to lead healthy and active lives.

A Cooperative Sport Environment

Sport clubs in North America have traditionally operated independently from one another as well as from schools and community (city) programming. This fiercely independent spirit has helped build strong nations but may be counterproductive within the sport context. This independent model results in coaches competing for good players, which often is not in the best interest of athletes. This approach is in contrast to the sport systems of other nations, in which sport organizations and coaches work together to develop athletes in the sport in which they may have the most success.

The European multisport club and Chinese sport school systems' success in developing Olympic and professional athletes challenge the North American single-sport club approach. At the root of the philosophical difference is the issue of sport clubs working together to put the interests of individual athletes' development above the results of the team or club at the early stages of development.

Consider a junior high school basketball coach who doesn't allow a "big kid" to dribble or come outside the key to shoot for fear of losing the ball and being scored against. Because the "big kid" does not dribble or shoot from a distance in the game, he has no reason to practice those skills. When the "big kid' grows to be only 6 feet 5 inches (195.6 cm), he is too small to be a "big man" and is left without the skills necessary for playing well at that height. This situation plays out across the gyms and fields of North America. It is for this reason that sport clubs need to review their programming and coaching practices relative to the LTAD model.

The LTAD model and philosophy first acknowledge that physical education, school sports, competitive sports, and recreational activities are mutually interdependent and contribute to healthy, active kids. Traditionally, physical education in schools, recreational sports, and elite sports have been developed separately. This approach is ineffective and expensive. It fails to ensure that all children, including those who may choose to become elite athletes, are given a solid foundation and knowledge base—physical, technical, tactical, and mental—on which to build their athletic abilities. LTAD is an inclusive model that encourages children to get involved in lifelong physical activity by connecting and integrating school physical education programs with elite sport club programs and recreational sport programs in the community. LTAD ensures that all children are introduced to fundamental movement skills during the optimum point in their physical development, prior to age 11 for girls and age 12 for boys.

Club Programming Based on Existing Models

Existing models of athlete development in North American exhibit a number of problems with training methods, trainers, and talent identification that are detrimental to the development of athletes. Clubs can do a better job of training athletes if these issues are addressed.

In the early stages of club play, athletes often overcompete and undertrain. As a result, they do not develop the skills and abilities necessary for reaching optimal performance levels in national and international competitions later in life. Sports programs have athletes specialize too early in an attempt to attract and retain participants with the misguided assumption that winning at an early age will result in long-term success. The result is that athletes do not enjoy being physically active and fail to reach their genetic potential and optimal performance level.

Imposing adult training and competition programs on developing athletes often takes the fun out of sport as well. Moreover, using training methods and competition programs designed for male athletes with female athletes results in their not reaching their potential. Finally, preparation that focuses on the short-term outcome (winning the next game or tournament) and not on the process of having fun and developing abilities often results in burnout.

Current athlete development models also do not consider the athletes themselves. Chronological age rather than developmental age is used in training and competition planning. Coaches largely neglect or do not even know about the sensitive periods of accelerated adaptation to training that vary by athlete. In the current system all 12-year-olds are doing the same things even though one may have matured earlier than another and some were born in January and others in November.

In existing models, fundamental movement skills and sport skills are either not being incorporated or not being taught properly. This is often because the most knowledgeable coaches work at the elite level, leaving athletes at the developmental level to be coached by volunteers when they are in need of quality, trained coaches. Inexperienced coaches tend to identify talent by looking for the biggest or strongest players rather than considering who will ultimately become the better athletes.

A further problem with current athlete development models is a lack of integration among school physical education programs, recreational community programs, and elite competitive programs. As a result, athletes are pulled in many directions as coaches promote their programs and denigrate others.

To address these issues, sport clubs and leagues should review their rules and schedules. A review of the rules may raise the question, Is it essential in youth sport to determine a clear winner? Although determining a winner in Olympic and professional sports is essential to the essence of competition, ranking children serves little value and often creates some negative effects. Take, for example, tie-breaker rules. In youth sport many parents, coaches, and administrators promote equal playing time for all players regardless of ability. Yet the tiebreaker rule is often used. This clearly rewards the team that has limited substitutions and always plays players in their strongest positions, allowing them to run up the score. This promotes early specialization.

SUCCESSFUL STRATEGY

Argument for Player Development

In a 2009 *Wall Street Journal* article, Miami Heat forward Michael Beasley, the number two pick in the 2008 National Basketball Association (NBA) draft, conceded that no one had ever asked him to play defense, particularly when he played for his club team.

In the same article, Stan Van Gundy, head coach of the NBA's Orlando Magic, stated "Our system isn't about developing players. The emphasis is to get exposure and play as many games as you can and show everybody how great you are. If I can win at 11- and 12-year-old league and tell all my friends about it, that is a whole lot more important than if my kid actually gets any better or learns anything about the game."

Van Gundy pointed to the European model of player development, in which the emphasis is on practice and not playing. "Those guys are doing five or six practices for every game," Van Gundy said, "They are spending a lot of time in the gym working on the individual skills. It is reversed here." It can be argued that this philosophy has been the reason the rest of the world has been catching up to the United States on the world basketball stage, and that an increasing number of players in the NBA come from foreign countries.

A product of that European model is NBA All-Star Peja Stojakovic from Serbia, who recalled spending hours dribbling through chairs and working on defense and other fundamental skills. In comparison, Beasley did not recall ever doing defensive drills with his club and commented that defense was not even played in club games.

The reality in the United States is that the development of players is left to high school and club coaches. It appears the model is, at worst, broken and, at best, severely flawed. The flawed system has not gone unnoticed. In 2008 the NBA and the National Collegiate Athletic Association announced a youth initiative called iHoops that they hope will improve the youth basketball structure. Jerry Colangelo, national director of USA Basketball, has called for high school coaches to have more time in the summer to work with players. Shoe companies such as Nike have developed summer programs for elite players that focus on instruction more than playing, and some clubs emphasize player development over playing for exposure.

Information from Clark, K. (2009). American kids flunk Basketball 101. *Wall Street Journal,* June 25, 2009. p. 7.

In terms of scheduling, many sports begin tiering children early. Research has shown that children in the top tiers are older and thus bigger and stronger, but not necessarily better. Compounding the bias is the fact that better coaching and more practice time are given to the higher tiers. Further, teams from different tiers within the same club are not given the opportunity to practice together, thus, limiting the opportunities for younger, less experienced, or less capable athletes to develop by playing with better players.

The LTAD model can help address all of these issues.

Long-Term Athlete Development Model

Long-term athlete development (LTAD) (Balyi, Way, Norris, Cardinal, & Higgs, 2005) is a practical model based on empirical coaching observations and experiences, coaching science, and pediatric exercise sciences and is supported by the emerging field of developing expertise in sport (Starkes & Ericsson, 2003). Harsanyi (1983) reviewed the literature of athlete development models from the 1950s to the 1980s and concluded that most of the models were characterized by a four-stage model: child, juvenile, junior, and adult (or basic, intermediate, advanced, and elite). All of the models were based on **chronological age** and did not consider biological or **developmental age.** Sanderson (1989) then introduced an LTAD model, which takes into consideration the growth and maturation processes of young, developing athletes.

The LTAD (Balyi et al., 2005) model is a seven-stage training, competition, and recovery model based on developmental age (maturation level) rather than chronological age. It is athlete centered; coach driven; and administration, sport science, and sponsor supported. Athletes who progress through the LTAD model experience training and competition programs that consider their biological and training ages when creating scheduled (periodized) plans specific to their development needs.

LTAD recognizes that people go through stages of growth and development from toddler to teen to adult and finally to senior. At each stage of development specific factors affect a person's participation in physical activity and ability to train and compete. Leaders of sport clubs who incorporate LTAD recognize their members' stages of development and design training and competition programs to meet their needs. They do this by following a stage-by-stage guide to developing athletes. As a result, athletes can reach their full potential, whether that be competing for the club's select teams, earning a college scholarship, competing in the Olympics or professionally, or simply enjoying a sport or several sports and remaining active for life.

LTAD's effectiveness is based on the belief in the **holistic development** of children and adolescents in terms of the physical, mental/cognitive, and emotional development. Each stage reflects a unique point in the athlete's development. Following this LTAD guide will ensure that children develop **physical literacy,** which is the development of fundamental movement and fundamental sport skills that permits them to move confidently and with control in a wide range of physical activity, rhythmic (dance), and sport situations. The sport club, therefore, is in the business of developing well-rounded athletes first and foremost. Physical literacy also includes the ability to read what is going on in an activity setting and react appropriately to those events. The goal of physical literacy in all children, from early childhood to late adolescence, is quality daily physical activity and a coordinated approach to developing physical abilities.

Seven Stages of LTAD

To implement the LTAD model, the club must understand the seven stages of LTAD. Club leaders must remember that moving from one stage to another is based on ability, not chronological age; however, chronological age is identified as a guide. Some stages also identify a developmental age, which is "the interrelationship between growth and maturation in relation to the passage of time. The concept of development also includes the social, emotional, intellectual, and motor realms of the child (Malina et al. 1991). Males and females develop at different rates, and ages are different through the stages for males and females. The following section is a brief overview of each stage.

---

chronological age—The number of years and days that have elapsed since the birth of an athlete.

developmental age—The physical, mental, and emotional level of an athlete.

holistic development—The development of children and adolescents that takes into account their physical, mental/cognitive, and emotional development.

physical literacy—The development of fundamental movement and sport skills that permits a child to move confidently and with control in a wide range of physical activity, rhythmic (dance), and sport situations.

Seven Stages of LTAD

Physical Literacy

1. Active start
2. FUNdamentals
3. Learning to train

Excellence

4. Training to train
5. Training to compete
6. Training to win

Lifelong Physical Activity

7. Active for life

Active Start   Chronological Age: Males and Females 0-6

Fun and physical movement should be a part of children's daily lives so they can develop fitness and movement skills. The club's programs in the active start stage should focus on proper movement skills such as running, jumping, twisting, kicking, throwing, and catching. Offering kids an active movement environment with well-structured gymnastics and swimming programs is recommended. The sport does not matter at this stage.

FUNdamentals   Chronological Age: Males 6-9 and Females 6-8

The FUNdamentals stage focuses on activities that address the ABCs of athleticism (agility, balance, coordination and speed) in practices and games rather than specific sports. (See the sidebar at the bottom of this page for activities that can't be enjoyed without the ABCs of athleticism.) Strength training at this stage should be exercises that use children's own body weight, medicine balls, or Swiss balls. At this stage children can be introduced to the simple rules of particular sports and fair play.

Learning to Train   Chronological or Developmental Age: Males 9-12 and Females 8-11

Because the learning to train stage is the major skill-learning stage, the focus should be on the development of overall sport skills by having children participate in three or four sports with sport-specific training three times per week and participation in other sports three times per week. This is in contrast to the common approach

ABCs of Athleticism

Children need the opportunity to master the ABCs of athleticism to enjoy the following activities:

Aerobics	Squash
Cricket	Badminton
Rounders	Dance
Baseball	Golf
Softball	Hockey
Rugby	Skateboarding
Basketball	Cycling
Netball	Athletics
Handball	Soccer
Football	Gymnastics
Sailing	Running
Canoeing	Swimming
Tennis	Walking

in single-sport clubs currently. Along with physical development, this stage should introduce mental preparation, proper nutrition, and recovery. After completing this stage, children should have acquired the fundamental movement and sport skills to enable them to be competent in one or several sports. It will also have encouraged them to be physically active for life. Those who choose to pursue a pathway to excellence progress through the following three stages.

Training to Train   Chronological or Developmental Age: Males 12-16 and Females 11-15

The training to train stage is a major fitness development stage in terms of endurance and strength. The biological markers are the onset of the growth spurt, the peak of the growth after growth decelerates, and the onset of menarche for female athletes; these are the key reference points in program design. Now is the time for athletes to concentrate on one sport, training six to nine times per week while using complementary sports to develop endurance and strength. This stage focuses further on mental preparation techniques, proper hydration, tapering, and peaking and, if desired, introduces free weights for strength training. These subjects can be addressed in education sessions with both athletes and parents.

Training to Compete   Chronological or Developmental Age: Males 16-23 +/– and Females 15-21 +/–

At the training to compete stage, the focus is on the sport; sporting events; position-specific physical conditioning; and technical, tactical, and mental preparation. Currently, this stage is initiated too early, sometimes to the detriment of athletes. At this stage the club should be offering sport-specific technical, tactical, and fitness training 9 to 12 times per week. Coaches can begin to test athletes' playing skills under relatively intense competitive conditions.

Training to Win   Chronological or Developmental Age: Males 19 +/– and Females 18 +/–

Athletes who reach this stage of development are competing at the highest levels (e.g., intercollegiate, professional, or international competition). Sport-specific technical, tactical, and fitness training occurs 9 to 15 times per week. All aspects of training and competition are now being refined or maintained. Variety in training allows for modeling all possible competition environments; however, the emphasis during this stage is quality over quantity with periodized plans that ensure proper breaks for recovery. Only a select few will reach this stage

Active for Life

Active for life athletes can enter this stage as early as their teen years or whenever they decide that they do not want to pursue the excellence pathway. Club leaders and coaches need to understand that at this stage people's goals change from skill refinement, development, and achieving victory to fun, fitness, and social interaction. People at this stage perform a minimum of 60 minutes of moderate daily activity (or 30 minutes of intense activity for adults). Also, they have the opportunity to transfer from one sport to another as well as to move to careers or volunteering in coaching, officiating, or administering sport. By catering to people in this stage, the sport club can meet the needs of all members. If it has done an

iStockphoto/Bob Ingelhart

Participants in the Active for Life stage are less interested in training to be a competitive athlete; instead, they are focused on the fitness and social aspect of sports.

effective job in the other stages, it will have cultivated participants in this stage. The best example of this is offering leagues for people over the ages of 30, 40, and 50, or offering free play times for these groups.

Key Factors Influencing LTAD

The LTAD model is built on the factors listed in the following section. (See the sidebar on page 193 for the ten factors of LTAD.) Any club interested in incorporating LTAD into its programming should appreciate these foundations and use these points when educating parents and participants on the benefits of the LTAD approach.

10-Year Rule

Scientific research has concluded that it takes a minimum of 10 years and 10,000 hours of training for a talented athlete to reach elite levels. For athlete and coach, this translates into slightly more than three hours of training or competition daily for 10 years. This factor is supported by Gibbons, Hill, McConnell, Forester, and Moore, the authors of *The Path to Excellence,* which provides a comprehensive view of the development of U.S. Olympians who competed between 1984 and 1998. This supports the contention that training is more important than competition, especially in the early stages of LTAD.

FUNdamentals: Physical Literacy

FUNdamental movements and FUNdamental sports skills should be introduced through fun and games. FUNdamental sport skills should include basic overall sport skills. Those, combined with movement skills, result in physical literacy,

Overview of a Sport-Specific LTAD Model

Stage	LTAD stage	Focus/age	Skill level	Program level	Coaching stage
1	Active start	• Basic movement • Females and Males 0-6	Fundamental movement and play	Play with parents and friends	Introduction to coaching course
2	FUNdamentals	• Fun and movement • Females and males 7-9	Fundamental movement and sport skills	• Entry-level program • Club teams	• Community coach • Children's courses
3	Learning to train	• Basic sport skills • Females 9-12 • Males 9-13	Developing sport skills and speed	• Club teams • School programs	• Community coach • Youth courses
4	Training to train	• Identifying the elite • Females 16 • Males 17	Building physical capacities and developing sport skills and tactics	• District and state teams • Sport schools: academies, national training centers	National coaching courses
5	Training to compete	• Developing professionals or Olympians • Females 18 • Males 19	• Refining skills and position play • Specific physical and mental training	• Universities • National training centers • Pro teams (minor leagues)	• National coaching • High-performance courses
6	Training to win	• Maintaining a professional or Olympian • Females 18+ • Males 19+	Perfecting performance	• Professional teams • National teams	• National coaching • High-performance courses
7	Active for life	• Sport and health • Males and females of all ages	Maintaining fitness and enjoyment	Moving from high-performance teams to competitive or recreational activity	• Community coach • Senior participants

This example is from Canadian Soccer.

Ten Factors of LTAD

10-year rule	Development
FUNdamentals	Planning and periodization
Specialization	Competition
Age	Alignment and integration
Trainability	Continuous improvement

which refers to competency in movement and sport skills. Physical literacy should be developed before the onset of the adolescent growth spurt. Movement skills should include traveling skills (e.g., running), object control skills (e.g., throwing, catching, dribbling), and balance movements (e.g., twisting). A wide variety of fundamental movement skills underpin physical literacy.

The basic movement skills of three activities provide the base for all other sports: track and field (running, jumping, and throwing), gymnastics (agility, balance, coordination, and speed), and swimming (water safety and balance in a buoyant environment). Without these basic movement skills, a child will have difficulty participating in any sport. For example, to enjoy baseball, basketball, cricket, football, netball, handball, rugby, and softball, a child must master the simple skill of catching (see figure 9.1). A common mistake youth coaches make is focusing on the tactics of a sport when the participants have not even mastered a basic skill such as catching or throwing. The coach gets frustrated over the breakdown of a play and focuses on the tactic when in many cases the skill breakdown was what led to the lack of success.

It is critically important that children with disabilities have the opportunity to develop their fundamental movement and sport skills as well. Failure to do so severely limits their lifelong opportunities for recreational and athletic success.

early specialization sports—Sports with very complex skills that are learned before maturation because they cannot be fully mastered if taught after maturation. They include artistic and acrobatic sports such as gymnastics, diving, and figure skating.

Specialization

Sports can be classified as either early or late specialization. **Early specialization sports** include artistic and acrobatic sports such as gymnastics, diving, and figure skating. Children learning these sports learn very complex skills before maturation because they cannot fully master them after maturation. Most sport clubs offer late specialization sports. However, all sports should be individually analyzed using

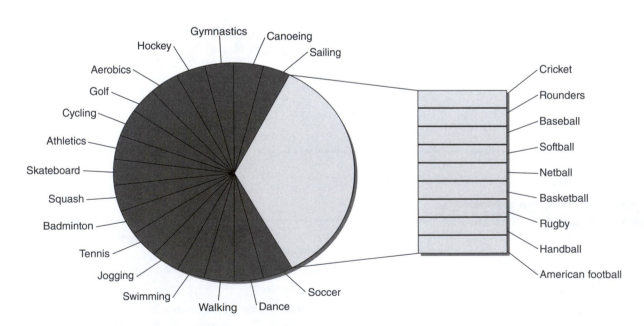

Figure 9.1   Many sports are unavailable to a child who can't catch a ball.
Reprinted, by permission, from R. Way. © Canadian Sport Centre Pacific. Adapted from Mike Jess, University of Edinburgh.

international and national normative data to decide whether they are early or late specialization. Athletes who acquire physical literacy before maturation can select a late specialization sport when they are between the ages of 12 and 15 and have the potential to excel at a high level in that sport.

Parents and clubs that promote specializing before the age of 10 in late specialization sports contribute to one-sided, sport-specific preparation; lack of ABCs (the basic movement and sport skill); overuse injuries; early burnout; and early retirement from training and competition. These occurrences are all too common in the current sport environment, resulting in shortcomings that are hard to correct later in an athlete's career. As a result, an athlete who had the natural ability to succeed is denied that opportunity. Sport clubs should encourage early involvement in the FUNdamentals stage for athletes interested in late specialization sports.

Age of an Athlete

When considering a training, competition, and recovery program for an athlete, regardless of the LTAD stage, club leaders and coaches must consider the age of the athlete. This is not done by checking the date of birth. A number of ages must be considered:

> ▶ Developmental age (physical, mental, and emotional)
> ▶ **General sport training age** (when the person started playing sports)
> ▶ **Sport-specific training age** (when the person started the sport)
> ▶ **Skeletal age** (bone development)
> ▶ Chronological age (the number of years and days that have elapsed since birth)

general sport training age—The age an athlete started training in and playing different sports.

sport-specific training age—The age an athlete began specializing in one sport.

skeletal age—The bone development of an athlete.

Training age refers to the age at which the athlete began planned, regular, serious involvement in training. The tempo of a child's growth has significant implications for athletic training because children who mature at an early age have a major advantage during the training to train stage compared to average or late maturers. However, after all athletes have gone through the growth spurt, late maturers often have greater potential to become top athletes provided they experience quality coaching throughout that period.

Determining all of these ages of an athlete is very important for a club committed to LTAD. However, age is often overlooked by other clubs and leagues, which use chronological age exclusively. This creates a bias for early maturers or athletes born early in the cutoff year. It discourages athletes who are late maturers, who are born later in the year, or who decide to take up the sport later than most. Coaches seldom are aware during selection that some children are almost a year younger than others. Sport clubs rarely offer programs to help children catch up on skills and enter the sport late. Instead, they are written off as not good enough to play, when in reality a catch-up course could enable them to compete.

In terms of chronological age, LTAD requires the identification of early, average, and late maturers. As stated earlier, most athletic training and competition programs are based on chronological age; however, athletes of the same age between

10 and 16 can be four to five years apart developmentally. Thus, chronological age is a poor guide to use to segregate adolescents for competitions. Also, understanding age is important for designing appropriate training and competition programs. The beginning and the peak of the growth spurt are very significant in LTAD applications to training and competition design.

Trainability

To create optimal training and competition programs (see figure 9.2), coaches and administrators need to be aware of the sensitive periods in which training stamina and strength, speed, skill, and suppleness is a better use of time than training some other systems. A **sensitive period** of development refers to the point in the development of a specific capacity when training has an optimal effect.

sensitive period— Accelerated adaption to training.

Trainability refers to the genetic endowment of athletes to respond to specific stimuli and adapt accordingly. Remember, all systems are always trainable! Sport clubs can hire strength and conditioning experts to work with coaches in the planning of training sessions as well as with individual athletes to capitalize on these important training times in their development.

trainability—The genetic endowment of athletes to respond to specific stimuli and adapt accordingly.

Physical, Mental, Cognitive, and Emotional Development

A club's training, competitive, and recovery programs should consider the mental, cognitive, and emotional development of each athlete in addition to addressing physical, technical, and tactical development—including decision-making skills. A major objective of LTAD is to take a holistic approach to athlete development. This includes emphasizing ethics, fair play, and character building throughout the various stages, an objective that reflects positive values. A sport club can include as part of its mission to use sport to develop these traits, which are as applicable off the playing field as they are on. Thus, a club's programming can consider athletes' cognitive ability to address these concepts.

Planning and Periodization (Time Management, Training and Competition Schedule)

Whether they realize it or not, parents of athletes are familiar with periodization through the scheduling of their children's sport and school commitments. Simply put, **periodization** is a time management technique that provides the framework for arranging the complex array of training processes into a logical and scientifically based schedule to bring about optimal improvements in performance. Periodization sequences the training components into weeks, days, and sessions. Periodization is situation-specific depending on priorities and the time available to bring about the required training and competition improvement. In the LTAD context, periodization connects the stage the athlete is in to the requirements of that stage. Proper planning and periodization must consider all aspects of the athletes to create the optimal environment for improved training performance.

periodization—A time management technique that provides the framework for arranging the complex array of training processes into a logical and scientifically based schedule to bring about optimal improvements in performance.

A club incorporating LTAD develops periodization models for all stages that consider the growth, maturation, and trainability principles unique to those stages and seamlessly integrate them with the subsequent stages of athletic performance

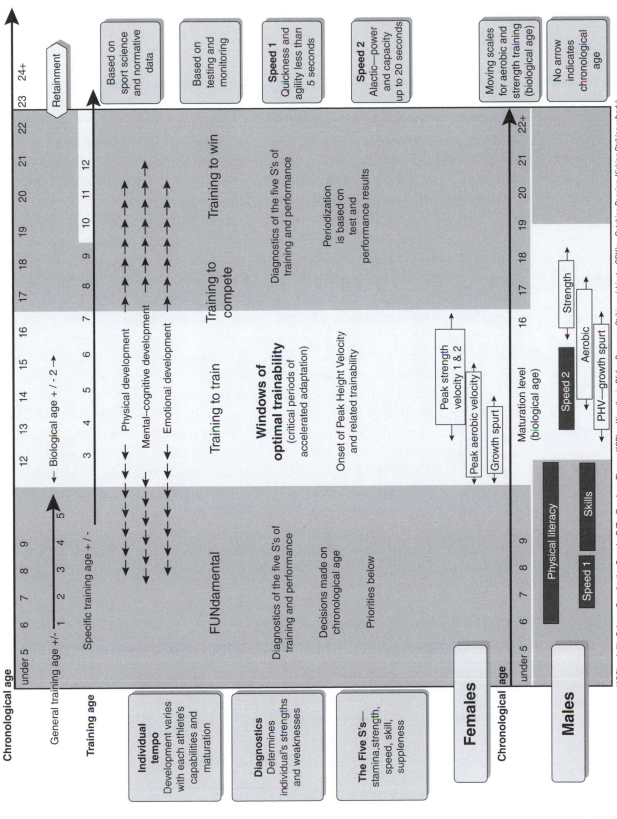

Figure 9.2 Optimal trainability program.

Reprinted, by permission, from R. Way. © Canadian Sport Centre Pacific. Adapted from Balyi and Way.

(ABC's = Agility Balance Coordination Speed + RJT = Run Jump Throw + KGB's + Kinesthesia Gliding Bouyance Striking w/object + CPK's = Catching Passing, Kicking Striking w/body)

ancillary capacities—
Lifetime health benefits
derived from physical activity.

and life. Incorporating LTAD is a commitment on the part of the club because it is typically a 10- to 12-year procedure that optimizes physical, technical, tactical (including decision-making), and mental preparation, as well as the supporting **ancillary capacities.** The LTAD model will drive the player development and competition philosophy of the club, but if followed, the benefits will be immense.

Calendar Planning for Competition

Optimal competition calendar planning at all stages is critical to athlete development. In the earlier stages, developing the physical and technical capacities of the athlete takes precedence over competition. At later stages, the ability to compete well becomes the focus. Table 9.1 outlines general recommendations for the ratio of training to competition and competition-specific training. Club leaders should consider how the quantity and quality of the training and competition program change as long-term plans progress.

The training-to-competition ratios presented in table 9.1 are general because each sport has optimal sport-specific competition ratios for all stages of LTAD. Club leaders must recognize that the level and length of the competitive season are aligned with the changing needs of the athlete progressing through the LTAD program. For example, overcompetition and undertraining at the learning to train and training to train stages can result in a lack of basic skills and fitness. Schedules for team sports are often set by leagues and organizations and not by the coach and athlete, making optimal training based on periodization difficult to implement. But the club can control the number of extra competitions such as tournaments.

For individual sports, the coach and athlete can select the competition schedules based on the athlete's developmental needs. Individual sports' training-to-competition ratios often have a much higher percentage of training than those of team sports. In general, not traveling and working on skills is better than going to yet another tournament; however, the coach needs to create fun, enjoyable practices that will help athletes develop their skills. The system of competition makes or breaks athletes; thus, the proper system of competition should be provided at all stages.

Table 9.1 Training-to-Competition Ratios

Stage	Recommended ratio
Active start	No specific ratios
FUNdamentals	All activity FUN based
Learning to train	70% training, 20% competition-specific training, 10% competition
Training to train	60% training, 20% competition-specific training, 20% competition
Training to compete	50% training, 25% competition-specific training, 25% competition
Training to win	40% training, 30% competition-specific training, 30% competition
Active for life	Based on the person's desire

These ratios are for team sports, and the ratios vary from sport to sport.

Competition-specific training includes scrimmaging, exhibition games, and so on.

Competition is sanctioned competition, league play, tournaments, playoffs, and so on.

Alignment and Integration

LTAD programs should be athlete centered; coach driven; and administration, sport science, and sponsor supported. LTAD can drive the core business of a club whether it be a swim club, soccer club, or multisport club, or even a national or state sport organization. After the LTAD design is completed, a sport-specific system of competition should be established that matches the competitive needs of athletes during the active start, FUNdamentals, learning to train, and training to train stages. LTAD can also have a strong impact on the coaching education curriculum. Developmental readiness replaces ad hoc decision making about programming preparation. LTAD can serve as the common thread that brings together school-based, community-based, and sport club programs in athlete development.

Continuous Improvement

The concept of continuous improvement, which permeates LTAD, is drawn from the respected Japanese industrial philosophy known as kaizen. Continuous improvement ensures that LTAD programs respond and react to new scientific and sport-specific innovations and observations and are subject to continuous research in all aspects. LTAD also reflects all emerging facets of physical education, sport, and recreation to ensure the systematic and logical delivery of programs to all ages. Finally, LTAD promotes the ongoing education of federal, state and local municipal governments; the mass media; sport and recreation administrators; coaches; sport scientists; parents; and educators about the interlocking relationships among physical education, school sport, community recreation, life-long physical activity, and high-performance sport.

Ten Ss of Training and Performance

A sport club can use the 10 Ss as the foundation when developing its training and competition plans. The first five address the physical capacities of athletes: stamina (endurance), strength, speed, skill, and suppleness (flexibility). Coaches monitor the remaining five Ss to provide holistic balance in each athlete's development: structure/stature, (p)sychology, sustenance, schooling, and sociocultural needs.

The following sections present the 10 Ss and a summary of factors that a club should consider in relation to ages and gender when implementing an LTAD program. These 10 items can drive the decisions a club makes in terms of what it

---

Ten Ss of Training and Performance

1. Stamina (endurance)
2. Strength
3. Speed
4. Skill
5. Suppleness (flexibility)

6. Structure/stature
7. (p)Sychology
8. Sustenance
9. Schooling
10. Sociocultural needs

is doing, with whom, and when. The Ss are presented in general terms; the club must incorporate them into individual sports. In the end athletes will benefit from a club that takes the time and effort to look at each athlete as an individual and that prescribes training and competition programs that address the uniqueness of individual athletes. Such a program enables athletes to reach their full potential.

Stamina (Endurance)   The sensitive period for training stamina occurs at the onset of the growth spurt. Players need increased focus on aerobic capacity training as they enter peak height velocity (PHV), and they should be progressively introduced to aerobic power as their growth rate decelerates. Sport-specific normative data define how much endurance is needed for excelling in a given sport (i.e., aerobic and anaerobic sports).

Strength   There are two sensitive windows of trainability for strength in girls: immediately after PHV and after the onset of menarche. Boys have one strength window that begins 12 to 18 months after PHV. Again, sport-specific normative data define how much strength is needed to excel in a given sport (i.e., speed and power sports versus aerobic sports).

Speed   In both boys and girls, there are two periods of trainability for speed. For girls, the first speed period occurs between the ages of 6 and 8, and the second period occurs between 11 and 13. For boys, the first speed window occurs between the ages of 7 and 9, and the second window occurs between 13 and 16. During the first speed window, training should focus on developing agility and quickness; during the second speed window, training should focus on developing the anaerobic alactic energy system.

Skill   Girls and boys both have one window for optimal skill training. For girls the window is between the ages of 8 and 11, whereas in boys it is between 9 and 12—more precisely, before the onset of the growth spurt. During this window, young athletes should be developing physical literacy—that is, competence in the fundamental movement and sport skills that are the foundation of all sports. Competence in these skills will make it easier for athletes to learn and excel later in all late specialization sports.

Suppleness   The sensitive period of trainability for suppleness occurs between the ages of 6 and 10 years in both girls and boys; however, special attention should also be paid to flexibility during PHV because of the rapid change in body size and structure.

Structure/Stature   This component describes the six stages of growth in the human body and links them to the windows of optimal trainability. Stature (height) is measured before, during, and after the growth spurt to help coaches and parents track developmental age. Using stature to track developmental age allows coaches to address the sensitive periods of physical (endurance, strength, speed, and flexibility) and skill development.

(p)Sychology   Sport is a physical and mental challenge. The ability to maintain high levels of concentration, yet remain relaxed with the confidence to succeed, is a skill essential to long-term successful performance in sport. This skill also has the potential to transcend sport and enhance the everyday lives of players.

Sustenance   **Sustenance** is defined as components that replenish the body, thereby preparing the player for the volume and intensity required to optimize training. Sustenance addresses several areas: nutrition, hydration, rest, sleep, and regeneration. Whereas overtraining and overcompetition can lead to burnout, improperly addressing sustenance can do the same.

sustenance—Components that replenish the body, thereby preparing the athlete for the volume and intensity required to optimize training.

Schooling   When designing training programs, club leaders must consider the demands of school— not just of school sports and physical education classes, but also of academic loads and exams. When possible, training camps and competition tours should not conflict with the timing of major academic events at school. Coaches should monitor overstress in their players as a result of schooling, exams, peer groups, family issues, and relationships, as well as increased training volumes and intensities. A good balance among all factors is necessary.

Sociocultural Needs   Sport exposes players to forces of socialization at the community level, and it can also lead to national and international experiences as players progress through the LTAD stages. The sociocultural aspect of sport can broaden the social perspective of players, including fostering an awareness of ethnicity and national diversity. Sociocultural development may be integrated into competition travel schedules by educating athletes about the history, geography, architecture, cuisine, literature, music, and visual arts of the competition location. Proper planning can allow sport to offer much more than simply commuting between the hotel room and the field of play.

Other Considerations in Trainability

Children often begin to play sports after the sensitive periods of trainability for speed, skill, and suppleness have passed. They are therefore dependent on schools, recreation programs, and other sports to provide timely training in these capacities. LTAD advocates that sport clubs build relationships with these organizations to promote and support appropriate training. If players miss these training periods entirely, coaches need to design individualized programs to remedy any shortcomings.

Summary

Clubs have a critical role in the development of athletes. The environment created by club administrators is critical to the enjoyment and sport expertise of all participants. As outlined in this chapter, the environment must be based on athletes' individual needs depending on their stages of development.

The LTAD model permits a sport club to make sound decisions about the best possible training, competition, and recovery programs for all members. Implementing a stage-by-stage LTAD approach can facilitate change in the culture of club sport because clubs develop their own LTAD programs and work with various partners in the community (schools and local government), with the goal of getting more people active and excelling in sport.

Clubs using the LTAD model have to educate the parents of participants because it is not business as usual. Such a model promotes the development of athletes and not sport-specific players at the early stages. It also considers not just the physical capabilities of the athlete in the moment, but the potential for an athlete in the future. Winning and sport-specific development is not the focus early on; these goals are achieved in the later stages of LTAD. For more information on LTAD, visit www.canadiansportforlife.ca.

Midtown reevaluated its club philosophy and incorporated LTAD into it. The focus shifted from winning tournaments and championships at the younger ages to athlete development. The club has already seen drastic improvements in the retention of players at the higher levels, and those players are better skilled and getting the opportunity to play in college. Midtown joined forces with a local basketball club to encourage players to play another sport as opposed to playing soccer year-round. Overall, the LTAD approach has made Midtown a more successful club in a number of areas.

By the end of the chapter, the sport club manager will be able to do the following:

- ▶ Explain the critical role ethics play in leading and managing a sport club.
- ▶ Appreciate the importance of values and principles in acting ethically within the sport club environment.
- ▶ Describe the major ethical theories that are applicable to managing a sport club.
- ▶ Appreciate the importance of morality in conducting oneself professionally.
- ▶ Recognize ethical behavior as defined by professional codes and standards established for the field.
- ▶ Assess their level of moral development as it applies to a career in sport club management.
- ▶ State the ethical theory to which they adhere.
- ▶ Appreciate professional situations that will arise that can potentially lead to an ethical dilemma.

10

Ethical Issues in Club Management

The Hotshot Basketball Club has been in existence for 15 years. Under new executive director Ken Henderson, the club is planning to renovate the existing facility to meet the increased needs of participants. Ken is looking to sell the naming rights of the facility to cover the majority of the costs associated with the renovation. A company is willing to sign a 10-year naming rights contract. The president and owner of the company has a son who aspires to be an elite basketball player, but he is not as talented as, nor does he have the work ethic of, the other players in his age group. The president of the company believes his son is good enough to start on the team. Ken and the coach disagree; they believe that placing the president's son on the team would displace a more deserving player. Ken has not had much luck with other naming rights prospects, and the president of the company has implied that that there are other clubs for which his son can play and who would also be interested in the additional funding. Should Ken place the son on the team to secure the funds that will benefit many others in the club at the expense of just one, the player displaced by the son, or should he tell the president, "Thanks but no thanks"? What is the right thing to do?

The majority of this text focuses on the technical aspects of operating a sport club from policies and procedures to mission statements to securing corporate sponsorship and understanding the legal ramifications of running a club. This chapter is not about what club leaders do, but rather how they do it. In the opening case, the question is, What is the right thing to do? Should Ken Henderson act to benefit the greatest number of people? If so, he should take the money and place the president's son on the team. Only one kid is harmed, and the club will have a renovated facility that will benefit many for years to come. On the other hand, Ken may wonder how he would feel if he were not included on a team even though he deserved to be, because his father did not have as much money as another player's father. If he looks at it this way, he may not take the money.

Many aspects of managing a sport club raise ethical questions. Sport club leaders address ethical issues when developing a philosophy for the club; dealing with the behavior of players, coaches, spectators, and parents; recruiting players; recruiting, hiring, and firing personnel; selecting players; addressing gamesmanship; distributing justice; dealing with the media and public relations; securing sponsorships; creating and enforcing rules; and addressing the well-being of athletes.

The Greek philosopher Heraclitus wrote: "Day by day what you choose, what you think, and what you do is who you become. Your integrity is your destiny." As a professional, a club manager will be judged as much on her professional ethics as on her professional competence. Integrity comes from knowing one's ethical beliefs and acting in accordance with those beliefs.

Laws and rules are created because people's ethical beliefs differ, thus leading to debates over what is actually right and wrong. Club leaders need to come to terms with their own ethical theories and try to understand the theories of others so they can understand the intent of their own and others' actions. How often does a club manger really consider the rightness of an action or the intent behind an action? The decision to recruit a player away from another club may be viewed by some as unethical, but a club manager may justify the action based on the ethical theory of self-interest. Another consideration for a club manager is who should matter most when a decision is being made—the player, the parent, the coach, or another club? There is no right answer, but the decision makes a statement about the club's leaders and the club's values and ethics.

Why Discuss Ethics?

Ethics has taken on increased importance in sport club management in recent years. The temptation for club managers and clubs to act unethically or immorally has become greater for several reasons. DeSensi and Rosenberg (2003) identified the following factors that have led to increase ethical digressions within the area of sport:

▶ *Overemphasis on success.* Several years ago Nike had a slogan, "Silver means first loser." In society, winning is paramount, and the pursuit of this goal by participants, coaches, parents, and society as a whole has led to ethical transgressions. Success is measured by extrinsic rewards such as trophies, scholarships, state and national championships, All-American status, and increased revenue. Cutting corners or outright cheating can help in attaining these goals. The use of performance-enhancing drugs, for example, stems from this emphasis on success. Athletes, coaches, and administrators see the goal of winning as paramount, even if it requires cheating. Thus, success has become the goal rather than a by-product of doing things the right way.

▶ *Pursuit of prestige and material rewards.* Along with success comes recognition. Gold medals can be worth millions of dollars in endorsement contracts; a college athletic scholarship can be worth more than $100,000; a club with successful teams and athletes can attract more and better players, improve facilities, and generate more sponsorship revenue; a winning coach can be duly compensated for that success; and parents can brag that their sons or daughters are national-level athletes or have earned scholarships. The pursuit of this prestige can lead to immoral or unethical actions. Does a club encourage its coaches to recruit players away from other clubs in order to be recognized as a great club? The question is, What price is a club or its leadership willing to pay to gain the prestige and material rewards associated with success?

▶ *Self-interest.* A question in sport as a whole seems to be, What's in it for me? People often make decisions that are in their best interests and disregard the ramifications or rightness of those decisions. An athlete leaves a club that introduced her to the game and worked with her on fundamental skills and academics so she would be prepared for the SAT exams, to go to a higher-profile club that claims it will get her noticed by major colleges. The athlete's self-interest is more important than demonstrating loyalty to the club that created the opportunity for her. Coaches and club managers may leave clubs for higher pay or generate revenue for themselves by training individual athletes rather than have those funds go to the club. In these cases, the people make decisions that are in their own best interests.

These factors have created a competitive environment with a great deal at stake for all involved. The higher the stakes, the greater the temptation is to disregard the rightness of actions. This highlights the importance of discussing ethics within the sport club environment.

Basic Ethical Concepts in Sport Club Management

A basic theoretical understanding of ethics is necessary for discussing the application of ethics in the sport club environment. This enables club managers to understand the intent of their actions and helps them make decisions that are consistent with their ethics.

Goree (2004) defined **ethical issues** as the questions, problems, situations, and actions that raise legitimate questions of right and wrong. When a club manager recognizes that an oversight has occurred regarding the age eligibility of an athlete that will allow that athlete to compete in a younger age classification, should she bring the oversight to the attention of the governing body, or let the athlete compete so that the club team has a competitive advantage? To address this situation, the

ethical issues—The questions, problems, situations, and actions that contain legitimate questions of right and wrong.

club manager must refer to her ethics. DeSensi and Rosenberg (2003) described ethics as the objective basis on which judgments are rendered regarding right and wrong, good and bad, authentic and inauthentic behavior.

Values

value—Anything a person assesses to be worthwhile, interesting, excellent, desirable, or important.

A person's ethics are based on values. A **value** is anything a person assesses to be worthwhile, interesting, excellent, desirable, or important (DeSensi & Rosenberg, 2003). These values can come in the form of virtues or moral values such as loyalty, integrity, honesty, compassion, courage, and perseverance. Values may also come in the form of tangible outcomes such as money and material objects or intangible outcomes such as fame, prestige, and reputation. Values are derived from a variety of sources such as family, friends, teachers, life experiences, and religion.

Principles

principles—Universal guides that tell what actions, intentions, or motives are prohibited.

Principles are universal guides that tell what actions, intentions, or motives are prohibited. Principles enable values to be translated in action. For example, if a club leader values honesty, he will develop a principle that he will not falsify the paperwork regarding the age of participants. If a coach values compassion, she will not disregard the well-being of an athlete and rush her back from an injury for the sake of winning a contest.

Action

action—The ultimate statement of a person's values and principles.

An **action** is the ultimate statement of ethics. A club manager can say he values honesty and develop a principle that he will not be dishonest in managing the club, but when asked to replace a player for one whose parents are influential in the club, what he does is the ultimate statement of his ethics.

Morality

morality—The debate over the rightness or wrongness of an action.

Morality is the debate over the rightness and wrongness of an action. A moral person does what is right. Consider a club's coach who recruits a player away from another club to improve her team for the upcoming season and further her reputation as a successful coach, and perhaps parlay that reputation into a position with a better club or the national team staff. In her recruiting, the coach fabricates false information about the player's current club that sways the player's decision. This coach can justify her action based on self-interest, arguing that she needs to stay employed or continue with her coaching career, or that she needs to support her family and must make more money to do so. Some may view her action, regardless of what appears to be a worthy intent, as morally wrong. Others may make normative judgments about the coach because she has benefited at the expense of another.

Moral Development

Morality is learned early in life from parents and others and then evolves throughout one's life. Thus, some have argued that the development of moral reasoning skills is a development process. Kohlberg (1987) quantified this process in his theory on moral development. He presented six stages of moral development (see the sidebar at the bottom of this page) that occur at three levels: preconventional, conventional, and postconventional. Each level includes two moral stages, one being more advanced than the other.

At the first stage of the preconventional stage, people obey rules to avoid punishment. A club coach does not use overage players for fear of being discredited professionally or dismissed from his position if discovered. At stage 2, people obey rules to obtain rewards and have favors returned. The coach does not use the overage player because he wants to continue in his career and reap the benefits that go along with practicing his profession in the right way. In both of these stages, self-interest and fear of punishment deter the person from acting in an unethical manner.

At stage 3 in the conventional stage, people obey rules to avoid others' disapproval; meeting the expectations of others is the most important element. The coach does not use the overage player because he does not want to be viewed as a cheat by his family, close friends, and mentors. At stage 4, the coach does what is deemed right to avoid guilt as well as to feel that he is a member of society. At this stage the coach does the right thing because he does not want to be discredited and viewed as a dishonest professional by his peers and society as a whole. In the conventional stages the incentive to do the right thing is based more on the person's desire to gain the approval of others.

At the postconventional stage 5, people obey rules for the sake of social and community welfare. In this case the coach does not use the overage player because if others do the same, a total breakdown of the integrity of competition as it is known could occur. By being honest, he is working within the social order and meeting his responsibility to his profession and the sport. At stage 6 in the postconventional stage, people obey rules to abide by universal ethical principles. At this stage, the coach does not use the overage player because it is not the right thing to do. He does not consider benefits or punishment or the judgments of

Kohlberg's Stages of Moral Development

Preconventional
Stage 1: Obey rules to avoid punishment
Stage 2: Obey rules to gain a reward

Conventional
Stage 3: Obey rules to avoid disappointing others
Stage 4: Obey rules to avoid guilt

Postconventional
Stage 5: Obey rules to promote social welfare
Stage 6: Obey rules to abide by universal ethical principles

others; he just believes that using the player is not the right thing to do. Kohlberg (1987) proposed that transitions from stage to stage are driven primarily by social interaction, especially at the higher levels of development.

Understanding and appreciating the stages of moral development are important in the club sport environment. A coach at stage 1 believes she can act immorally as long as she doesn't get caught, whereas a coach at a higher stage will do the right thing because it is the right thing to do. Club leaders should consider the stages of moral development when hiring staff. Ethical clubs hire people with similar values and principles.

Social Responsibility

social responsibility—A club's obligation to act in a manner that recognizes and accepts the consequences of each action and decision.

Social responsibility is the obligation to act in a manner that recognizes and accepts the consequences of each action and decision, whether it is at the state, government, corporation, organization, or individual level (DeSensi & Rosenberg, 2003). Upholding this conviction can be a challenge considering the extrinsic and intrinsic rewards associated with success in sport for players, coaches, teams, and clubs.

Participants are at the center of the sport club environment. Professionals are working with athletes, in most cases young athletes. The club and its staff have the social responsibility to respect the rights of participants. Whether participants are elite athletes, beginners, or seniors, club personnel must consider issues such as gender, race, and special needs and ensure that all participants are treated in a morally appropriate way that meets the codes and standards established by society as a whole and the profession.

Ethical Theories

teleological theories— Ethical theories that focus on the consequences of actions.

deontological theories— Ethical theories that do not consider the consequences of actions.

When making a decision, to what degree does a person consider the consequences of the action? The response indicates the ethical theory to which the person adheres. Ethical theories can be broken down into two broad categories: those that focus on the consequences of actions (**teleological theories**) and those that do not (**deontological theories**).

Teleological Theories

Teleological theories are characterized by a focus on consequences. Thus, decisions are made based on what will result from those decisions. Actions that lead to good and valuable consequences are right, whereas actions that lead away from them are wrong. Thus, teleology is the "science of ends." Teleological theories include egoism, utilitarianism, and situation ethics which focus on consequences but differ in intent.

Egoism

egoism—The belief that all people act in self-interest.

Egoism is the belief that all people act in self-interest. Egoists may act on behalf of another, but ultimately they are concerned about themselves and not about making sacrifices on behalf of others. An egoist club manager will develop a topflight club program not for the benefit of the participants but for her own benefit (e.g., monetary reward, enhanced reputation, personal glory). Egoists are often viewed in the negative, but they argue that the pursuit of their personal goals benefits many. Members of the club benefit from the egoist's pursuit of personal ambition. The negatives associated with egoists stem from the pursuit of personal ambition to the detriment of others. Either way, egoists will not hear the critics who make normative judgments about their acts, because they are acting in accordance with their belief system.

Utilitarianism

Utilitarianism contends that the only moral duty is to promote the greatest amount of happiness, and that pleasure and happiness are the only goods worth pursuing. From a utilitarian perspective, the end justifies the means and behavior must be practical and useful. A utilitarian sport club manager will make decisions that will be of the most benefit to the greatest number of people within the club. He may rent the facility to generate significant revenues for the club at the expense of club members, who do not have access to the facilities during the rental period. If the revenue generated ultimately provides more services or better facilities for the members, the club manager believes there is utility in renting the facility.

utilitarianism—The belief that the only moral duty is to promote the greatest good for the greatest number of people.

Utilitarians can justify their actions based on the fact that they accrue the most benefits to the greatest number of people. The situation in the opening scenario can demonstrate the utilitarian perspective. On the surface, placing the company president's son on the team may be viewed as wrong, but doing so will bring major sponsorship revenue to the club. Does the action have utility? Some would argue yes, because the funds from the sponsorship will enhance the quality of the club for all of the members. The club manager in this case sees utility in selecting the less talented player over the more talented player in terms of benefiting the greatest number. This decision, however, is open to the normative judgments of others.

Situation Ethics

Situation ethics do not take into account overriding moral principles or rules. Those practicing situation ethics evaluate acts in light of the situational context. In the opening scenario, Ken Henderson may decide that the situation dictates that he place the company president's son to bring in sponsorship dollars. In another situation he may place the more skilled player because he is more deserving and the less skilled player's parent is not a potential major sponsor. Each situation is unique, and the consequences dictate what actions to take.

situation ethics—The belief that the situational context should dictate the actions to take.

Deontological Theories

Club managers who practice deontological ethics believe they have an obligation to do right without considering the outcomes of their decisions. Consequences do not determine the rightness of actions. A club manager with this ethical orientation will not recruit a player away from another club because it is wrong. Doing the right thing supersedes the positive consequences associated with the action. In this case the athlete stays with his current club and that club wins the regional competition.

One of the most well-known deontological principles is the Golden Rule: Do unto others as you would have them do unto you. The Golden Rule is based on the assumption that all people want to be treated well. A club manager will not try to recruit an athlete away from another club because she would not want that done to her club. A coach would not abuse an athlete in training because he would not want be abused.

Emmanuel Kant, a Western philosopher, proposed that ethics has no relation to fulfilling an end; rather, it is an obligation that comes from a sense of duty. **Kantian ethics** asserts that people should take stands and restrain their actions based on principles. The ultimate good is not the action that results in the most pleasure, but the action that leads to a person (in this case, a club professional) leading a life of virtue. Club managers with a Kantian ethics orientation do the right thing because it is the right thing to do. They do not believe they can do something simply because someone else did it. They create in their minds a vision of a moral club manager and aspire to attain that status.

Kantian ethics—The belief in doing the right thing because it is the right thing to do.

Applied Ethics in Sport Clubs

Because ethics are involved in every aspect of a club, each chapter in this book can be viewed through ethical lenses. Applied ethics entails taking ethical theories into the real world, in this case, running a sport club from an ethical perspective.

Club Philosophy

As stated in chapter 1, the philosophy of the club should be driven by the club's values, principles, and ultimately, ethics. A philosophy is a statement of values in terms of what is important to the club and what it will and won't do. Honesty, integrity, fair play, and commitment are values; not cheating and not practicing poor sporting behavior are principles.

A sound philosophy permeates the club's missions, goals, and policies and procedures. A mission statement that includes "the development of the whole person through sport" encourages fair play and the appropriate treatment of athletes. The club should revisit its mission statement on a regular basis to be sure that the philosophy drives the decisions and actions of the club.

Behavior of Players, Coaches, and Spectators

A club's ethics should drive the actions of all of those associated with the club. Exhibiting poor sporting behavior, disrespecting an opponent or game official, cheating in competition, violating administrative or game rules, and using foul language should not be condoned from staff, coaches, parents, and participants. How the club responds to these actions will be the ultimate statement of its ethics and reveal whether the talk of ethical behavior is just that, talk.

Inappropriate behavior is not limited to club personnel and players. How spectators, often the parents of players, present themselves also makes a statement about the club. Home court or field advantage can take on a number of meanings. Does the advantage just constitute the players' familiarity with the surroundings? Does the behavior of spectators make the visiting team uncomfortable? The club leaders must determine what constitutes inappropriate spectator behavior. Is making fun of a young athlete's physical appearance as inappropriate as yelling loudly during a foul shot in a basketball contest? Should the club only allow calls of encouragement from its spectators and prohibit negative chants against an opponent? By answering questions such as these, club leaders can address the sometimes difficult issue of spectator behavior.

Recruiting Players

The success of a club and its teams is often dictated by the talent of the athletes participating. Questions arise over the rightness of a club coach recruiting a player away from another club. The ethical theory a club and its staff adhere to determines the overall attitude toward recruiting. There are many stories of clubs that develop a player over several years, only to have a rival club entice the player away with promises of more exposure, better coaching, and more travel opportunities. The club that gets the talented player meets its needs, but what about the club that invested time and effort in developing that player? The club that loses the player can make a normative judgment on the rival club for stealing the player. The rival club can justify its action based on self-interest—the player will improve the performance of the other players on the team, and more players may decide to join the club as a result of the success the new player brings to the club.

Governing organizations have established guidelines on player transfers to deter the practice of switching players. Most apply to changes in season, but not between seasons. As stated before, laws and rules are created because the rightness of actions is open to debate. In the case of recruiting, a club needs to develop a policy or view that is consistent with its values, and its representatives must act in accordance with those values. A club that does not want its players recruited away should not recruit. If a club's goal is to be the best and to do that it must have the best players, then recruiting players away from other clubs is consistent with its values. The club leaders may not be viewed as ethical by their peers in other clubs, but if they are living up to their ethical beliefs, they can justify their actions to themselves.

Recruiting, Hiring, and Evaluating Personnel

Chapter 3 presents strategies for recruiting, hiring, and evaluating employees. Ethics should play an important part in these processes. During an interview process both the applicant and the club should discuss ethical views. Will a coach's actions be consistent with the values of the club? If there is a disconnect between the two, trouble will most likely follow. A coach who puts the well-being of the athlete above on-field success may not be a good fit for a club that values success and winning above all other values.

As mentioned in chapter 3, recruiting staff from other clubs is a potential strategy for a sport club, although some question the ethics of such a strategy. Would a club manager like the manager of another club to tempt one of his staff members away? If not, why should he do it to another club?

When evaluating staff members, club leaders should consider the degree to which they act in accordance with the ethics and values of the club. Should a coach who cheats or promotes extreme gamesmanship remain with a club that in its mission states the importance of good sporting behavior? If the coach's actions have led to championships and a higher profile for the club and club leaders are happy with those results, they should revisit their mission statement and reassess their values.

Selecting Players

Developing policies for player selection is important. Such policies, however, do not guarantee that the most deserving players will be selected. A club's selection process may include tryouts and a matrix to assess athletes' strengths and weaknesses, but even with these policies in place, the most deserving may be slighted. Factors such as the financial or political influence of the parents of an athlete or the relationship of the coach to the parents of an athlete should not matter in the selection of players, but they sometimes do.

Club leaders who adhere to deontological theories would believe that selecting an athlete who is not as deserving as another is wrong and would not consider the consequences of damaging a friendship or forgoing potential sponsorship revenue. They would not slight the deserving player because they would not like same to be done to them. Club leaders who adhere to teleological theories may believe that the greater good is served by selecting the less talented player or that doing so is in the best interest of the coach.

Club leaders with a situational ethics approach may look at each situation in a different light. In one situation, all of the deserving players make the team; but in another, two players who are more deserving are not selected. Instead, the coach selects his best friend's son as well as the son of the president of the club's board of directors.

Each club must determine its player selection strategy. Ideally, a club will reward those who are most deserving, but the reality is it is not always that clean. The process should be consistent with the values of the club. Player selection decisions are often the most difficult and controversial in the overall management of a club.

Treatment of Participants

Chapter 5 addresses the legal responsibility a club has to its participants. This chapter addresses the moral and ethical responsibility the club has to ensure the safety and well-being of those participants. Parents of participants trust that a club will do everything in its power to provide safe facilities for competition and practice, that qualified and moral coaches will train the athletes, that the participants will face equitable competition, and that every precaution will be taken to ensure that participants are not placed in dangerous situations.

Clubs should not need laws to require that they ensure the safety of their participants. Doing so is simply the right thing to do. If the club does not live up to its moral responsibility, in most cases the courts will address the situation in the form of a lawsuit. But even if this is the case, it cannot repair the damage done to a participant by the action or nonactions of club personnel.

SUCCESSFUL STRATEGY

Determining Rightness

The sport club environment presents many situations that are open to ethical debate. The competitive environment, the things at stake for clubs and the professionals who run them, the hopes and desires of the players and their parents, and the codes of conduct of governing bodies create an environment for much debate over the rightness of actions. Some may argue that the following example highlights a successful strategy, whereas others may argue the opposite; nevertheless, it's an important issue that many clubs face and so warrants inclusion.

The firing of a former director of coaching at the Sereno Soccer Club in Arizona is an example of differing ethical views. On one side of the issue is the former director of coaching, who takes great pride in the success of the club during the 20 years he led it. That success includes numerous players receiving athletic scholarships and playing for the U.S. women's national team and the club winning state cups. It can be argued that the results justified the means of achieving them, and many former players and parents praise the approach the director and club took.

On the other side of the issue are the parents who believed that the club director was abusive and controlling of players. These parents paid the Sereno Soccer Club $10,000 a year with many having hopes that their sons or daughters would earn college scholarships. The club director demanded that players focus solely on club soccer and discouraged them from playing for high school teams or participating in other activities. Some parents were disappointed when their son or daughter's playing time was taken by a player who received a scholarship to join the club. The scholarship the parents had hoped for never materialized.

The board of the Sereno Soccer Club believed that the direction the club had taken was unhealthy. A member of the club resigned stating that the environment was unhealthy at best and potentially abusive. In relieving the director of coaching of his position, the leadership of the board stated that the club wanted to remain competitive but to be about more than just winning.

Finally, the U.S. Youth Soccer National Championship board revoked a Sereno state and regional championship based on findings that Sereno replaced a player on the team by having him sign a form agreeing to give up his spot on the team. The player said he never signed the form. He was replaced by a more talented player. The Arizona Youth Soccer Association conducted its own investigation and concluded that the director had ordered a forgery of the signature on the form. The Arizona board suspended the individual from coaching soccer for five months.

Who is right in the situation is open for debate. Determining rightness is based on the ethical views to which one adheres.

Information from Dickerson, J. (2008). Arizona club soccer produces scholarship-backed players, but at what cost? *Phoenix New Times*, December 16, 2008.

Gamesmanship

Where is the line between playing smart and cheating? This question raises the issue of gamesmanship. In sport an athlete may act in a manner that is legal, but may not be right. Gamesmanship can take the form of trash talking, intimidating, using stalling tactics, faking injuries, or using fouls for a benefit. In each case, the rules of the game are not broken. However, the competitor is seeking to alter the outcome of the contest by trying to unsettle an athlete, taking away a team's momentum, or giving themselves a break.

In soccer and basketball, professional fouls were often used to the advantage of the person committing the foul. Soccer players were often instructed to take an opponent down from behind if that player was on a breakaway. The penalty was

Celebrating after a win can be a healthy form of gamesmanship, but athletes must be led by example from coaches, parents, and other club personnel.

a lesser punishment than having one's opponent score a goal. Soccer has since instituted a rule that gives a red card to the person committing the act. In basketball flagrant fouls were used in much the same manner. Now the consequences include awarding two foul shots as well as possession of the ball to the person fouled. In both of these cases, the sport governing bodies established new rules following debates over the rightness of these gamesmanship strategies.

Clubs should revisit their values to determine which actions on the part of athletes, coaches, and supporters are inconsistent with those values. Some clubs encourage these types of acts in the name of competiveness and gaining the edge. Others believe that because they would not like such actions done to them, they will not do them to others. They believe that contests won using such strategies are undeserved victories. Each club must decide how it views gamesmanship.

Distributive Justice

distributive justice—The allocation of rewards and punishment and the means and criteria for such decisions.

Distributive justice addresses the allocation of rewards and punishment and the means and criteria for such decisions. Clubs have many things to distribute: playing time to players, promotions and raises to employees, field or court time to teams, and work schedules and responsibilities to employees. The question that always arises is, What is fair? Why did one staff coach get a $2,000 raise while another got only $500? On what basis was this determined? Was it merit or need? Should it have been distributed equally?

Those involved with the club evaluate their treatment based on the treatment of others. "Why did Johnny play three quarters of the game and my son only half?"

"Why did Steve get promoted to director of coaching over me?" "Why did Bill get the same raise as me even though my teams were more successful and I spend much more time at the club than he does?" These are the kinds of questions sport club managers face.

The answers to these questions are based on the criteria the club uses to distribute rewards. Rewards can be based on merit. Those who meet their goals, enable the club to achieve its overall goals, and contribute greatly to the club's success are rewarded to a greater degree than those who don't. This is the classic method used for allocating playing time, but it also can be used throughout the club.

Rewards can also be based on need. A staff member who is not as productive as another may get a larger raise because that person has a larger family to support and only one income. The other staff member, who is more productive, is single and has other business interests, and so club leaders decide that she may not need the raise as much. Is it fair to give to the one that needs over the one that has earned? The same can occur with playing time. A more talented player may not play the whole game because the coach believes that a less talented player needs the experience to grow as a player or to improve his self-esteem. Is that fair? Finally, a coach who regardless of the situation or the outcome of a game plays all players the same amount of time, and an executive director who distributes annual raises equally to all employees regardless of performance may be viewed as being fair, but are they?

Because those receiving rewards will compare their treatment to that of others, club leaders need to be prepared to justify the rewards they distribute. One strategy is to state the criteria up front so that everyone is prepared. A coach who says at the start of the season that the goal is to win a state championship and that the best players will play and there is no guarantee of playing time has been clear about rewarding playing time based on merit. Knowing this, parents can choose whether to sign their children up for the team.

The rewards system may vary across the club. Competitive teams often reward based on merit. In-house recreation and development programs often base rewards on need and advocate for equal treatment. The club leadership should consider the ramifications of the system it will implement and be prepared to refer to it when questions arise about the allocation of playing time, team selection, raises, and promotions.

Media and Public Relations

Chapter 6 addresses the importance of public and media relations to the branding and growth of the club. How a club interacts with the media is based on its ethics. A common strategy when dealing with the media is to highlight the positive and ignore the negative. If a player is selected for a national team or earns an athletic scholarship, the club will hold a press conference, send out a press release, and post the news on its Web site. But when a coach has been caught serving alcohol to the underage members of his traveling team, the club will quietly dismiss the coach and not issue a press release or post the news on the Web site. Is this ethical?

Does a sport club owe it to the public to give as much attention to negative news as it does to positive news? Is it the club leaders' responsibility to let parents know of issues and concerns, or should they hide them and let them find out for themselves? Parents may have joined the club based on all of the positive things they have seen, but because the negatives were not disclosed, they were not able to make an informed decision. The club has acted in its self-interest and for the greater good by attracting more members, but was hiding its negative news the right thing to do? How would club leaders feel if they were not presented all of the facts when making a decision?

Sponsorship

Selecting sponsors has ethical ramifications. At its most basic level, sponsorship can be seen as a business exploiting the club and its participants for financial gain. Club leaders need to decide whether they want that to occur or whether sponsorship is against its values. Chapter 7 explains what a sponsor seeks from a club. A club may determine that certain wants of the business are appropriate and others are not. Club leaders may be willing to put a company logo on the club's uniforms, but may not feel good about sharing the e-mail addresses of club members with that company.

If club leaders decide to pursue sponsorship, the next question is what product categories and companies they will purse. Are they willing to have a beer company or a local bar or tavern sponsor a youth sport complex or program? In accepting sponsor dollars from a beer company, the club may be seen as endorsing the use of alcohol. Is that an appropriate message to send to youths? Several years ago members of the sport community called for a boycott of Nike products and sponsorships because of allegations of human rights violations. The sponsors of the club make a statement about the values of the club.

Rule Creation and Enforcement

The policies, procedures, and rules of the club are extensions of its values, principles, mission, and vision and provide the framework for the club to fulfill its mission and vision. Policies dictate what club participants should do, and procedures communicate how they will do it.

Rules are statements about prohibited behavior in competition and the management and operation of the club. Some rules are mandates of the external organization of which the club is a member and are created to ensure equitable competition, to ensure the safety of the participants, and to promote the spirit of the game. Clubs should agree to follow these rules without question, but many look for ways to circumvent rules or interpret them in a way that is beneficial to the club. The conscious choice to break a rule constitutes cheating. If a club is caught, it will suffer the established consequences.

The way a club enforces the rules makes a statement about the club itself. Some clubs follow rules and policies strictly regardless of the consequences. For others, the rules are just window dressings that sound good on paper but are rarely enforced. If a rule gets in the way of achieving success, it is not enforced. Other clubs enforce the rules selectively—in one situation but not in another. If a rule is broken by a top player or coach, there may be no consequences, but that may not be the case for a less talented player or staff person.

Participation Opportunities

Society has come a long way in ensuring that all have the opportunity to participate in sport. Females are as encouraged to play sport as males; special needs children are offered participation opportunities as well, and seniors are encouraged to pursue an active lifestyle. Many countries have enacted laws to ensure that these opportunities are presented, thus eliminating the ethical debate. Despite such progress, issues still arise over the allocation of financial and human resources and the use of facilities. Clubs may view a particular population as second tier and assign the best coaches and the ideal practice times and facilities to the talented teams. The rightness of these actions can be a source of debate. Should all members of a club be treated equally, or should some be treated better than others? Each club must determine how it will treat those associated with the club.

Codes of Ethics

To enforce ethical and moral behavior, codes of ethics have been established by individuals, clubs, and professional organizations. The purpose of a **code of ethics** is to establish moral guidelines to monitor the behavior of those under its authority. When faced with an ethical dilemma, a person can refer to a code of ethics for guidance.

code of ethics—Moral guidelines that monitor the behavior of those under its authority.

Professional organizations establish codes of ethics to dictate which actions are ethical and which are unethical. A professional code of ethics should address issues that present the greatest dilemma for professionals and should be revised based on current issues in the field. The code can address issues such as player recruitment, treatment of players, treatment of officials, dealing with parents, treatment of visiting teams, sponsorship, relations with other clubs, and media relations. (See the sidebar on pages 220-221 for a sample code of ethics.)

A sport club should refer to the codes of ethics established by international, national, and state federations and develop one that is consistent with those codes, keeping in mind specific issues the club wants to address. The code should state that it is consistent with the codes of the governing organizations. A sport club's code of ethics can be more stringent than the state, national, or international codes, but should not be less stringent.

Sample Code of Ethics

The Tornado Sport Club will conduct the club with the highest ethical standards that reflect the elements of the code of the ethics for the state, national, and international federation of the sport. The club recognizes its role in the development of athletes and human beings and will abide by its founding values and principles in carrying out its business. Specifically, the Tornado Sport Club has established a code of ethics specific to the following categories:

Player Recruitment

The Tornado Sport Club board of directors, staff, coaches, parents, and players will do the following:

- Refrain from initiating communication for the purpose of enticing or recruiting a player from a competing club to join the Tornado Sport Club.
- Refrain from speaking negatively about other clubs to recruit a player to the Tornado Sport Club.

Treatment of Players

The Tornado Sport Club board of directors, staff, coaches, and parents will do the following:

- Respect the rights of all who are associated with the club and offer equal opportunities to all.
- Place the emotional and physical well-being of the players ahead of all other considerations.
- Treat each player as an individual, remembering the large range of emotional and physical development of participants.
- Offer a safe playing environment for all players and never place anyone in a situation that may risk injury.

Treatment of Officials

The Tornado Sport Club board of directors, staff, coaches, parents, and players will do the following:

- Offer the utmost respect to game officials.
- Refrain from verbally berating officials during a contest.

Parent Relations

The Tornado Sport Club board of directors, staff, and coaches will do the following:

- Respect the interest and views of all parents in terms of the policies and procedures of the club.
- Be honest and forthright in all communications with parents.
- Respect the confidentiality of all conversations between parents and club representatives.
- Provide multiple channels of communication between the club and coaches and parents.

Treatment of Visiting Teams

The Tornado Sport Club board of directors, staff, coaches, parents, and players will do the following:

- Treat all visiting team players, coaches, and spectators as guests at the Tornado Sport Club facility.
- Provide visiting teams access to the club facilities and offer ample warm-up time and space and spectator space.

Sponsorship

The Tornado Sport Club board of directors, staff, and coaches will do the following:

- Refrain from entering into any sponsorship agreements that are not consistent with the high ideals, values, and morals of the club. The image and values of the club supersede revenue generation.

Relations With Other Clubs

The Tornado Sport Club board of directors, staff, coaches, parents, and players will do the following:

- Conduct themselves in a professional and courteous manner when interacting with other clubs.
- Respect the rights and views of other clubs and work with them to grow the sport and benefit all those involved with the sport.

Enforcement

All club participants and representatives will be held accountable to this code, and failure to comply may lead to expulsion from the club via a hearing with the Tornado Sport Club's leadership and board of director's committee on ethics.

With many professional codes, there is no punishment associated with not following them, other than the normative judgments of others in the profession. Kultgen (1988) believed that professional codes of ethics are instruments of persuasion for both members of a profession and the public. (See the sidebar below for elements of a code of ethics.) They enhance the sense of community among members and of belonging to a group with common values and a common mission. Goree (2004) argued that an effective code of ethics maintains a sense of professionalism, offers guidance to those facing ethical dilemmas in the profession, and gives the public a standard to which it can hold those in the profession.

Elements of a Code of Ethics

Kultgen (1988) identified four basic elements that comprise a code of ethics:

- *Ethical code.* This component brings legitimacy to the field by creating standards.
- *Model laws.* This component regulates the action by stating minimum professional standards and disciplinary actions for those who do not follow the laws.
- *Basic ideals.* This component expresses the values and what is viewed as moral behavior.
- *Rationale.* This component allows for the interpretation of the code.

A code of ethics provides guidelines on both a professional and personal level. It facilitates decision making when a person is faced with a difficult ethical dilemma. The first step, of course, is agreeing to abide by the code.

A sport club can develop a code of ethics based on its philosophy, vision, values, and principles. It is an extension of it mission statement and makes definite statements about what the club views as ethical behavior in specific areas. All those associated with the club should be expected to follow the code. There may not be a punishment associated with breaking the code, but peer pressure within the club may entice a person to follow the code.

Finally, a person may want to establish a personal code for ethics based on her own values and principles. This would be a self-imposed code that would require self-discipline to follow. She may want to share her personal code of ethics with the club she works for or one with which she is interviewing.

Ethical Decision Making

Theodore Roosevelt stated that he would rather have one person practice good sportsmanship than hundreds talk about it. Mission statements and codes of ethics may be written and posted for all to see, but the ultimate test is the actions the people involved with the club take. Decisions are based on judgments and involve choice. To make a decision that would be morally appropriate within the club sport environment, a person should develop a strategy. Following are concepts that will help a person move in the direction of making an ethical decision.

Kidder (1995) provided a rather simplistic method for determining the rightness of an action. He proposed that before acting a person should consider, first, how she would feel if the action she is about to do were reported on the front page of a newspaper, and second, how she would feel if her grandmother discovered she had done the act. In both cases, Kidder appealed to the person's moral development: if she does not want to be held up to public scorn or to let down a significant other, she should not do the act. The club manager who is about to use an ineligible player in competition could use Kidder's approach by asking herself how would she feel if grandma found out she had used the ineligible player, or if it were published on the front page of the local news.

Cavanaugh (1990) proposed a model in which the person asks whether an action is acceptable based on utility (Does it optimize benefits?), rights (Does it respect the rights of those involved?), and justice (Is it fair?). If the answer is no to all three, the action is unethical; if the answer is yes to all three, the action is ethical. If two of the three answers are yes or no, then overriding factors must be considered: whether one criterion is more important than the other, whether the action is freely taken, and whether the undesirable effects are outweighed or uncontrollable. This will enable the person to determine whether the action is ethical or unethical. Ultimately, the person's values and principles will determine his views of utility, rights, and justice and therefore dictate whether he considers the action ethical or unethical.

Right Versus Right Decision Making

Many choices are not between right and wrong but between two rights. Kidder (1995) proposed that resolution results from selecting the action that is the most right for the circumstance and offers an ends-based resolution, the greatest good for the greatest number; a care-based resolution, which follows the golden rule; and a rule-based resolution, which states that we should act in a manner that we hope the rest of the world would act if placed in the same situation.

Summary

A sport club manager has the professional and moral responsibility to know the law and to create an environment that is as safe as possible for the participants. A sport club and its leadership will be judged more on ethics than on professional competence. There are many cases of people who have careers full of accomplishments tarnished by making one unethical decision. Knowing their ethics and acting in accordance with their beliefs while respecting the rights of others is important for all involved in the management of club sport.

Club managers inevitably bring their own personal life experience to the club. How they manage the ethical issues that arise at the club depends largely on their personal experience in both ethical and unethical life situations.

A club's ethics should drive the actions of all of those associated with the club. Poor sporting behavior, disrespecting an opponent or game official, cheating in competition, violating administrative or game rules, and using foul language are behaviors that should not be condoned in employees, coaches, and participants. How the club responds to these types of actions will be the ultimate statement of its ethics and reveal whether the talk of ethical behavior is just that, talk. Team members should apply the team standards of ethics to their dealings with each other as well as to their dealings with spectators, referees, and members of opposing teams.

Codes of ethics are established by individuals, clubs, and professional organizations to enforce ethical and moral behavior. The purpose of a code of ethics is to establish moral guidelines to monitor the behavior of those under its authority. A person facing an ethical dilemma can refer to a code of ethics for guidance.

A sport club can develop a code of ethics based on its philosophy, vision, values, and principles. It is an extension of its mission statement and makes definite statements about what the club views as ethical behavior in specific areas. All those associated with the club would be expected to follow the code. There may not be a punishment associated with breaking the code, but peer pressure within the club may entice a person to follow it.

Ken decides not to select the company president's son for the team because he would not want to be treated that way if he were the more deserving player. Ken realizes that the sponsorship may go to the club who accepts the son, but he believes he is acting in accordance with his values and principles. There will be other sponsorship opportunities in the future, and he will keep working toward them while living up to what he believes is right and leading his club in a manner that respects the rights of its members.

Epilogue: The Club Sport Scene in 2029

• • •

The year is 2029. Mario Patrick Robinson is ecstatic. The BlueStar Sports Club of Pennsylvania, where Mario serves as general manager, has had another banner year. Of the 10 sports that it offers for both males and females, it captured state championships in seven sports and three national championships. BlueStar had equal success in the 21 other states in which it has franchises. In total, BlueStar-franchised clubs won 54 state championships and 11 national championships across seven sports. On five occasions BlueStar state clubs faced each other in national championship games.

BlueStar's CEO and senior management staff have invited the general managers of all 22 franchises to come to the BlueStar corporate headquarters in Charlotte, North Carolina, for the club's annual retreat. Seminars at the retreat will be on topics such as new marketing strategies and how to implement the new standard practices for facility management that each franchise will initiate in the coming year. Also, the national staff will work with franchises that are due for reaccreditation from the National Club Sport Accreditation Agency (NCSAA), which is required of clubs every 10 years.

Another important development in the last year is that BlueStar has been designated a club of excellence by USA Basketball based on the fact it has produced five male Olympians and three female Olympians over the past five years. BlueStar has had players at all age groups chosen as representatives for national teams that will compete or have competed in the FIBA World Championships. By placing athletes on the teams, BlueStar receives an annual financial bonus. BlueStar has achieved similar results with athletes in swimming, lacrosse, soccer, track and field, tennis, and men's and women's volleyball and has received similar bonuses from the national governing bodies of these sports and the U.S. Olympic Committee.

The BlueStar men's senior basketball team has captured the USA National Championship the past two years and will compete for the World Club championship in Madrid, Spain, in the summer. The team recently transferred the rights of three players who had played on the BlueStar development team to Bayern Munich of the German Professional Basketball League. The transfer fee will be used to pay its top player, whose contract is up at the end of the year. There were rumors that Real Madrid had wanted to sign him as well.

During the annual retreat in Charlotte, all of the head basketball coaches from the franchise clubs will attend a four-day coaching clinic lead by the BlueStar national basketball staff. Even though BlueStar requires that all of its head coaches have a USA Basketball A license and all of its other coaches a USA Basketball B License, BlueStar holds these clinics to teach the "BlueStar way." The clinic will be held at the same time as the under-16 select training camp for the top players at each of the 22 clubs. This will be held in the McDonald's BlueStar Arena and Training Complex, home of the BlueStar professional team.

BlueStar's upper management team as well as franchise general managers and coaches consist of many former BlueStar athletes. While training as athletes with BlueStar, they earned their business degrees at universities that are partnered with BlueStar. The universities waive the tuition for college-aged athletes in exchange for the opportunity to advertise in BlueStar arenas and stadiums and during the telecasts of their games.

● ● ●

Is BlueStar—a multisport club franchised across the country that receives funds from the national governing bodies of its sports and the Olympic Committee for developing world-class athletes—the model sport club for the future? Only the future will tell, but if current trends continue, this scenario may not be that far off.

The overview of sport club management presented in this book is valuable because the future of club sport appears to be bright and will only be getting brighter. Sport clubs can contribute to this bright future by offering quality programs that meet the needs of all participants, socialization opportunities for participants and families, and high-quality coaching. But along with opportunities for growth comes responsibility. Club leaders need to be aware of the dangers of overtraining athletes to the point of burnout, mismanaging club finances, misrepresenting the qualifications of staff and programs, and focusing only on sport performance and not the other benefits participation in sport can offer.

Although sport clubs have been the norm in the majority of the world, they are becoming increasingly popular in North America. Club sport can provide strong athletic as well as social opportunities for a community, thereby bringing the community together. In the past, youth were introduced to sport through community organizations (e.g., Boys & Girls Clubs, recreation councils) and faith-based organizations, (e.g., YMCA, Jewish community centers). Those who excelled were given the opportunity to compete in the education environment (e.g., high school and intercollegiate programs).

The U.S. sport community is now moving more toward the sport club model, and it appears that the trend will continue for the future. Market forces are at work in which clubs with paid, professional coaches and modern facilities are attracting parents who are willing to pay for their sons and daughters to have first-class athletic experiences. Following are some trends that are emerging within the club sport environment.

Accreditation of Clubs

A criticism of sport clubs is that there is no established standard to help consumers distinguish a good club from a poor club, or a club that trains elite athletes from one that focuses only on participation opportunities. Accreditation, either voluntary or mandatory, would serve as an incentive for clubs to meet professionally accepted standards. Those who earn accreditation could highlight it in their marketing efforts, and those who do not will be at a disadvantage in the marketplace.

In the United States, national governing bodies such as USA Swimming have established criteria for club levels. USA Swimming's Club Recognition Program is a voluntary program that recognizes clubs that demonstrate a commitment to long-term club growth, development, and stability. These clubs must meet markers measuring business and organizational success, parent and volunteer development, coach development and education, and athlete development and performance. The requirements for recognition are based on the club's designation as coach owned, institutionally owned, or parent governed. To learn more, visit www.usaswimming.org.

In 2002 Sport England, the government agency responsible for developing a world-class community sport system in England, introduced Clubmark. The purpose of Clubmark was to ensure that accrediting partners apply common criteria to ensure that consistent good practice and minimum operating standards are delivered through all club development and accreditation schemes across multiple sports. The goal of the program is to empower parents who are choosing clubs for their children, to ensure that Clubmark-accredited clubs are recognized through a common approach to branding, and to provide a focus around which all organizations involved in sport can come together to support good practice in sport clubs working with children and young people. For more information, visit www.clubmark.org.uk/about/about-clubmark.

Many clubs are already doing things the right way, and if a sport or governing organization had accreditation standards, many clubs would probably meet them. Clubs that are not doing things the right way would be most affected by an accreditation system. Such clubs would need to change the way they work with athletes, their business practices, or their staffing policies to meet accreditation standards. Clubs that meet those standards could advertise the fact that they are accredited, thus giving customers the option to choose between an accredited club and a nonaccredited club.

Clubmark certification is based on the club's playing program, duty of care and safeguarding and protection of children and young people, sport equity and ethics, and club management. The benefits of certification are increased membership, member retention, continuous improvement, increased funding, increased use of facilities, use of coach development programs, greater interest from volunteers, links with schools, a raised profile, help with marketing and communications, and club development (www.clubmark.org.uk/benefits).

Accreditation and certification programs benefit both clubs and customers. Clubs have standards toward which to strive, and customers can distinguish among clubs. Athletes benefit, and in the long term, so do sports.

Licensing and Educating Club Coaches

Sport club customers have high expectations about the quality of club coaching. To succeed, clubs must hire the most qualified coaches, be willing to compensate them and treat them as professionals, and provide the resources for them to continue to grow professionally. Clubs that rely on volunteer coaches must recruit, train, and supervise them to ensure that participants have positive experiences.

In the United States some sports, such as soccer, swimming, and track and field, have implemented coaching education and certification programs. Certification is a statement of the proficiency of the coach. The licensing of coaches ties into accreditation because one criterion for accreditation is usually the quality of coaching. The sport consumer is an educated consumer and will be looking for the qualifications of the coaching staff in selecting a club.

Certification is also helpful to coaches in marketing themselves for positions. A coach with an A license from U.S. Soccer has demonstrated a high level of competence by passing the course. This coach may not be necessarily a better coach than one without an A license, or with no license at all, but the proficiency of the coach with the license is quantified.

Opinions differ on whether coaches should be required to participate in coaching education and certification programs. It is understood that a volunteer working with youth must have some sort of coaching education to be granted voluntary immunity. But the more compelling debate surrounds whether a coach working with elite athletes must have certification. Does certification make a great coach?

Consider the fact that the majority of coaches in the National Basketball Association have no formal coaching education. Most of them have played the game at a high level (e.g. college, professional), served as assistant coaches or scouts, attended a variety of coaching clinics, observed other coaches' training sessions, read sport-specific or general coaching books, relied on outside sport influences (e.g., Phil Jackson, coach of the Los Angeles Lakers, the Zen Warrior), and participated in informal discussions with peers. These experiences may not meet the standards of a coaching certification curriculum, but are they less valuable?

Those who support coaching education refer to the fact that coaches who participate in some form of coaching education program coach longer than those who do not. The argument is that they are better trained and in turn have a positive experience and see the impact they are making whether it be in victories or in player development.

Coaches need an understanding of the sport so that they teach athletes, especially at young ages, the right things the right way. Irreparable damage to developing athletes can occur from a coach who teaches the fundamentals incorrectly or applies too much pressure to win too early. The future debate is on the degree to which licensing and certifying coaches will be required.

Professionalization of Clubs and Coaches

When a person pays for something, he has high expectations about the quality of service, whether it is a meal in a restaurant or the training of his son or daughter in a sport. The reality in sport today is that parents are willing to pay for their children to have quality sport experiences in high-quality facilities, and the opportunity to compete at the highest levels. Sport clubs run by volunteers cannot always meet these high expectations, and therefore the attractiveness of sport opportunities offered by volunteers has diminished.

Consider the difference between a club run by a person who has another full-time job and works at the club on the weekends and a few weeknights, and one that has a full-time executive director who works five to seven days a week developing the club and making sure it operates at high levels in terms of coaching, facility management, and athlete development. Now consider the volunteer coach who only wants to coach his own child (or worse, is coaching because no one else wanted to) versus a licensed coach who is trained to work with youth of that age group and is evaluated on a seasonal basis by club management on whether he is meeting club standards (and whose employment is based on meeting those standards). These comparisons highlight the importance of professionalism in the club sport environment.

This is not to discount the importance of volunteers to a club. Parents should be encouraged to help the club achieve its goals. Volunteers are needed to help host tournaments and assist with the social aspects of the club, and to be involved with the learn-to-play levels with youth. The use of volunteers eliminates expenses for a club. Club members are willing to donate their time if it helps keeps some of the costs of membership down.

Increased Respect for the Youth Club Coach

In years past the youth coach was usually a volunteer whose son or daughter played on the team. Coaches had little training and no aspirations to turn a hobby or what they viewed as quality time with their sons or daughters into a career. Those who did view coaching as a career either stayed clear of the youth environment or saw it as a starting point for their climb up the coaching ladder. Most were always looking to coach at the next level of competition. Prestige and the opportunity to make a career out of coaching did not exist at the youth level but at the high school, college, professional, and national levels.

Recent years have seen an increased recognition of the importance of the youth coach in the development of athletes. The youth coach provides the foundation for the overall development of an elite athlete. Those who teach the fundamental skills in a way that is challenging but fun so that skilled athletes are not burned out at age 13, who put the long-term development of athletes ahead of winning trophies, and who train athletes the right way at an early age develop the fundamental skills that enable those athletes to excel at higher levels.

Coaches of well-trained athletes at the higher levels benefit from quality coaching at the youth level. Parents look to send their kids to coaches who have produced the athletes who are competing at the higher levels. It is often the case that coaches at the higher levels have received the credit while the hard work of youth club coaches is overlooked.

Youth club coaches are not well compensated for their skills and rarely are recognized for their efforts by those in their sport community. In the United States, USA Swimming has instituted a program that awards the youth coach of a medal winner in the Olympic Games. Such positive steps will lead to coaches who excel at developing young athletes staying in that environment as opposed to looking to work with older or more experienced athletes.

Moving Away From School-Based Athletics

As stated earlier, the U.S. model of sport has relied on the educational setting. In recent years clubs and schools have often been in competition for the loyalty of athletes. School-based teams played during the traditional sport season, and the club was relegated to a nontraditional season. Clubs that did offer in-season opportunities were often left with athletes who did not make a school team. In the case of a quality club team playing during the traditional season, athletes were forced to choose between the club team and the school team.

School-based athletics programs have faced several challenges in recent years. At both the high school and intercollegiate levels, athletic budgets have been cut, and the departments have either had to find ways to generate revenues or cut sports. At the intercollegiate level, the need to meet Title IX requirements has led to a number of intercollegiate athletic departments dropping men's programs. Many intercollegiate athletic departments have taken the position of offering fewer programs as well.

In the high school setting, the cost of programs is a concern. Sport clubs can often offer higher-quality coaching than high schools can. Some high school teams are coached by people with limited backgrounds in the sport, whereas sport clubs can hire professionals. This is especially common in individual sports such as swimming, tennis, golf, and gymnastics. Athletes train from an early age with a club or a professional teacher and then represent their schools in interscholastic competition. To this day it is still not uncommon at the college level for the head coach in a primary sport to be assigned a coaching position in a second sport that she is not qualified to coach. In high schools, teachers often take on the responsibility of coaching a sport for which they are unqualified because they can earn a few thousand dollars for doing so.

In the United States, school-based sports are an institution. They build school spirit and pride, and athletes relish the opportunity in representing their schools. Also, there are great high school coaches who are well trained and develop outstanding athletes. However, the future may be that schools and clubs form partnerships in terms of the use of facilities and staff. Rather than competing with a club, the school can contract out to the club to train athletes instead of hiring unqualified coaches. In the end, the goal is to give athletes experiences and help them reach their potential.

Merging of Clubs

As in other businesses, mergers are sometimes a viable option for sport clubs. Two competing clubs may realize that collaboration makes more sense than competition, or a club may recognize that its weakness is another club's strength. In either scenario, by coming together, two or more clubs can reduce expenses and pool resources to meet the needs of customers. Mergers are often easier said than done, but if planned, negotiated, and executed well, they can be successful both for the clubs and the customers.

Rise of the Multisport Clubs

The move toward multisport clubs and the merging of single-sport clubs into multisport clubs make great sense on a number of levels. Clubs can consolidate their assets while limiting their liabilities, increase the number of available facilities, offer one-stop shopping to customers, and prevent the overtraining and burnout that often occur in younger athletes who take part in year-round single-sport training.

A single-sport club has a vested interest in having athletes compete in the sport year-round. The clubs are in business and need the cash flow. The downside of this model is that youth are specializing too early, which can lead to burnout as well as overuse injuries. If an athlete wants to do multiple sports, it creates financial hardships on parents and can result in the athlete having two training sessions or competitions in one day and being forced to choose between sports.

The ideal structure is a sport club that offers several sports in a multisport facility. Club leaders coordinate the scheduling of programs and facilities to prevent conflicts between sports and eliminate the necessity of parents traveling from one site to the next in a night. In addition, the club can have a consistent training methodology across sports. Coaches from different sports can communicate about the fundamental skills athletes can work on to improve performance across sports.

The multisport club can also better use its staff. If the club follows the long-term athlete development (LTAD) model presented in chapter 9, at the youth levels, one coach can coach multiple sports because the focus would be on developing athletes rather than sport-specific players. At the higher levels of competition, sport-specific coaches can be used. For example, ideally, the club would have an A-licensed coach working with the soccer players on its under-17 club team that has several players who have the potential to play at the intercollegiate level and a well-trained basketball coach who works with those athletes out of soccer season. It is also not out of the realm of possibility for the A-licensed coach to work with the youth program in soccer or perhaps have an interest in another sport that she can coach as well.

Franchising Clubs

McDonald's success is based on a customer getting the same product at the same level of quality at the same price and in the same facility no matter where that customer may be. This concept is known as franchising, and McDonald's is the most recognized franchise in the world. A sport club has the potential to franchise as well. It can be argued that Clubmark standards of accreditation are a step in the direction of franchising because they are promoting consistency across clubs, even as the clubs keep their unique identities.

A club that wishes to expanded its business beyond one location or geographic region can take the franchise approach. It has been successful in the fitness club industry with franchises such as Bally Total Fitness and Gold's Gym. A club interested in doing this would develop its brand, set operating procedures, and then either approach existing clubs in other cities with a franchise proposal or sell the franchising rights to an individual or group in an area and then support the entity with materials and assistance to start and then operate the club.

Training Elite Athletes

If the opportunities for athletes to train and develop in education-based programs are eliminated or decreased, other environments will have to serve as the training areas for the elite athletes of a country. National governing bodies (NGBs) and national olympic committees can financially support clubs that can serve as sites for elite athlete training. These sites can be existing sport clubs or newly created clubs. The NGBs and national olympic committees can financially support those sites so that they can continue to attract and train athletes who have the ability to represent the country and excel at the international level. This support can come in the form of scholarships for athletes to live near and train at those clubs or funds that will improve the existing training facilities or pay outstanding coaches.

Conclusion

The club sport model has thrived around the globe and appears to have the potential to become the norm in the United States. Athletes and the parents of athletes are seeking and willing to pay to get the best athletic experience possible, and through quality clubs and excellent coaches, the club sport environment can meet those needs. In the end, the athletes and the sports will benefit.

References

Ammon, R., & Brown, M. (2007). Risk management process. In D.J. Cotton & J.T. Wolohan (Eds.), *Law for recreation and sport managers* (4th ed.). Dubuque, IA: Kendall-Hunt.

Balyi, I., Way, R., Norris, S., Cardinal, C., & Higgs, C. (2005). *Canadian sport for life: Long-term athlete development resource paper.* Vancouver, BC: Canadian Sport Centres.

Bridges, F., & Roquemore, L. (1996). *Management for athletic/sport administration: Theory and practice* (2nd ed.). Decatur, IL: ESM.

Caughron, R.L. (2007). Employment contracts. In D.J. Cotton & J.T. Wolohan (Eds.), *Law for recreation and sport managers* (4th ed.). Dubuque, IA: Kendall-Hunt.

Cavanaugh, G.F. (1990*). American business values*, 3rd ed. Englewood Cliffs, NJ: Prentice Hall.

Chelladurai, P. (2001). *Managing organizations for sport and physical activity: A systems perspective.* Scottsdale, AZ: Holcomb Hathaway.

Cote, J., Baker, J., & Abernethy, B. (2003). From play to practice: A developmental framework for the acquisition of expertise in team sport. In J. Starkes & K.A. Ericsson (Eds.), *Recent advances in research of sport expertise* (pp. 89-114). Champaign, IL: Human Kinetics.

Cote, J., & Fraser-Thomas, J. (2007). Youth involvement in sport. In P.R.E. Cricker (Ed.), *Introduction to sport psychology: A Canadian perspective* (pp. 266-295). Boston: Allyn & Bacon.

Cotton, D. (2007a). Defenses against liability. In D.J. Cotton & J.T. Wolohan (Eds.), *Law for recreation and sport managers* (4th ed.). Dubuque, IA: Kendall-Hunt.

Cotton, D. (2007b). Which parties are liable. In D.J. Cotton & J.T. Wolohan (Eds.), *Law for recreation and sport managers* (4th ed.). Dubuque, IA: Kendall-Hunt.

Cotton, D.J. & Cotton, M.B. (2005). Waivers & release of liability (5th ed.) Sport risk consulting. www.lulu.com.

DeSensi, J.T., & Rosenberg, D. (2003) *Ethics and morality in sport management.* Morgantown, WV: Fitness Information Technology.

Drucker, P. (1954). *The practice of management.* New York: Harper & Row.

Fayol, H. (1949). *General and industrial management.* London: Pitman. (First published in French in 1916).

Fraser-Thomas, J., Cote, J., & Deakin, J. (2008). Understanding dropout and prolonged engagement in adolescent competitive sport. *Psychology of Sport and Exercise, 9,* 645-662.

French, J.R.P., & Raven, B. (1959). The bases of social power. In D. Cartwright (Ed.), *Studies in social power* (pp. 150-167). Ann Arbor: University of Michigan Press.

Fried, G., Shapiro, S.J., & DeSchriver, T.D. (2003). *Sport finance.* Champaign, IL: Human Kinetics.

Gardell, B. (1982). Scandinavian research in stress and working life. *International Journal of Health Service, 12,* 31-41.

Gibbons, T., Hill, R., McConnell, A., Forester, T., & Moore, J. (2000). *The path to excellence: A comprehensive view of development of U.S. Olympians who competed from 1984-1998.* Colorado Springs, CO: USOC.

Goree, K. (2004) *Ethics applied* (4th ed.). Boston: Pearson Education.

Gould, D., Lauer, L., Rolo, C., Jannes, C., & Penniski, N. (2006). Understanding the role parents play in tennis success. *British Journal of Sports Medicine, 40,* 632-636.

Hackman, J. R., & Oldham, G. R. (1980) Work redesign. Reading, MA: Addison-Wesley.

Ham, L. (2005). Accounting and budgeting. In B. Parkhouse (Ed.), *The management of sport: Its foundation and application* (4th ed.). Boston: McGraw-Hill.

Harsanyi, L. (1983). *Preparation model for the 10-18 year old athletes.* Budapest: Utanpotlas-neveles, No.10.

Hickson, D.J., Hinings, C.R., Lee, C.A., Schneck, R.E., & Pennings, J.M. (1971). A strategic contingencies theory of interorganizational power. *Administrative Science Quarterly, 14,* 378-397.

Hums, M. (2007). Assault and battery. In D.J. Cotton & J.T. Wolohan (Eds.), *Law for recreation and sport managers* (4th ed.). Dubuque, IA: Kendall-Hunt.

Katz, R.L. (1974). Skills of an effective administrator. *Harvard Business Review, 52,* 90-102.

Kidder, R. (1995). *How good people make tough choices.* New York: Harper.

Kohlberg, L. (1987). *Child psychology and childhood education: A cognitive-development view.* New York: Longman.

Kultgen, J. (1988). *Ethics and professionalism.* Philadelphia: University of Pennsylvania Press.

Locke, E.A. (1976). The nature and causes of job satisfaction. In M.D. Dunnette (Ed.), *Handbook of industrial and organizational psychology* (pp. 1297-1349). Chicago: Rand McNally.

Malina, R.M., Bouchard, C. and Bar-Or, O. (1991). Growth, maturity, and physical activity. Champaign, IL.: Human Kinetics.

McGregor, D. (1960). *The human side of enterprise.* New York: McGraw-Hill.

McMillen, J.D. (2007). Game, event and sponsorship contracts. In D.J. Cotton & J.T. Wolohan (Eds.), *Law for recreation and sport managers* (4th ed.). Dubuque, IA: Kendall-Hunt.

Miller , L.K. (1997). *Sport business management.* Gaithersburg, MD: Aspen.

Mondy, R.W., Shaplin, A., & Premeaux, S.R. (1991). *Management: Concepts, practices and skills* (5th ed.). Needham Height, MA: Allyn & Bacon.

Moyer, R.C., McGuigan, J.R., & Kretlow, W.J. (2003). *Contemporary financial management* (9th ed.).

Mullin, B., Hardy, S., & Sutton, W. (2007). *Sport marketing* (3rd ed.). Champaign, IL: Human Kinetics.

National Center for Nonprofit Boards. (1988). *Ten basic responsibilities of nonprofit boards.* Washington, DC: National Center for Nonprofit Boards.

Olson J. (1997). *Facility and equipment management for sport directors.* Champaign, IL: Human Kinetics.

Pajares, M.F. (1992). Teachers' beliefs and educational research: Cleaning up a messy construct. *Review of Educational Research, 62* (3), 307-332.

Regan, T. (1997). Financing facilities. In M. Walker & D. Stotlar (Eds.), *Sport facility management.* Boston: Jones & Bartlett.

Robbins, S.P., & Stuart-Kotze, R. (1990). *Management concepts and applications* (Canadian 2nd ed.). Englewood Cliffs, NJ: Prentice Hall.

Rushing, G. (2007). Other intentional torts: Invasion of privacy-breach of fiduciary duty, tortuous interference with contract. In D.J. Cotton & J.T. Wolohan (Eds.), *Law for recreation and sport managers* (4th ed.). Dubuque, IA: Kendall-Hunt.

Sanderson, L. (1989). Growth and development for design and training plans for young athletes. Ottawa, *CACS SPORTS, 10* (2).

Sawyer, T. (2002). *Facilities planning for health, fitness, physical activity, recreation and sports: Concepts and applications* (10th ed.). Champaign, IL: Sagamore Press.

Seigrist, J. (1996). Adverse health effects of high-effort/low-reward conditions. *Journal of Occupational Health Psychology, 1,* 27-41.

Sharpe. L. (2007). Contract essentials. In D.J. Cotton & J.T. Wolohan (Eds.), *Law for recreation and sport managers* (4th ed.). Dubuque, IA: Kendall-Hunt.

Slack, T. (1997). *Understanding sport organizations: The application of organization theory.* Champaign, IL: Human Kinetics.

Smith, P.C., Kendall, L.M., & Hulin, C.L. (1969). *The measurement of satisfaction in work and retirement.* Chicago: Rand McNally.

Starkes, J., & Ericsson, E. (2003). *Expert performance in sport: Recent advances in research on sport expertise.* Champaign, IL: Human Kinetics.

Taylor, F.W. (1911). *The principles of scientific management.* New York: Harper & Brothers.

Tort. (1991). In *Black's law dictionary* (6th ed., p. 1036). St. Paul, MN: West.

van der Smissen, B. (2007). Elements of negligence. In D.J. Cotton & J.T. Wolohan (Eds.), *Law for recreation and sport managers* (4th ed.). Dubuque, IA: Kendall-Hunt.

White, H & Karabetsos, J. (2002) Planning and Desiging. In Sawyer, T. *Facilities planning for health, fitness, physical activity, recreation and sports: Concepts and applications* (10th ed.). Champaign, IL: Sagamore Press.

Index

Note: The italicized *f* and *t* following page numbers refer to figures and tables, respectively.

About the Author

Matthew Robinson, EdD, is associate professor and director of the sport management program at the University of Delaware. He also is a member of the legal studies faculty, has a secondary appointment with the School of Education, and serves as director of the International Coaching Enrichment Certificate Program funded by the United States Olympic Committee and the International Olympic Committee's Olympic Solidarity fund. Robinson also serves as director of management education for the National Soccer Coaches Association of America and developed the organization's director of coaching course.

Robinson earned his EdD in athletic administration from Temple University. He is the author of another successful sport management text, has written over 25 articles, and has delivered over 100 national and international scholarly and professional presentations. He is president of CPTM Sport Enterprise, a sport consulting firm.

You'll find
other outstanding
sport management resources at

www.HumanKinetics.com

In the U.S. call

1-800-747-4457

Australia..08 8372 0999
Canada 1-800-465-7301
Europe..+44 (0) 113 255 5665
New Zealand...0800 222 062

HUMAN KINETICS
The Information Leader in Physical Activity & Health
P.O. Box 5076 • Champaign, IL 61825-5076 USA